SAINT MARY'S COLLEGE OF CALIFORNIA
COLLEGIATE SEMINAR 103

WESTERN
TRADITION II

Acknowledgments:

pp. 48–69: From *Discourse on Method and Meditations on First Philosophy,* 4th edition,
by René Descartes, translated by Donald A. Cress. Copyright © 1998 by Hackett
Publishing Company, Inc. Reprinted by permission.
pp. 97–129: From *The Turkish Embassy Letters* by Mary Wortley Montagu, edited by
Teresa Heffernan and Daniel O'Quinn. Copyright © 2003 by Teresa Heffernan and
Daniel O' Quinn. Reprinted by permission of Broadview Press.
pp. 139–140: As appeared in *German Feminist Writings*, edited by Patricia A.
Herminghouse and Magda Mueller, translated by Melanie Archangeli and Patricia A.
Herminghouse. Copyright © 2001 by Bloomsbury Academic, U.S. Reprinted by permission of the publisher via the Copyright Clearance Center.
pp. 141–155: From *The Social Contract* by Jean-Jacques Rousseau, translated by
Maurice Cranston. Copyright © 1968 by Maurice Cranston. Reprinted by permission
of Peters, Fraser & Dunlop Ltd. (www.petersfraserdunlop.com) on behalf of the Estate
of Maurice Cranston.
pp. 214–242: Copyright © Libreria Editrice Vaticana. Reprinted by permission.

530 Great Road
Acton, MA 01720
800-562-2147
www.xanedu.com

Contents

Collegiate Seminar Goals and Outcomes

Collegiate Seminar Vision Statement

The Collegiate Seminar Program seeks to engage Saint Mary's students in a critical and collaborative encounter with the world of ideas as expressed in great texts of the Western tradition in dialogue with and exposure to its encounter with other traditions. Thereby students become part of the Great Conversation. The Program seeks to help them develop as curious, thoughtful members of an intellectual community. Designed to serve the College's goals of a liberal education, the Program strives to put students in possession of their powers to think clearly, critically, and collaboratively, and articulate their ideas effectively—powers that will serve them for the rest of their lives.

Goals of the Collegiate Seminar Program

The Collegiate Seminar Program fosters a genuine sense of collegiality and intellectual community by providing an authentic forum for students to meet and partake of a common experience—the reading and discussion of shared texts under the guidance of faculty from all disciplines. Its participants engage in collaborative dialogue with texts whose ideas shape our world. Through careful reading, shared inquiry, and writing, students improve their skills of analysis and communication. During this process students will develop increased appreciation for these great ideas, and grow in their intellectual curiosity, becoming life-long learners and thinkers. Students will be exposed to a variety of ways of knowing, encouraged in their search for meaning, and learn to accept ambiguity while aiming for clarity.

Seminar Specific Learning Outcomes

As a result of their participation in the Collegiate Seminar Program, students will grow in their ability to:

1. Understand, analyze, and evaluate challenging texts from different genres and periods.
2. Comprehend the intellectual threads that connect works both backward and forward through history.

3. Relate the works studied to their own experience and to notions of authentic humanity.
4. Reflect on prior knowledge and assess one's own process of learning.

Critical Thinking

Critical thinking within Seminar is grounded on the processes of analysis, synthesis and evaluation necessary to read with understanding. Through careful reading, listening, and reflection, which lead to a solid understanding of the texts, critical thinking allows students to make perceptive insights and connections between texts, Seminars and ultimately their life experiences. Critical thinking within Seminar also includes skills that allow for sound judgments to be made when multiple, competing viewpoints are possible. Seminar is a place where reading critically is transformed and integrated into a habit of mind, providing students with the tools to question the authority of the text and the foundations of their own assumptions. In short, critical thinking allows students to recognize, formulate and pursue meaningful questions, which are not only factual but also interpretive and evaluative, about the ideas of others as well as their own.

Critical Thinking Learning Outcomes

As a result of their participation in the Collegiate Seminar Program, students will grow in their ability to:

1. Distinguish the multiple senses of a text (literal and beyond the literal).
2. Identify and understand assumptions, theses, and arguments that exist in the work of authors.
3. Evaluate and synthesize evidence in order to draw conclusions consistent with the text. Seek and identify confirming and opposing evidence relevant to original and existing theses.
4. Ask meaningful questions and originate plausible theses.
5. Critique and question the authority of texts, and explore the implications of those texts.

Written and Oral Communication

A mind is not truly liberated until it can effectively communicate what it knows. Thus the Collegiate Seminar Program seeks to develop strong written and oral communication skills in its students. Students will develop skills that demonstrate an understanding of the power of language to shape thought and experience. They will learn to write and speak logically, with clarity, and with originality, and grow in their intellectual curiosity through the process of writing.

Written and Oral Communication Learning Outcomes

As a result of their participation in the Collegiate Seminar Program, students will grow in their ability to:

1. Recognize and compose readable prose, as characterized by clear and careful organization, coherent paragraphs and well-constructed sentences that employ the conventions of Standard Written English and appropriate diction.
2. Recognize and formulate effective written and oral communication, giving appropriate consideration to audience, context, format, and textual evidence.
3. Analyze arguments so as to construct ones that are well supported (with appropriate use of textual evidence), are well reasoned, and are controlled by a thesis or exploratory question.
4. Use discussion and the process of writing to enhance intellectual discovery and unravel complexities of thought.

Shared Inquiry

Shared inquiry is the act of reasoning together about common texts, questions, and problems. It is a goal of Collegiate Seminar to advance students' abilities to develop and pursue meaningful questions in collaboration with others, even in the context of confusion, paradox, and/or disagreement. Through the habits of shared inquiry students will carefully consider and understand the perspectives and reasoned opinions of others, reconsider their own opinions, and develop rhetorical skills.

Shared Inquiry Learning Outcomes

As a result of their participation in the Collegiate Seminar Program, students will grow in their ability to:

1. Advance probing questions about a common text or other objects of study.

2. Pursue new and enriched understandings of the texts through sustained collaborative inquiry.
3. Reevaluate initial hypotheses in light of evidence and collaborative discussion with the goal of making considered judgments.
4. Engage in reflective listening and inclusive, respectful conversation.

Honor Code and Seminar

The Student Honor Council (of academic 2004–2005) has requested that all Seminar sections discuss the proper use of other persons' opinions in Seminar classes. The Governing Board of Collegiate Seminar proposes the following list of good practices:

Authentic engagement in seminar classes requires that—

1. Students read only the assigned texts in preparation;
2. Students give their own thoughts about the assigned readings;
3. Students do not introduce opinions of experts into the conversation;
4. Student essays present the student's own thoughts on the agreed-upon topic;
5. Instructors advise whether and how essays should respond to, use, or cite opinions which other students have voiced in class.

(CSGB, 5/19/04)

Collegiate Seminar Guidelines for Grading Oral Participation

The following criteria shall be considered in evaluating the oral participation of seminar students:

- Good listening and close attention to the discussion.
- Frequency of contribution to discussion.
- Quality of contributions in terms of forwarding the conversation.
- Clear evidence of reflection upon the reading.
- Ability, with respect to the reading, to describe, propose insights, analyze, see alternatives, compare, and evaluate.
- Ability to counter questions and/or challenge other discussants (including the seminar leader) respectfully.
- Seriousness of engagement, degree of interest in the ideas under discussion, and spontaneity.
- Sense of responsibility for the group's understanding of the text and for the progress of the conversation.

Seminar leaders and students are encouraged to use these criteria to evaluate perfomance as follows:

The student who earns a grade of "A" for oral participation is one who:

1) Is rarely if ever absent from class and is likely to inform the instructor in advance.
2) Is always excellently prepared and demonstrates her/his preparation by consistently offering text-related contributions throughout the discussion.
3) Is self-motivated, entering the discussion with pertinent and useful contributions as appropriate.
4) Is engaged and active in pursuing questions and in testing opinions.

5) Regularly forwards the discussion by drawing comparisons, analyzing problems and questions, offering opinions on interpretations, and responding critically and respectfully to the contributions of others.

6) Listens with active interest to the comments of others; questions others in an effort to understand not only what they are saying but also the reasons and implications of what they are saying.

7) Takes responsibility for the "health and well-being" of the seminar.

The student who earns a grade of "B" for oral participation is one who:

1) Is rarely, if ever, absent from class and is likely to inform the instructor in advance.

2) Is nearly always well prepared and demonstrates her/his preparation by often offering text-related contributions to the discussion.

3) Is often self-motivated, entering the discussion with pertinent and useful contributions as appropriate.

4) Is sometimes engaged and active, sometimes more passive, in pursuing questions and in testing opinions.

5) Sometimes forwards the conversation, sometimes takes a less active role, supporting or questioning the more positive contributions of others.

6) Listens with active interest to the comments of others.

7) Does not obstruct or retard the "health and well being" of the seminar.

The student who earns a grade of "C" for oral participation is one who:

1) Is seldom absent from class.

2) Is generally prepared and demonstrates her/his preparation by offering text-related contributions at some point in the discussion.

3) Regularly contributes to discussion but takes a follower's rather than a leader's role in forwarding the conversation.

4) Listens respectfully to the comments of others.

5) Does not obstruct or retard the "health and well-being" of the seminar.

The student who earns a grade of "D" for oral participation is one who:

1) May be absent from class more than three or four times per semester.
2) May be unprepared for discussion or fail to demonstrate preparation by pertinent text-related contributions to the discussion.
3) Often does not contribute, even as a follower, in the seminar discussion.
4) May fail to listen to others; may engage in disruptive "side conversations."
5) May obstruct or retard the "health and well-being" of the seminar.

The student who earns a grade of "F" for oral participation is one who:

1) May be often absent from seminar.
2) Is unprepared for the majority of classes.
3) Rarely, if ever, contributes to the discussion.
4) Does not listen to others or follow the course of the discussion; may engage in disruptive behavior.
5) May obstruct or retard the seminar.

Saint Mary's College Grading Standards
Collegiate Seminar Program
Seminar 02/14

	The C essay is competent, exhibiting no serious or frequent deficiencies.	*The B essay* is strong in most areas.
Thesis/ Purpose/ Controlling Idea	The C essay addresses the topic and offers a thesis. The thesis, however, may not explore the topic with sufficient complexity or take on a significant intellectual challenge.	The B essay exhibits intellectual engagement. It has a narrowly focused thesis, with a clear sense of purpose and audience. It explores the topic in some depth and with some complexity.
Structure, Organization, and Development	The C essay offers support for its thesis; however, this support may not be evaluated or analyzed thoughtfully, or may tend toward plot summary. The C essay has an introduction, body, and conclusion, generally unified paragraphs, and transitions between paragraphs. However, it may proceed formulaically or mechanically. (e.g. listing examples). The conclusion may not move much beyond the initial thesis.	The B essay proceeds logically and offers appropriate support for its thesis. It is a generally unified essay, with a clear introduction, coherent paragraphs, and effective transitions. Its conclusion does not merely restate the argument, but attempts to draw together preceding insights in a new way.
Language, Style, and Syntax	The C essay employs readable prose, but the sentences may be simple and lack variety. Language may be overly general and wordy.	In the B essay, sentences are sufficiently varied. Language is generally concise and appropriate.
Grammar, Spelling, Punctuation, Formatting, and Documentation of Sources	The C essay employs generally correct grammar, punctuation, formatting, spelling, and documentation. Errors, however, may be serious enough to detract from the effectiveness of the essay.	The B essay employs generally correct grammar, punctuation, formatting, spelling, and documentation. Errors, when they appear, do not detract from the overall effectiveness of the essay.

The F essay is seriously deficient. It may exhibit a poor grasp of the assignment or a lack of familiarity with assigned texts. It may be deficient in one or more of the following areas: purpose, organization and development, language, and mechanics. It may lack a clear thesis or fail to support its thesis.

	The A essay excels in all areas.	*The D essay* is deficient in one or more areas.
	The A essay has a clearly defined, intellectually challenging focus and a strong sense of purpose and audience. It exhibits depth and complexity in its analysis and originality in its thought.	The D essay may lack a clear thesis, or the thesis may be weak or overly general.
	The A essay is distinguished by sound logic. It offers sufficient and appropriate support for the thesis in the form of concrete, specific, and relevant evidence. It is a unified essay that proceeds coherently with an effective introduction, well-developed and unified paragraphs, graceful transitions, and a conclusion that, rather than summarizing previous points, explores the implications of the preceding analysis.	The D essay may fail to provide adequate support for its thesis in the form of textual analysis or other evidence; it may substitute repetition for development or make inaccurate claims. It may lack a clear structure and paragraphs may lack coherence. Transitions may be awkward or nonexistent.
	In the A essay, sentences are skillfully crafted and effectively varied; langauge is fresh, precise, and economical. It maintains a consistent and appropriate tone.	The D essay often lacks variety in sentence structure and suffers from inappropriate diction and akward syntax. Language tends to be vague, imprecise, or rambling.
	The A essay is almost entirely free of errors in grammar, punctuation, formatting, spelling, and documentation.	A D essay is often characterized by grammatical errors such as fragments, comma splices, agreement errors, or inappropriate shifts in tense, voice, mood, or person. It may also be rife with spelling, punctuation, or formatting errors. It may lack documentation or be improperly documented.

Other common features of failing essays are: faulty logic, ineffective organization, incoherent paragraphs, misreadings, incorrect diction, and so many syntactic and grammatical errors that the essay becomes unreadable.

Kinds of Questions

Questions of Fact

To a question of fact there will be only one answer which can be supported using evidence from the text; this answer may, however, take some effort to discover.

Example: In "The Analogy of the Cave", why do philosophers (those with "beatific vision") appear foolish in the everyday world (such as in the law courts)?

Questions of Interpretation

Your purpose is to make sense of the text. You might ask what conclusions we can draw about the author's meaning, purpose, or basic assumptions. Or you might question the relationship of two statements which seem to be in contradiction. To questions of interpretation, attentive readers can give differing answers, each of which can be supported using evidence from the text.

Example: According to Socrates, the prisoners of "The Analogy of the Cave" are "like us." How does the reading support this view?

Questions of Evaluation

Judge what is presented in the reading. Is what is written true? False? Neither true nor false? Likely? Unlikely? Wrong? Right? Fair? Unfair? Insightful? Obvious? Of course, these categories of judgment (and others like them) are often themselves the very subject of the readings.

Example: Is "The Analogy of the Cave" a good and useful image of human existence? (And what do I mean by "good" or by "useful" or by "image"?)

Timeline for Seminar 103

Current (Christian) Era (CE)

1492	First New World contact by Christopher Columbus
1517	Martin Luther posts 95 Theses, starting Protestant Revolution
1520	Martin Luther publishes *On Christian Liberty*
1532	Nicoló Machiavelli, posthumous publication of *The Prince*
1532	Brother Franciscus de Vitoria publishes "On the Indians Lately Discovered"
1534	England splits from Roman Catholic Church, establishes Church of England
1545–1563	Council of Trent, Catholic response to Protestantism
1550	Bartholomew de las Casas publishes *The Destruction of the Indies*
1562–1598	French Wars of Religion, between Catholics and Huguenots (Protestants)
1559	Marguerite de Navarre publishes *The Heptameron*
1603	William Shakespeare, first performance of *Measure for Measure*
1609	Galileo manufactures telescope for astronomical observation
1618–1648	Thirty Years War between Catholic & Protestant forces in Central & Northen Europe
1620	Pilgrims land at Plymouth Rock
1637	Rene Descartes publishes *Discourse on Method*
1651	Thomas Hobbes publishes *Leviathan*
1687	Isaac Newton publishes *Principia Mathematica*, setting forth laws of motion and gravity
1688	English "Glorious Revolution"
1691	Sor Juana Inés de la Cruz writes *The Answer*
1703	Construction begins on St. Petersburg, Russia
1716	Lady Mary Wortley Montagu writes *Turkish Letters*
1759	Voltaire publishes *Candide*
1760–1840	Industrial Revolution; starts in Great Britain, spreads through Europe

1762	Jean-Jacques Rousseau publishes *The Social Contract*
1776	American Continental Congress adopts *The Declaration of Independence*
1789	Start of the French Revolution
1792	Mary Wollstonecraft publishes *A Vindication of the Rights of Women*
1794–1820	Poems by Wordsworth, Blake, Shelley, Byron, and Keats
1815	Fall of Napoleon
1848	Democratic revolutions in numerous European countries
1848	Karl Marx publishes *The Communist Manifesto*
1851	Louise Otto-Peters publishes "The Lace Makers"
1852	Frederick Douglass gives the speech "What to the Slave Is the Fourth of July?"
1854	Charles Dickens publishes *Hard Times*
1859	Charles Darwin publishes *The Origin of Species*
1861	Russia emancipates its serfs, allowing peasants to own land and move without restriction
1861–1865	American Civil War
1864	Fyodor Dostoevsky publishes *Notes from Underground*
1891	Pope Leo XIII issues *Rerum Novarum*

WESTERN TRADITION II

The Good-Morrow

John Donne

I wonder, by my troth, what thou and I
Did, till we loved? Were we not weaned till then?
But sucked on country pleasures, childishly?
Or snorted we in the Seven Sleepers' den?
'Twas so; but this, all pleasures fancies be.
If ever any beauty I did see,
Which I desired, and got, 'twas but a dream of thee.

And now good-morrow to our waking souls,
Which watch not one another out of fear;
For love, all love of other sights controls,
And makes one little room an everywhere.
Let sea-discoverers to new worlds have gone,
Let maps to other, worlds on worlds have shown,
Let us possess one world, each hath one, and is one.

My face in thine eye, thine in mine appears,
And true plain hearts do in the faces rest;
Where can we find two better hemispheres,
Without sharp north, without declining west?
Whatever dies, was not mixed equally;
If our two loves be one, or, thou and I
Love so alike, that none do slacken, none can die.

from *On the Indians Lately Discovered*

Francisco de Vitoria
Translated by John Pawley Bate

[What follows are the summary from the second section of the first set of arguments ("Reconsiderations"), along with the full discussion of the final nine articles (that is, articles 8 through 16) of that section. The author is Fray Francisco de Vitoria, a sixteenth-century Dominican priest and professor at the University of Salamanca in Spain.]

The passage to be discussed is from St. Matthew's Gospel: "Teach all nations, baptizing them in the name of the Father and Son and Holy Spirit," last chapter.

Summary of the Second Section

On the illegitimate titles for the reduction of the aborigines of the New World into the power of the Spaniards.

1. The Emperor is not the lord of the whole world.

2. Even if the Emperor were the lord of the world that would not entitle him to seize the provinces of the Indian aborigines and to erect new lords and put down the former lords or to levy taxes.

3. The Pope is not civil or temporal lord of the whole world, in the proper sense of civil lordship and power.

4. Even if the Supreme Pontiff had secular power over the world, he could not give that power to secular princes.

5. The Pope has temporal power, but only so far as it subserves things spiritual.

6. The Pope has no temporal power over the Indian aborigines or over other unbelievers.

7. A refusal by these aborigines to recognize any dominion of the Pope is no reason for making war on them and for seizing their goods.

8. Whether these aborigines were guilty of the sin of unbelief, in that they did not believe in Christ, before they heard anything of Christianity.

9. What is required in order that ignorance may be imputed to a person as, and be, sin, that is, vincible ignorance. And what about invincible ignorance?

10. Whether the aborigines are bound to hearken to the first messengers of Christianity so as to commit mortal sin in not believing Christ's Gospel merely on its simple announcement to them.

11. If the faith were simply announced and proposed to them and they will not straightway receive it, this is no ground for the Spaniards to make war on them or to proceed against them under the law of war.

12. How the aborigines, if they refuse when asked and counselled to hear peaceably preachers of religion, can not be excused from mortal sin.

13. When the aborigines would be bound to receive Christianity under penalty of mortal sin.

14. In the author's view it is not sufficiently dear whether Christianity has been so proposed and announced to these aborigines that they are bound to believe it under the penalty of fresh sin.

15. Even when Christianity has been proposed to them with never so much sufficiency of proof and they will not accept it, this does not render it lawful to make war on them and despoil them of their possessions.

16. Christian princes can not, even on the authority of the Pope, restrain these aborigines from sins against the law of nature or punish them therefor.

It being premised, then, that the Indian aborigines are or were true owners, it remains to inquire by what title the Spaniards could have come into possession of them and their country.

And first, I shall advert to the titles which might be alleged, but which are not adequate or legitimate.

[*Articles 1 through 7 are omitted here.*]

8. By way of answer let my first proposition be: Before the barbarians heard anything about Christianity, they did not commit the sin of unbelief by not believing in Christ. This proposition is precisely that of St. Thomas in *Secunda Secundae*, qu. 10, art. 1, where he says that in those who have not heard of Christ unbelief does not wear the guise of sin,

but rather of punishment, such ignorance of things divine being a consequence of the sin of our first parent. "Such unbelievers as these," says he, "are indeed open to condemnation for other sins, . . . but not for the sin of unbelief." Accordingly our Lord says (St. John, ch. 15): "If I had not come and spoken unto them, they had not had sin." St. Augustine, in his exposition of this passage, says it refers to the sin of unbelief in Christ. St. Thomas says the same (*Secunda Secundae*, qu. 10, art. 6, and qu. 34, art. 2, on obj. 2) . . .

The conclusion above stated is entirely in accord with St. Thomas's doctrine. The proof of it is as follows: Such as have never heard anything, however much they may be sinners in other respects, are under an invincible ignorance; therefore, their ignorance is not sin. The antecedent is evident from the passage (Romans, ch. 10): "How shall they believe in him of whom they have not heard, and how shall they hear without a preacher?" Therefore, if the faith has not been preached to them, their ignorance is invincible, for it was impossible for them to know. And what Paul condemns in unbelievers is not that they have not done what in them lies in order to receive illumination from God, but that they do not believe after they have heard. "Have they not heard?" says he, "Yes, verily, their sound went into all the earth." That is the ground of his condemnation, inasmuch as the Gospel has been preached over all the earth; he would not otherwise condemn them, whatever other sins they might have.

9. . . . For the aborigines to whom no preaching of the faith or Christian religion has come will be damned for mortal sins or for idolatry, but not for the sin of unbelief, as St. Thomas (*Secunda Secundae*, as above) says, namely, that if they do what in them lies, accompanied by a good life according to the law of nature, it is consistent with God's providence and He will illuminate them regarding the name of Christ, but it does not therefore follow that if their life be bad, ignorance or unbelief in baptism and the Christian faith may be imputed to them as a sin.

10. Second proposition: The Indians in question are not bound, directly the Christian faith is announced to them, to believe it, in such a way that they commit mortal sin by not believing it, merely because it has been declared and announced to them that Christianity is the true religion and that Christ is the Saviour and Redeemer of the world, without miracle or any other proof or persuasion. This proposition is proved by the first . . .

11. From this proposition it follows that, if the faith be presented to the Indians in the way named only and they do not receive it, the Spaniards

can not make this a reason for waging war on them or for proceeding against them under the law of war. This is manifest, because they are innocent in this respect and have done no wrong to the Spaniards. And this corollary receives confirmation from the fact that, as St. Thomas lays it down (*Secunda Secundae*, qu. 40, art. 1), for a just war "there must be a just cause, namely, they who are attacked for some fault must deserve the attack." Accordingly, St. Augustine says (Liber 83 *Quaestionum*): "It is involved in the definition of a just war that some wrong is being avenged, as where a people or state is to be punished for neglect to exact amends from its citizens for their wrongdoing or to restore what has been wrongfully taken away." Where, then, no wrong has previously been committed by the Indians, there is no cause of just war. This is the received opinion of all the doctors, not only of the theologians, but also of the jurists, such as Hostiensis, Innocent, and others. Cajetan (*Secunda Secundae*, qu. 66, art. 8) lays it down clearly and I know of no doctor whose opinion is to the contrary. Therefore this would not be a legitimate title to seize the lands of the aborigines or to despoil the former owners.

12. Third proposition: If the Indians, after being asked and admonished to hear the peaceful preachers of religion, refused, they would not be excused of mortal sin. The proof lies in the supposition that they have very grave errors for which they have no probable or demonstrable reasons. Therefore, if any one admonishes them to hear and deliberate upon religious matters, they are bound at least to hear and to enter into consultation. Further, it is needful for their salvation that they believe in Christ and be baptized (St. Mark, last ch.), "Whoso believeth," etc. But they can not believe unless they hear (Romans, ch. 10). Therefore they are bound to hear, otherwise if they are not bound to hear, they would, without their own fault, be outside the pale of salvation.

13. Fourth proposition: If the Christian faith be put before the aborigines with demonstration, that is, with demonstrable and reasonable arguments, and this be accompanied by an upright life, well-ordered according to the law of nature (an argument which weighs much in confirmation of the truth), and this be done not once only and perfunctorily, but diligently and zealously, the aborigines are bound to receive the faith of Christ under penalty of mortal sin. This is proved by our third proposition, for, if they are bound to hear, they are in consequence bound also to acquiesce in what they hear, if it be reasonable. This is abundantly clear from the passage (St. Mark, last ch.): "Go ye out into all the world, preach the Gospel to every

creature; whoso believeth and is baptized shall be saved, but whoso believeth not shall be damned"; and by the passage (Acts, ch. 4): "No other name is given unto man whereby we can be saved."

14. Fifth proposition: It is not sufficiently clear to me that the Christian faith has yet been so put before the aborigines and announced to them that they are bound to believe it or commit fresh sin. I say this because (as appears from my second proposition) they are not bound to believe unless the faith be put before them with persuasive demonstration. Now, I hear of no miracles or signs or religious patterns of life; nay, on the other hand, I hear of many scandals and cruel crimes and acts of impiety. Hence it does not appear that the Christian religion has been preached to them with such sufficient propriety and piety that they are bound to acquiesce in it, although many religious and other ecclesiastics seem both by their lives and example and their diligent preaching to have bestowed sufficient pains and industry in this business, had they not been hindered therein by others who had other matters in their charge.

15. Sixth proposition: Although the Christian faith may have been announced to the Indians with adequate demonstration and they have refused to receive it, yet this is not a reason which justifies making war on them and depriving them of their property. This conclusion is definitely stated by St. Thomas (*Secunda Secundae*, qu. 10, art. 8), where he says that unbelievers who have never received the faith, like Gentiles and Jews, are in no wise to be compelled to do so. This is the received conclusion of the doctors alike in the canon law and the civil law. The proof lies in the fact that belief is an operation of the will. Now, fear detracts greatly from the voluntary (*Ethics*, bk. 3), and it is a sacrilege to approach under the influence of servile fear as far as the mysteries and sacraments of Christ. Our conclusion is also proved by the canon de Judaeis (can. 5, Dist. 45), which says: "The holy synod also enjoins concerning the Jews that thenceforth force be not applied to any of them to make him believe; 'for God has compassion on whom He wills, and whom He wills He hardens.'" (Romans, ch. 9, v. 18) There is no doubt about the doctrine of the Council of Toledo, that threats and fears should not be employed against the Jews in order to make them receive the faith. And Gregory expressly says the same in the canon qui sincera (can. 3, Dist. 45): "Who with sincerity of purpose," says he, "desires to bring into the perfect faith those who are outside the Christian religion should labor in a manner that will attract and not with severity; . . . for whosoever does otherwise and under cover of the latter would turn them from their accustomed

worship and ritual is demonstrably furthering his own end thereby and not God's end."

Our proposition receives further proof from the use and custom of the Church. For never have Christian Emperors, who had as advisors the most holy and wise Pontiffs, made war on unbelievers for their refusal to accept the Christian religion. Further, war is no argument for the truth of the Christian faith. Therefore the Indians can not be induced by war to believe, but rather to feign belief and reception of the Christian faith, which is monstrous and a sacrilege. And although Scotus (Bk. 4, dist. 4, last qu.) calls it a religious act for princes to compel unbelievers by threats and fears to receive the faith, yet he seems to mean this to apply only to unbelievers who in other respects are subjects of Christian princes (with whom we will deal later on). Now, the Indians are not such subjects. Hence, I think that Scotus does not make this assertion applicable to their case. It is clear, then, that the title which we are now discussing is not adequate and lawful for the seizure of the lands of the aborigines.

Another, and a fifth, title is seriously put forward, namely, the sins of these Indian aborigines. For it is alleged that, though their unbelief or their rejection of the Christian faith is not a good reason for making war on them, yet they may be attacked for other mortal sins which (so it is said) they have in numbers, and those very heinous. A distinction is here drawn with regard to mortal sins, it being asserted that there are some sins, which are not against the law of nature, but only against positive divine law, and for these the aborigines can not be attacked in war, while there are other sins against nature, such as cannibalism, and promiscuous intercourse with mother or sisters and with males, and for these they can be attacked in war and so compelled to desist therefrom. The principle in each case is that, in the case of sins which are against positive law, it can not be clearly shown to the Indians that they are doing wrong, whereas in the case of the sins which are against the law of nature, it can be shown to them that they are offending God, and they may consequently be prevented from continuing to offend Him. Further they can be compelled to keep the law which they themselves profess. Now, this law is the law of nature. Therefore. This is the opinion of the Archbishop of Florence (pt. 3, tit. 22, ch. 5, § 8), following Augustinus Anconitanus, and of Sylvester (under the word Papa, § 7); and it is the opinion of Innocent in X, 3, 34, 8, where he expressly says: "I hold that if the Gentiles who have no other law than the law of nature break that law, they can be punished by the Pope. This is shown by the case of the men of Sodom, who were punished by God (Genesis, ch. 19). Now, the judgments of God are examples unto us, and so I do not see why the Pope, who is the vicar of Christ, can not do this." This is what Innocent said. And on the same principle the Indians can be punished by Christian princes under the authority of the Pope.

16. I, however, assert the following proposition: Christian princes can not, even by the authorization of the Pope, restrain the Indians from sins against the law of nature or punish them because of those sins. My first proof is that the writers in question build on a false hypothesis, namely, that the Pope has Jurisdiction over the Indian aborigines, as said above. My second proof is as follows: They mean to Justify such coercion either universally for sins against the law of nature, such as theft, fornication, and adultery, or particularly for sins against nature, such as those which St. Thomas deals with (*Secunda Secundae*, qu. 154, arts. 11, 12), the phrase "sin against nature" being employed not only of what is contrary to the law of nature, but also of what is against the natural order and is called uncleanness in II Corinthians, ch. 12, according to the commentators, such as intercourse with boys and with animals or intercourse of woman with woman, whereon see Romans, ch. 1. Now, if they limit themselves to the second meaning, they are open to the argument that homicide is just as grave a sin, and even a graver sin, and, therefore, it is clear that, if it is lawful in the case of the sins of the kind named, therefore it is lawful also in the case of homicide. Similarly, blasphemy is a sin as grave and so the same is clear; therefore. If, however, they are to be understood in the first sense, that is, as speaking of all sin against the law of nature, the argument against them is that the coercion in question is not lawful for fornication; therefore not for the other sins which are contrary to the law of nature. The antecedent is clear from I Corinthians, ch. 5: "I wrote to you in an epistle not to company with fornicators," and besides "If any brother among you is called a fornicator or an idolater," etc.; and lower down: "For what have I to do to judge them also that are without?" Whereon St. Thomas says: "The prelates have received power over those only who have submitted themselves to the faith." Hence it clearly appears that St. Paul declares it not his business to pronounce judgment on unbelievers and fornicators and idolaters. So also it is not every sin against the law of nature that can be clearly shown to be such, at any rate to every one.

Further, this is as much as to say that the aborigines may be warred into subjection because of their unbelief, for they are all idolaters. Further, the

Pope can not make war on Christians on the ground of their being for-nicators or thieves or, indeed, because they are sodomites; nor can he on that ground confiscate their land and give it to other princes; were that so, there would be daily changes of kingdoms, seeing that there are many sinners in every realm. And this is confirmed by the consideration that these sins are more heinous in Christians, who are aware that they are sins, than in barbarians, who have not that knowledge. Further, it would be a strange thing that the Pope, who can not make laws for unbelievers, can yet sit in judgment and visit punishment upon them.

A further and convincing proof is the following: The aborigines in ques-tion are either bound to submit to the punishment awarded to the sins in question or they are not. If they are not bound, then the Pope can not award such punishment. If they are bound, then they are bound to rec-ognize the Pope as lord and lawgiver. Therefore, if they refuse such recog-nition, this in itself furnishes a ground for making war on them, which, however, the writers in question deny, as said above. And it would indeed be strange that the barbarians could with impunity deny the authority and jurisdiction of the Pope, and yet that they should be bound to sub-mit to his award. Further, they who are not Christians can not be sub-jected to the judgment of the Pope, for the Pope has no other right to condemn or punish them than as vicar of Christ. But, the writers in ques-tion admit—both Innocent and Augustinus of Ancona, and the Archbishop and Sylvester, too—that they can not be punished because they do not receive Christ. Therefore not because they do not receive the judgment of the Pope, for the latter presupposes the former.

The insufficiency alike of this present title and of the preceding one, is shown by the fact that, even in the Old Testament, where much was done by force of arms, the people of Israel never seized the land of unbelievers either because they were unbelievers or idolaters or because they were guilty of other sins against nature (and there were people guilty of many such sins, in that they were idolaters and committed many other sins against nature, as by sacrificing their sons and daughters to devils), but because of either a special gift from God or because their enemies had hindered their passage or had attacked them. Further, what is it that the writers in question call a profession of the law of nature? If it is mere knowledge, they do not know it all; if it is a mere willingness to observe the law of nature, then the retort is that they are also willing to observe the whole divine law; for, if they knew that the law of Christ was divine, they would be willing to observe it. Therefore, they make no more a profession of the law of nature than they make of the law of Christ. Further, we certainly possess clearer proofs whereby to demonstrate that the law of Christ is From God and is true than to demonstrate that fornication is wrong or that other things which are also forbidden by natural law are to be shunned.

Therefore, if the Indians can be compelled to observe the law of nature because it admits of proof, they can therefore, be compelled to observe the Gospel law. There remains another, a sixth title, which is put forward, namely, by voluntary choice. For on the arrival of the Spaniards we find them declaring to the aborigines how the King of Spain has sent them for their good and admonishing them to receive and accept him as lord and king; and the aborigines replied that they were content to do so. Now, "there is nothing so natural as that the intent of an owner to transfer his property to another should have effect given to it" (Inst., 2, 1, 40). I, however, assert the proposition that this title, too, is insufficient. This appears, in the first place, because fear and ignorance, which vitiate every choice, ought to be absent. But they were markedly operative in the cases of choice and acceptance under consideration, for the Indians did not know what they were doing; nay, they may not have understood what the Spaniards were seeking. Further, we find the Spaniards seeking it in armed array from an unwarlike and timid crowd. Further, inasmuch as the aborigines, as said above, had real lords and princes, the populace could not procure new lords without other reasonable cause, this being to the hurt of their former lords. Further, on the other hand, these lords themselves could not appoint a new prince without the assent of the populace. Seeing, then, that in such cases of choice and acceptance as these there are not present all the requisite elements of a valid choice, the title under review is utterly inadequate and unlawful for seizing and retaining the provinces in question.

There is a seventh title which can be set up, namely, by special grant from God. For some (I know not who) assert that the Lord by His especial judgment condemned all the barbarians in question to perdition because of their abominations and delivered them into the hands of the Spaniards, Just as of old He delivered the Canaanites into the hands of the Jews. I am loath to dispute hereon at any length, for it would be hazardous to give credence to one who asserts a prophecy against the common law and against the rules of Scripture, unless his doctrine were confirmed by miracles. Now, no such are adduced by prophets of this type.

Further, even assuming that it is true that the Lord had determined to bring the barbarians to perdition, it would not follow, therefore, that he who wrought their ruin would be blameless, any more than the Kings of Babylon who led their army against Jerusalem and carried away the children of Israel into captivity were blameless, although in actual fact all of this was by the especial providence of God, as had often been foretold to them. Nor was Jeroboam right in drawing Israel away from Rehoboam, although this was done by God's design, as the Lord had also threatened by his prophet. And, would that, apart from the sin of unbelief, there might be no greater sins in morals among certain Christians than there are among those barbarians! It is also written (I St. John, ch. 4): "Believe not every spirit, but try the spirits whether they be of God;" and as St. Thomas says (*Prima Secundae*, qu. 68), "Gifts are given by the Holy Spirit for the perfecting of virtues." Accordingly, where faith or authority or providence shows what ought to be done, recourse should not be had to gifts.

Let this suffice about false and inadequate titles to seize the lands of the Indians. But it is to be noted that I have seen nothing written on this question and have never been present at any discussion or council on this matter. Hence it may be that others may found a title and base the justice of this business and overlordship on some of the passages cited and not lack reason in so doing. I, however, have up to now been unable to form any other opinion than what I have written. And so, if there be no other titles than those which I have discussed, it would certainly be of ill omen for the safety of our princes, or rather of those who are charged with the discovery of these matters; for princes follow advice given by others, being unable to examine into these matters for themselves. "What is a man advantaged" so saith the Lord, "if he gain the whole world and lose himself, or be cast away?" (St. Matthew, ch. 16; St. Mark, ch. 8; St. Luke, ch. 9)

from *The Heptameron*

Marguerite d'Angoulême, Queen of Navarre
Translated by Walter K. Kelly

From the Introduction

*On the 1st of September, when the baths of the Pyrenees begin to have effi-
cacy, several persons from France, Spain and other countries were assembled at those
of Cauterets, some to drink the waters, some to bathe in them, and others to be
treated with mud; remedies so marvelous, that patients given over by physicians go
home cured from Cauterets. My intention is not to speak to you either of the situation or the virtue of the baths; but only to recount what is pertinent to the matter
I am about to write. The patients remained at these baths until they found themselves sufficiently improved in health; but then, as they were preparing to return
home, there fell such excessive and extraordinary rains, that it seemed as though
God had forgotten his promise to Noah that he would never again destroy the world
with water.*

• • •

Editorial Notes:

The Heptameron tells the story (and stories) of ten French travelers per-
ilously returning from the baths, who are stranded at a monastery during the
flood. The characters include:

- **Oisille**: a pious, aged widow, who puts trust in her faith to survive
  the flooded roads, but loses most of her servants and horses
- **Hircan** and **Parlemente**: a married couple, attacked by bandits en
  route home
- **Longarine**: a young wife, made a widow by that same bandit attack
- **Dagoucin** and **Saffredent**: two gentlemen, who save the persons
  above from the bandits, whom they have been following at a distance as admirers of the two wives

- **Ennasuite** and **Nomerfide**: young ladies, whose entourage has been killed by bears
- **Geburon**: a companion of Hircan, who joins the party at mass in only his night shirt, having been forced to flee his bed by a group of attackers
- **Simontault**: a knight, who is in love with Parlemente

At the news that the party was to be stranded for ten to twelve days, Oisille suggests they use the time reading the Holy Scriptures. Hircan objects that they are not so morally in peril as to require a full day of religious observation, and offers a compromise of reading the Bible in the morning, but spending the afternoons dedicated to "some pastime which may be agreeable to the body and not prejudicial to the soul." His wife, Parlemente, is embarrassed by the sexual innuendo that followed and instead suggests that they emulate the work of Boccaccio's *Decameron*, which had recently been translated into French and praised by their king, Francis I (Marguerite de Navarre's brother). Thus, each of the ten characters is tasked with offering one story per day for ten days. [*Only seventy-two of the proposed one hundred tales were completed in Marguerite's lifetime; most were probably composed in the 1540s.*] The stories roughly follow daily themes [*see "Contents" below*], but are often taken in different directions by the narrators in response to previous stories or according to their own interests. The only rule is that they should tell the stories gracefully but without allowing art, scholastic learning, or the "flowers of rhetoric" to prejudice against the "truth of history." Generally, the stories are intended to prompt reflection and discussion from the group about the social and moral values and practices of men and women in the mid-sixteenth century.

• • •

Contents

Day One: *Bad Turns Done by Women to Men and Vice Versa* (Novels I–X)

Day Two: *The First Striking Thing that Comes to Mind* (Novels XI–XX)

Day Three: *Honorable Ladies and Hypocritical Monks* (Novels XXI–XXX)

Day Four: *Patient Women and Prudent Men, in Wooing and Marriage* (Novels XXXI–XL)

Day Five: *Virtuous, Wanton, and Simpleminded Women* (Novels XLI–L)

Day Six: *Deceits Practiced by Men and Women* (Novels LI–LX)

Day Seven: *People Who Have Done What They Least Desired* (Novels LXI–LXX)
Day Eight: *Cases of Lechery* (Novels LXXI–LXXII)

• • •

From the First Day

As soon as the morning broke they all went to the chamber of Madame Oisille, whom they found already at prayers. She read to them for a good hour, after which they heard mass, and at ten o'clock they went to dinner. Every one then retired to his own chamber, and attended to what he had to do. At noon all were punctually assembled in the meadow, which was so beautiful and agreeable, that it would need a Boccaccio to depict all its charms: enough for us to say that there never was its like.

The company being seated on the green turf, so soft and delicate that no one had need of floor or carpet, "Which of us," said Simontault, "shall have the command over the rest?"

"Since you have been the first to speak," said Hircan, "it is right you should have the command; for in sport all are equals."

"God knows," replied Simontault, "I could desire nothing better in the world than to command such a company."

Parlamente, who knew very well what that meant, began to cough, so that Hircan did not perceive she had changed color, and told Simontault to begin his tale, for all were ready to hear him. The same request being urged by the whole company, Simontault said: "I have been so ill-requited for my long services, ladies, that to revenge myself on love and on the fair one who treats me with so much cruelty, I am about to make a collection of misdeeds done by women to men, in the whole of which I will relate nothing but the simple truth." . . .

"It seems to me, ladies, that the last speaker has cast such a slur upon our sex by the true story he has narrated of a wretched woman, that I must run back through all the past years of my life in order to call to my mind one woman whose virtue was such as to belie the bad opinion he has of our sex. . . .

The ladies were so touched by the sad and glorious death of the muleteer's wife, that there was not one of them but shed tears, and promised herself that she would strive to follow such an example should fortune expose her to a similar trial. At last, Madame Oisille, seeing they were losing time in praising the dead woman, said to Saffredent, "If you do not say something to make the company laugh, no one will forgive me for the fault I have committed in making them weep." Saffredent, who was really desirous to say something good and agreeable to the company, and especially to one of the ladies, replied that this honor was not due to him, and that there were others who were older and more capable than himself who ought to speak before him. "But since you will have it so," he said, "the best thing I can do is to despatch the matter at once, for the more good speakers precede me, the more difficult will my task be when my turn comes."

NOVEL III.

A King of Naples, having debauched the wife of a Gentleman, at last wears horns himself.

As I have often wished I had shared the good fortune of one about whom I am going to tell you a tale, I must inform you that in the time of King Alfonso, the scepter of whose realm was lasciviousness, there was at Naples a handsome, agreeable gentleman, in whom nature and education had combined so many perfections, that an old gentleman gave him his daughter, who for beauty and engaging qualities was in no respects inferior to her husband. Great was their mutual love during the first months of their marriage; but the carnival being come, and the king going masked into the houses, where every one did his best to receive him well, he came to this gentleman's, where he met with a better reception than anywhere else. Confections, music, concerts, and other amusements were not forgotten; but what pleased the king most was the wife, the finest woman, to his thinking, he had ever seen. After the repast she sang with her husband, and that so pleasingly, that she seemed still more beautiful. The king, seeing so many perfections in one person, took much less pleasure in the sweet harmony of the husband and wife than in thinking how he might break it. Their mutual affection appeared to him a great obstacle to his design; therefore he concealed his passion as well as he could; but to solace it in some manner, he frequently entertained the lords and ladies of Naples, and did not forget the husband and his wife.

As one readily believes what one desires, the king thought that the lady's eyes promised him something agreeable, if only those of the husband were not in the way. To put his conjecture to the proof, he sent the husband to Rome with a commission which would occupy him a fortnight or three weeks. When he was gone, his wife, who never before had lost sight of him, so to speak, was in the deepest affliction. The king went to see her frequently, and did his best to console her by obliging words and presents. In a word, he played his part so well, that she was not only consoled, but even very well pleased with her husband's absence. Before the end of three weeks she was so much in love with the king, that she was quite as distressed at her husband's return as she had been at his departure. That she might not be deprived of the king's presence, it was settled between them, that whenever the husband went to the country she should give notice to the king, who then might come to see her in perfect security, and so secretly, that her honor, which she respected more than her conscience, should not be hurt; a hope which the fair lady dwelt on with great pleasure.

The husband, on his return, was so well received by his wife, that even had he been told that the king fondled her during his absence, he never could have believed it. But in course of time this fire, which such pains were taken to conceal, began gradually to make itself visible, and became at last so glaring, that the husband, justly alarmed, set himself to observe, and with such effect, that he had scarcely any room left for doubt. But as he was afraid that he who wronged him would do him a still worse mischief if he made any noise about the matter, he resolved to dissemble, thinking it better to live with grief at his heart, than to expose his life for a woman who did not love him. Nevertheless, he longed, in the bitterness of his resentment, to retaliate on the king, if it were possible; and as he knew that spite will make a woman do more than love, especially such as are of a great and honorable spirit, he took the liberty one day to say to the queen how grieved he was that the king her husband treated her with indifference. The queen, who had heard of the king's amour with his wife, replied that she could not have honor and pleasure both together. "I know well," she added, "that I have the honor whereof another receives the pleasure; but then she who has the pleasure has not the same honor as is mine."

Well knowing to whom these words applied, the gentleman responded, "Honor is born with you, madam. You are of so good a lineage, that the rank of queen or empress could add nothing to your nobility; but your beauty, your graces, and your winning deportment, merit so much pleasure, that she who robs you of that which is your due does more harm to herself than to you, since for a glory which turns to shame she loses as much pleasure as you or any woman in the kingdom could enjoy. And I can tell you, madam, that the king, the crown apart, is not more capable than I of contenting a woman. Far from it, I am certain that to satisfy a woman of your merit the king ought to wish that he was of my temperament."

"Though the king is of a more delicate complexion than you," replied the queen, laughing, "the love he has for me gratifies me so much, that I prefer it to any other thing."

"If that be so, madam," returned the gentleman, "I no longer pity you. I know that if the king had for you a love as pure as that you have for him, you would literally enjoy the gratification you speak of; but God has determined that it should be otherwise, in order that, not finding in him what you desire, you should not make him your god on earth."

"I own to you," said the queen, "that the love I have for him is so great, that no heart can love with such passion as mine."

"Allow me, if you please, to tell you, madam, that you have not fathomed the love in every heart. I dare assure you, madam, that there is one who loves you with a love so perfect and impassioned, that what you feel for the king cannot be compared with it. His love grows stronger as that of the king grows weaker, and it only rests with yourself, madam, if you think proper, to be more than compensated for all you lose."

By this time the queen began to perceive, both from the gentleman's words and his manner, that his tongue was the interpreter of his heart. She now recollected that for a long time past he had been seeking opportunities to do her service, and seeking them with such eagerness that he had become quite melancholy. At first she had supposed that his wife was the cause of his sadness; but now she made no doubt that it was all on her own account. As love never fails to make itself felt when it is real, the queen had no difficulty in unriddling what was a secret for every one else. The gentleman, therefore, appearing to her more amiable than her husband, considering, besides, that he was forsaken by his wife, as she was by her husband, and animated with resentment and jealousy against her husband, "My God!" she exclaimed with a sigh, and with tears in her eyes, "must it be that vengeance shall effect upon me what love has never been able to effect?"

"Vengeance is sweet, madam," observed the now hopeful suitor, "when, instead of killing one's enemy, one bestows life on a real friend. It is high time, methinks, that the truth should cure you of an unreasonable love you entertain for a person who has none for you and that a just and well-founded love should expel the fear which is very ill-lodged in a heart so great and so virtuous as yours. Let us put out of consideration, madam, your royal quality, and let us contemplate the fact that you and I, of all persons in the world, are the two who are most basely duped and betrayed by those whom we have most perfectly loved. Let us avenge ourselves, madam, not so much for sake of retaliation as for the satisfaction of love, which on my side is such that I could not bear more and live. If your heart is not harder than adamant, you must feel some spark of that fire which augments in proportion as I labor to conceal it, and if pity for me, who am dying for love of you, does not incite you to love me, at least you should do so out of resentment. Your merit is so great, that it is worthy of the love of every honest heart; yet you are despised and abandoned by him for whom you have abandoned all others."

These words caused the queen such violent transports, that in order to conceal the commotion of her spirits, she took the gentleman's arm, and went with him into a garden adjoining her chamber, where she walked up and down a long while without being able to speak a single word to him. But the gentleman, seeing her half-conquered, no sooner reached the end of an alley where no one could see them, than he plied her to good purpose with his long-concealed passion. Being both of one mind, they revenged themselves together; and it was arranged between them that whenever the king went to visit the gentleman's wife, the gentleman should visit the queen. Thus, the cheaters being cheated, four would share the pleasure which two imagined they had all to themselves. When all was over, the queen retired to her chamber, and the gentleman went home, both of them so well contented, that they thought no more of their past vexations. The gentleman, far from dreading lest the king should visit his wife, on the contrary desired nothing better; and to afford him opportunity for doing so, he went to the country oftener than he had been used. When the king knew that the gentleman was at his village, which was but half a league from the city, he went at once to the fair lady; whilst the gentleman repaired by night to the queen's chamber, where he did duty as the king's lieutenant so secretly that no one ever perceived it.

Things went on in this way for a long while; but whatever pains the king took to conceal his amour, all the world was aware of it. The gentleman was much pitied by all good-natured people, and ridiculed by the ill-natured, who used to make horns at him behind his back. He knew very well that they did so, and he laughed in his sleeve, for he thought his horns were as good as the king's crown. One day when the royal-gallant was at the gentleman's, casting his eyes on a pair of antlers hung up in the hall, he could not help saying, with a laugh, in presence of the master of the house himself, "These antlers very well become this place." The gentleman, who had as much spirit as the king, had this inscription put up beneath the antlers after the king was gone:

Io porto le corna, ciascun lo vede;
Ma tal le porta, chi no lo crede.

I wear the horns as all men know;
He wears them too who thinks not so.

On his next visit the king observed this inscription, and asked the meaning of it. "If the stag," replied the gentleman, "does not know the king's secret, it is not just that the king should know the stag's secret. Be satisfied with knowing, sire, that it is not every one who wears horns who has his cap lifted off his head by them; some horns are so soft that a man may wear them without knowing it."

It was plain to the king from this reply that the gentleman knew something of his own affair, but he never suspected either him or the queen. That princess played her part extremely well; for the more pleased she was with her husband's conduct, the more she pretended to be dissatisfied. So they lived as good friends on both sides until old age put an end to their mutual pleasures.

This, ladies, is a story which I have great pleasure in proposing to you by way of example, to the end that when your husbands give you horns you may do the same by them.[1]

"I am very well assured, Saffredent," said Ennasuite, laughing, "that if you were as much in love as you have formerly been, you would endure horns as big as oaks for the sake of bestowing a pair as you pleased; but now that your hair is beginning to turn gray, it is time to put a truce to your desires."

"Though she whom I love, mademoiselle, allows me no hope," replied Saffredent, "and age has exhausted my vigour, my desires remain still in full force. But since you reproach me with so seemly a passion, you will, if you, please, relate to us the fourth novel; and we shall see if you can find some example which may refute me."

One of the ladies present, who knew that she who had taken Saffredent's words to herself was not the person he loved so much as to be willing to wears horns of her making, could not help laughing at the manner in which she had taken them up. Saffredent, who perceived that the laughing lady had guessed right, was very glad of it, and let Ennasuite talk on. "To prove, ladies," she said, "to Saffredent and all the company that all women are not like the queen of whom he has told us, and that the audacious are not always successful, I will relate to you the adventure of a lady who deemed that the vexation of failing in love was harder to bear than death itself. I shall not name the persons, because the story is so recent that I should be afraid of offending some of the near relations if I did so."

• • •

From the Third Day:

Early as it was next morning when the company assembled in the refectory, they found Madame Oisille already there. She had been meditating for half an hour on what she was to read to them; and so intent were they on listening to her that they did not hear the bell, and a monk had to come and tell them that high mass was about to begin. After hearing mass and dining soberly, in order to have their memories more clear, they all retired to their chambers to review their several repertories of tales previously to the next meeting in the meadow. Those who had some droll story to tell were already so merry, that one could not look in their faces without being prepared beforehand for a hearty laugh. When all were seated, they asked Saffredent to whom he addressed his call. "The fault I committed yesterday," he said, "being as you say so great, and knowing not how to repair it, I call on Parlamente. Her excellent sense will enable her to praise the ladies in such a manner as will make you forget the truth I have told you."

"I do not undertake to repair your faults," replied Parlamente; "but I will take good care not to imitate them. To this end, without departing from the truth we have pledged ourselves to speak, I will show you that there are ladies who in their love have had no other end in view than virtue and honor. As the lady of whom I have to speak is of a good family, I will change nothing in her story but the names. You will see, ladies, from what I am going to narrate, that love can make no change in a chaste and virtuous heart."

NOVEL XXI.

Virtuous love of a young lady of quality and a bastard of an illustrious house—hindrance of their marriage by a queen—Sage reply of the demoiselle to the queen—Her subsequent marriage.

There was a queen in France who had in her household several young ladies of good birth, and among the rest, one named Rolandine, who was her near relation. But the queen being displeased with this young lady's father, punished the innocent for the guilty, and behaved not very well to Rolandine. Though this young lady was neither a great beauty nor the reverse, such was the propriety of her demeanor and the sweetness of her disposition, that many great lords sought her in marriage, but obtained no reply, for Rolandine's father was so fond of his money that he neglected the establishment of his daughter. On the other hand, she was so little in favor of her mistress, that she was not wooed by those who wished to ingratiate themselves with the queen. Thus, through the negligence of her father and the disdain of her mistress, this poor young lady remained long unmarried. At last she took this sorely to heart, not so much from eagerness to be married, as from shame at not being so. Her grief reached such a pitch that she forsook the pomp and mundane pursuits of the court to occupy herself only with prayer and some little handiworks. In this tranquil manner she passed her youth, leading the most blameless and devout of lives.

When she was approaching her thirtieth year, she became acquainted with a gentleman, a bastard of an illustrious house, and one of the best-bred men of his day, but ill endowed by fortune, and of so little comeliness that no one but herself would have readily chosen him for a lover. As this poor gentleman had remained solitary like herself, and as the unfortunate naturally seek each other's society, he one day accosted Rolandine. There being a strong similitude between them in point of temperament and fortune, they poured their griefs into each other's ears, and that was the beginning of a very intimate friendship between them. Seeing that they both labored under the same misfortune, they everywhere sought each other out for mutual consolation, and thus they became more and more attached to each other to an extraordinary degree. Those who had known Rolandine so coy that she would hardly speak to any one, were shocked to see her every moment with the bastard, and told her gouvernante that she ought not to permit such long conversations. The gouvernante spoke to Rolandine on the subject, telling her that it was taken amiss that she should be on such familiar terms with a man who was neither rich enough to marry her, nor good-looking enough to be loved. Rolandine, who had hitherto been reproved for her austerity, rather than for her mundane ways, replied, "You see, mother, that I cannot have a husband of my own quality. I have hitherto always attached myself to the young and good-looking; but as I am afraid of falling into the pit into which I have seen so many fall, I now attach myself to this gentleman, who, as you know, is so correct and so virtuous that he never talks to me but of seemly things. What harm, then, do I do to you, and to those who make a talk about it, consoling my sorrows by means of an innocent converse?"

The poor woman, who loved her mistress more than herself, made answer, "I see plainly, mademoiselle, that you are right, and that your father and your mistress do not treat you as you deserve. But since this acquaintance gives rise to remarks which are not to the advantage of your honor, you ought to break it off, though the man were your own brother."

"I will do so, since such is your advice," replied Rolandine, weeping, "but it is very hard to have no consolation in the world."

The bastard came to see her as usual, but, with tears in her eyes, she related to him in detail all that her gouvernante had said to her, and begged him not to visit her any more until this tattle should have subsided; and he complied with her entreaty. Both of them having lost their consolation through this separation, they began to feel an uneasiness such as neither had ever before experienced. Her whole time was spent in prayer, fasting, and journeying; for the sentiment of love, so totally new to her, caused her such agitation that she did not know a moment's rest. The bastard was not in a much better plight; but as he had made up his mind to love her and try to obtain her for a wife, and saw that it would be a very glorious thing for him to succeed in the attempt, his only thought was how he should press his suit, and how he should secure the gouvernante in his interest. To this end he represented to her the deplorable condition of her mistress, who was wilfully deprived of all consolation. The good woman thanked him with tears for the interest he took in her mistress's welfare, and cast about with him for means to enable him to have an interview with her. It was arranged between them that Rolandine should pretend to be troubled with a headache, which made all noise insupportable to her; and that when her companions left her in her chamber, the bastard and she might remain alone, and converse together without restraint. The bastard, delighted with the expedient, gave himself up entirely to the guidance of the gouvernante, and in this way he was enabled to talk with his mistress whenever he pleased.

But this pleasure was not of long duration; for the queen, who disliked Rolandine, asked what she was doing in her chamber. Some one replied that she had a headache; but somebody else; either disliking her absence or wishing to cause her annoyance, said that the pleasure she took in conversing with the bastard would be sure to cure her headache. The queen, who regarded as mortal sins in Rolandine what would have been venial sins in others, sent for her, and forbade her ever to speak to the bastard, except in her own chamber or hall. Rolandine professed obedience, and replied, that had she known that the bastard, or any one else, was displeasing to her majesty, she would never have spoken to him. At the same time she was inwardly resolved to find out some other expedient, of which the queen should know nothing. As she fasted on Wednesdays, Fridays, and Saturdays, and did not quit her chamber, she took care to be visited on those days by the bastard, whom she was beginning to love greatly, and had time to talk with him in presence of her gouvernante whilst the others were at supper. The less time they had at their disposal, the more fervid and impassioned was their language; for they stole the time for mutual conversation, as the thief steals something precious. But there is no secret which is not found out at last. A varlet, having seen the bastard come in one day, mentioned it in a place where it failed not to be repeated, till it reached the ears of the queen, who put herself into such a towering passion, that the bastard never afterwards durst enter the chamber of the demoiselles. He often pretended to go a journey, in order to have opportunity to see the object of his affections, and every evening he used to return to the chapel of the château, dressed sometimes as a Cordelier, sometimes as a Jacobin, and always so well disguised that no one knew him except Rolandine and her gouvernante, who failed not at once to accost the good father.

The bastard, feeling assured that Rolandine loved him, did not scruple to say to her one day, "You see, mademoiselle, to what I expose myself for your service, and how the queen has forbidden you to speak to me. You see, too, that nothing is further from your father's thoughts than disposing of you in marriage. He has refused so many good offers, that I know no one far or near who can have you. I know that I am poor, and that you could not marry a gentleman who was not richer than myself; but if to have a great deal of love were to be rich, I should think myself the most opulent man in the world. God has given you great wealth, and the expectation of still greater. If I were so happy as to be chosen by you for your husband, I would be all my life your spouse, your friend, and your servant. If you marry one who is your own equal—and such a one, I think, will not easily be found—he will insist on being the master, and will have more regard to your wealth than to your person, to beauty than to virtue; he will enjoy your wealth, and will not treat you as you deserve. My longing to enjoy this contentment, and my fear that you will have none with another, oblige me to entreat that you will make me happy, and yourself the best-satisfied and best-treated wife in the world."

Rolandine, hearing from her lover's lips the declaration she had made up her mind to address to him, replied with a glad face, "I rejoice that you have anticipated me, and have said to me what I have long resolved to say to you. Ever since I have known you, now two years, not a moment has passed in which I have not thought over all the arguments that could be adduced in your favor and against you; but at last, having resolved to engage in matrimony, it is time that I should make a beginning, and choose the man with whom I think I can pass my life with most quiet and satisfaction. I have had as suitors men of good figure, wealthy and of high birth; but you are the only one with whom it seems to me that my heart and mind can best agree. I know that in marrying you I do not offend God, but that, on the contrary, I do what he commands. As for my father, he has so much neglected the duty of establishing me, and has rejected so many opportunities, that the law empowers me to marry without his having a right to disinherit me; but even should I have nothing but what belongs to myself, I shall esteem myself the happiest woman in the world in having such a husband as you. As for the queen my mistress, I need make no scruple of disobeying her to obey God, since she has not scrupled to frustrate all the advantages that offered themselves to me during my youth. But to prove to you that my love for you is founded on honor and virtue, I require your promise, that in case I consent to the marriage you propose, you will not ask to consummate it until after the death of my father, or until I shall have found means to obtain his consent."

The bastard having promised this with alacrity, they gave each other a ring in pledge of marriage, and exchanged kisses in the church before God, whom they called to witness their mutual promise; and never afterwards was there anything between them of a more intimate nature than kisses. This slight satisfaction quite contented these two perfect lovers, who were a long time without seeing each other, or ever giving way to mutual suspicion. There was hardly a place where honor was to be acquired to which the bastard did not repair, being assured that he could never be poor, since God had bestowed on him a rich wife; and she during his absence so faithfully preserved that perfect affection for him, that she made no account of any other man. There were some who sought her in marriage, and had for answer, that having been so long unmarried, she was resolved to remain so for ever. This reply obtained such publicity that it reached the ears of the queen, who asked her the reason of such language. Rolandine replied that it was dictated by obedience; that she well knew her majesty had never chosen to marry her when very advantageous matches had offered; and that age and patience had taught her to be content with her present condition. Whenever marriage was mentioned to her, she always replied to the same effect.

The war being ended, and the bastard having returned to court, she did not speak to him before others, but always in the church under pretext of confession, for the queen had forbidden both of them, on pain of their lives, ever to converse except in public. But virtuous love, which fears no prohibitions, was more ingenious in suggesting to them means and opportunity to meet and converse than their enemies in hindering them. There was no monastic habit which the bastard did not successively assume; and by that means their intercourse was always agreeably maintained, until the king went to one of his country seats near Tours, which was so situated that the ladies could not go on foot to any other church than that of the château, which had such an exposed confessional, that the confessor would have easily been recognized. But as often as one opportunity failed them, love furnished them with another. At that very time there came to the court a lady nearly related to the bastard. She and her son were lodged in the king's residence; and the young prince had a projecting chamber, detached as it were from the king's apartments, and so placed, that from his window one could see and speak to Rolandine, their windows being exactly at the angle of the main building and the wing. The chamber which was over the king's hall was that of Rolandine and the other ladies of honor. Rolandine having frequently seen the young prince at the window, sent word of the fact by her gouvernante to the bastard. The latter having reconnoitered the ground, pretended to take great pleasure in reading the book of the Knights of the Round Table, which was one of those belonging to the prince; and towards dinner-hour he used to beg a valet de chambre to let him in, and leave him shut up in the chamber to finish reading his book. The valet, knowing him to be his master's relation, and a gentleman to be trusted, let him read as much as he pleased. Rolandine, on her part, used to come to her window, and in order to be free to remain there the longer, she pretended to have a sore leg; and she took her meals so early that she had no need to go to the table of the ladies of honor. She also bethought her of working at a crimson silk coverlet, which she hung at the window where she was very glad to be left alone to converse with her husband, who spoke in such a manner that no one could overhear them. When she saw any one coming she coughed and made signs to the bastard to retire. Those who had orders to watch them were persuaded that there was no love between them, for she never quitted a chamber in which he certainly could not see her, the entrée being forbidden him.

The mother of the young prince being one day in her son's chamber, placed herself at the window where lay the big book. Presently one of Rolandine's companions in office, who was at the window of their chamber, saluted the lady. The latter asked her how Rolandine was. The other replied that she should see her if she pleased, and made her come to the window in her nightcap. After some conversation about Rolandine's illness, both parties retired. The lady, casting her eyes on the big book of the Round Table, said to the valet de chambre who had charge of it, "I am astonished that young people give up their time to reading such follies." The valet de chambre replied that he was still more surprised that persons of ripe years, and who passed for sensible people, were more attached to them than the young; and thereupon he told her, as a curious fact, how the bastard, her relation, spent four or five hours every day in reading that book. The lady at once guessed the reason, and ordered the valet de chambre to conceal himself, and watch narrowly what the bastard did. The valet de chambre executed his commission, and found that, instead of reading, the bastard planted himself at the window, and that Rolandine came and talked with him. He even overheard many expressions of their love, which they thought they had so well concealed. Next day, the valet having told his mistress what he had seen and heard, she sent for her cousin, the bastard, and after some sharp remonstrances, forbade him ever more to place himself at that window. In the evening she spoke to Rolandine, and threatened she would inform the queen if she persisted in that foolish attachment. Rolandine, without losing her presence of mind, replied, that whatever the lady might have been told, she had not spoken to the bastard since she had been prohibited from doing so by her mistress, as her companions, and her servants, could witness. As for the window of which the lady spoke, she had never talked there with the bastard.

The lover now fearing lest his intrigue should be exposed, withdrew from the danger, and absented himself for a long time from court, but not without writing to Rolandine, which he managed to do with such address, that, in spite of all the queen could do, Rolandine heard from him twice a week. In the first instance he employed a monk to convey his letters; but this means failing, he sent a little page, dressed sometimes in one color, sometimes in another. The page used to post himself at the places through which the ladies passed, and, mingling with the other servants, found means always to deliver his letters to Rolandine. The queen going into the country, one of those persons whom she had charged to be on the watch regarding this affair recognized the page, and ran after him; but the page, who was a cunning lad, darted into the house of a poor woman, who was boiling her pot, and instantly thrust his letters into the fire. The gentleman who pursued him having caught and stripped him naked, searched him all over, but, finding nothing, let him go. When the page was gone, the good woman asked the gentleman why he had searched the poor boy in that manner. He replied, that it was because he believed the boy had letters about him. "You were not likely to find them," she said; "he had hidden them too well." "Where, pray?" inquired the gentleman who now made sure of having them. He was quite confounded when he heard that they were burnt, and saw that the page had been too clever for him. However, he went at once, and told the queen what he had ascertained.

The bastard not being able to employ the page any more, sent in his stead an old domestic, who, without caring for the threats of death which he well knew the queen had proclaimed against all who should meddle in this affair, undertook to convey the letters to Rolandine. Having entered the château, he stationed himself at a door which was at the foot of a great staircase used by all the ladies; but a valet, who had formerly known him, recognized him at once, and denounced him to the queen's maître d'hôtel, who gave orders for his instant arrest. The wary servant, seeing that he was watched, turned to the wall, under a certain pretence, tore his letters into the smallest possible pieces, and threw them behind the door. Immediately afterwards he was arrested and searched, but nothing being found on him, he was interrogated upon oath as to whether he had not carried letters. Nothing was left untried in the way of promises or threats to make him confess the truth, but, in spite of all they could do, they could never get anything out of him. This unsatisfactory result was reported to the queen; but some one having thought of looking behind the door, found there the fragments of the letters. The king's confessor was sent for; and having arranged all the pieces on a table, he read the whole of the letter, in which the secret marriage was plainly revealed, for the bastard called Rolandine his wife. The queen, who was not of a humor to conceal her neighbor's fault, made a great noise about the matter; and insisted on every means being employed to make the man confess the truth respecting the letter, the identity of which he could not deny; but say to him or show him what they would, there was no possibility of making him avow anything. Those who had been commissioned in this matter took him to the edge of the river, and put him into a sack, telling him that he lied to God and the queen, contrary to the proved truth. Choosing rather to die than to betray his master, he asked for a confessor, and after having set his conscience right, he said to them, "I pray you, Sir, to tell the bastard my master, that I commend to him my wife and my children, and that I die with a good heart for his service. Do with me what you please and be assured that you will never extract anything from me to my master's disadvantage." Then, to frighten him more, they threw him into the water, shut up as he was in the sack, and shouted to him that his life should be saved if he would speak the truth; but seeing that he made no reply, they took him out of the water, and reported his firm behavior to the queen. "Neither the king nor myself," said her majesty, "is so fortunate in servants as the bastard, who has not wherewithal to reward them." She did all she could to engage the worthy fellow in her service, but he would never quit his master, until the latter permitted him to enter the service of the queen; in which he lived happy and contented.

Having discovered the secret marriage by means of the intercepted letter, the queen sent for Rolandine, and with great violence of manner called her several times wretch instead of cousin, upbraiding her with the dishonor she had done to her house, and to her who was her mistress, in having thus married without her consent. Rolandine, who was long aware of the little kindness the queen entertained for her, fully returned that feeling. As there was no love between them, fear no longer availed; and as Rolandine saw plainly that a reprimand so publicly given was prompted less by regard for her than by the wish to put her to shame, and that the queen was more pleased in mortifying her than grieved to find her in fault, she replied with an air as calm and composed as that of the queen was agitated and passionate, "If you did not know your own heart, madam, I would set before you the bad feeling you have long entertained towards my father and me; but you know it so well, that you will not be surprised to hear that it is not a secret for anybody. For my part, madam, I have seen and felt it to my cost. If you had been as kind to me as to those who are not so nearly related to you, I should now be married in a manner that would do honor both to you and to me; but you have forsaken me, and not shown me the least mark of favor, so that I have missed all the good offers I have had through my father's negligence and the little account you have made of me. This unkind treatment threw me into such despair, that if my health had been strong enough to endure the austerities of a convent, I would gladly have entered one to escape from the continual vexations which your harshness caused me. In the midst of this despondency I became acquainted with one who would be of as good a house as myself, if the love of two persons was as much esteemed as the matrimonial ring; for you know that his father would take precedence of mine. He has long loved and cheered me; but you, madam, who have never forgiven me the least fault, or praised any good act I may have done, though you knew by experience that it was not my wont to talk of love and mundane vanities, and that I lived a more religious life than any other of your servants, you have not hesitated from the first to take offence at my speaking to a gentleman as unfortunate as myself, and in whose friendship I sought nothing else than consolation of mind. When I saw that I was entirely deprived of this, my despair was so great that I resolved to seek my repose with as much solicitude as you took to deprive me of it. From that very hour we interchanged promises of marriage which were sealed with a ring. It seems to me, then, madam, that you wrong me in calling me wicked. The great and perfect friendship which subsists between the bastard and myself would have given me occasion to do wrong if I had been so disposed, yet we have never gone further than kissing, it being my conviction that God would do me the grace to obtain my father's consent before the consummation of our marriage. I have done nothing against God or against my conscience. I have waited till the age of thirty to see what you and my father would do for me; and my youth has been passed in such chastity and virtue that no one in the world can justly cast the least reproach upon me in that respect. Finding myself on the decline, and without the hope of obtaining a husband of my own rank, reason determined me to take one according to my taste, not for the lust of the eyes, for, as you know, he whom I have chosen is not comely; nor yet for that of the flesh, since there has been no consummation; nor for the pride and ambition of this life, for he is poor, and of little preferment; but I have had regard purely and simply to the virtue and good qualities he possesses, as to which all the world is constrained to do him justice, and to the great love he has for me, which affords me the hope of enjoying quiet and contentment with him. After having maturely considered the good and the evil which might result to me, I took the course which appeared to me the best, and finally resolved, after two years' examination, to end my life with him; and this I so fully resolved, that no torments which could be inflicted upon me, nor death itself, could make me change my purpose. So, madam, I beseech you to excuse in me what is highly excusable, as you very well know, and leave me to enjoy the peace and quiet I expect to find with him."

The queen, unable to make any reasonable reply to language so resolute and so true, could only renew her passionate chiding and abuse, and, bursting into tears, "Wretch," she said, "instead of humbling yourself, and testifying repentance for the fault you have committed, you speak with audacity, and, instead of blushing, you do not so much as shed one tear; thereby giving plain proof of your obstinacy and hardness of heart. But if the king and your father do as I would have them, they will put you in a place where you will be constrained to hold other language."

"Since you accuse me, madam, of speaking with audacity," replied Rolandine, "I am resolved to say no more, unless you are pleased to permit me to speak." The queen having given her permission, she continued: "It is not for me, madam, to speak to you with audacity. As you are my mistress, and the greatest princess in Christendom, I must always entertain for you the respect which is your due; and it has never been my intention to depart from it. But as I have no advocate but the truth, and as it is known to myself alone, I am obliged to speak it boldly, in the hope that if I have the good fortune to make you thoroughly cognizant of it, you will not believe me to be such as you have been pleased to call me. I am not afraid that any mortal creature should know in what manner I have conducted myself in the affair which is laid to my charge, for I know that I have not done anything contrary either to God or to my honor. This, madam, is what makes me speak without fear, being well assured that He who sees my heart is with me; and with such a judge on my side, I should be wrong to fear those who are subject to His judgment. Wherefore should I weep, madam, since honor and conscience do not upbraid me? As to repentance, madam, I am so far from repenting of what I have done, that were it to be done again, I would do it. It is you, madam, who have great reason to weep, both for the wrong you have done me in the past, and for that which you now do me in censuring me publicly for a fault of which you are more guilty than I. If I had offended God, the king, you, my kindred, and my conscience, I ought to testify my repentance by my tears; but I ought not to weep for having done an act that is good, just, and holy, which would never have been spoken of but with honor, if you, madam, had not prematurely divulged it, and given it an air of culpability; thereby plainly showing that you are more bent on dishonoring me than on preserving the honor of your house and your kindred. But since it is your pleasure, madam, to act thus, it is not for me to gainsay you. Innocent as I am, I shall feel no less pleasure in submitting to the punishment you may choose to inflict upon me, than you in imposing it. You and my father, madam, have but to say what you desire that I should suffer, and you shall be promptly obeyed. I reckon upon it, madam, that he will not be backward in this; and I shall be very glad if he will share your sentiments, and if, after having agreed with you in the negligence he has shown in providing for my welfare, he imitates your activity now that the question is how to do me harm. But I have another Father in heaven, who, I hope, will give me patience enough to endure the evils I see you are preparing for me; and it is in Him alone I put my whole trust."

The queen, bursting with rage, gave orders that Rolandine should be taken out of her sight, and shut up alone in a chamber where she should not be allowed to speak to any one. Nevertheless, her gouvernante was left with her, and through her it was that Rolandine made known her present condition to the bastard, asking his advice at the same time as to what she should do. The bastard, believing that the services he had rendered to the king would be counted for something, repaired at once to the court. He found the king at the chase, told him the truth of the matter, reminded him of his poverty, and besought his majesty to appease the queen and permit the consummation of the marriage. The king made no other reply than to say, "Do you assure me that you have married her?"

"Yes, sire," replied the bastard, "by words and by presents only; but if your majesty pleases, the ceremony shall be completed."

The king looked down, and without saying another word returned to the château. On arriving there, he called for the captain of his guards, and ordered him to arrest the bastard. However, one of the friends of the latter, who guessed the king's intention, sent him warning to get out of the way and retire to one of his houses which was not far off, promising, that if the king should send in search of him, as he expected would be the case, he should have prompt notice, so that he might quit the kingdom; and that should matters be more favorable, he would send him word to return. The bastard took his friend's advice, and made such good speed that the captain of the guards did not find him.

Meanwhile, the king and queen having conferred together as to what should be done with the poor lady who had the honor to be their relation, it was decided, at the queen's suggestion, that she should be sent back to her father, who should be made acquainted with the truth of the matter. Before she went away, several ecclesiastics and people of sage counsel went to see her, and represented to her that, being engaged only by word of mouth, the marriage could easily be dissolved, provided both parties were willing, and that it was the king's pleasure she should do so, for the honor of the house to which she belonged; but she replied, that she was ready to obey the king in all things, provided conscience was not implicated; but what God had joined men could not put asunder. She besought them not to ask of her a thing so unreasonable. "If the love and the good-will which are founded only on the fear of God," she added, "are a true and solid bond of marriage, then am I so closely bound that neither steel, nor fire, nor water can loose me. Death alone can do so, and to it alone will I surrender my ring and my oath; so, gentlemen, I beg you will say no more to me on the subject." She had so much steadfastness, that she would rather die and keep her word, than live after having broken it.

This resolute reply was reported to the king, who, seeing that it was impossible to detach her from her husband, gave orders that she should be taken away to her father's; and thither she was carried with such little ceremony or regard to her quality, that none who saw how she was treated could restrain their tears. She had transgressed, indeed; but her punishment was so great and her fortitude so singular, that they made her fault seem a virtue. Her father, on hearing this disagreeable news, would not see his daughter, but sent her away to a castle situated in a forest, and which he had formerly built for a reason well worthy to be narrated. There she was for a long time a prisoner, and every day she was told, by her father's orders, that if she would renounce her husband he would treat her as his daughter, and set her at liberty. But nothing could shake her constancy. One would have thought she made pleasant pastime of her sufferings, to see how cheerfully she bore them for the sake of him she loved.

What shall I say here of men? The bastard, who was under such obligations to her, fled to Germany, where he had many friends, and showed by his inconstancy that he had attached himself to Rolandine through avarice and ambition, rather than through real love; for he became so enamored of a German lady, that he forgot to write to her who was suffering so much for his sake. However cruel fortune was towards them, she yet left it always in their power to write to each other; but this sole comfort was lost through the bastard's inconstancy and negligence; whereat Rolandine was distressed beyond measure. The few letters he did write were so cold and so different from those she had formerly received from him, that she felt assured some new amour had deprived her of her husband's heart, and done what vexations and persecutions had been incapable of effecting. But her love for him was too great to allow of her taking any decisive step on mere conjectures. In order, therefore, to know the truth, she found means to send a trusty person, not to carry any letters or messages to him, but to observe him, and make careful inquiries. This envoy, on his return, informed her that the bastard was deeply in love with a German lady, and that it was said she was very rich, and that he wished to marry her. So extreme was poor Rolandine's affliction on learning this news, that she fell into a dangerous illness. Those who were aware of its cause told her, on the part of her father, that since the bastard's inconstant and dastardly behavior were known, she had a perfect right to abandon him; and they tried hard to persuade her to do so. But it was in vain they tormented her; she remained unchanged to the end, displaying alike the greatness of her love and of her virtue. In proportion as the bastard's love diminished, Rolandine's augmented, the latter gaining as it were all that the former lost. Feeling that in her bosom alone was lodged all the love that had formerly dwelt in two, she resolved to cherish it until the death of the one or the other.

The divine goodness, which is perfect charity and true love, took pity on her sorrows, and had so much regard for her patience, that the bastard died soon after in the midst of his wooing of another woman. The news being brought her by persons who had been present at his burial, she sent to her father, begging he would be so good as to allow her to say a few words to him.

Her father, who had never spoken to her during the whole time of her captivity, went to her forthwith. After having heard her plead her justification at very great length, instead of condemning and thinking of killing her, as he had often threatened, he embraced her, and said, with swimming eyes, "You are more just than I, my daughter; for if you have committed a fault, I am the principal cause of it. But since it has pleased God that things should happen thus, I will try to make amends for the past." Accordingly, he took her home, and treated her as his eldest daughter.

A gentleman who bore the name and the arms of the family at last sought her in marriage. This gentleman, who was very prudent and virtuous, often saw Rolandine, and conceived so much esteem for her, that he praised her for what others blamed, persuaded as he was that she acted only upon virtuous principles. The chevalier being liked both by the father and the daughter, the marriage was forthwith concluded. It is true that a brother she had, and who was the father's sole heir, would never give her a portion of the family wealth, under pretext that she had been wanting in obedience to her father; after whose death he treated her so cruelly, that she and her husband, who was a younger son, found it a hard matter to subsist. But God provided a remedy, for the brother, who wished to retain all, died, leaving behind him both his own wealth and that of his sister, which he unjustly retained. By this means Rolandine and her husband were raised to great affluence. They lived honorably, according to their quality, were grateful for the favors bestowed on them by Providence, had much love for one another, and, after they had brought up two sons, with whom it pleased God to bless their marriage, Rolandine joyfully yielded up her soul to him in whom she had always put her whole trust.[2]

Ladies, let the men who regard us as inconstancy's very self show us a husband like the wife of whom I have been telling you, one who had the same goodness, fidelity, and constancy. I am sure they will find the task so very hard, that I will acquit them of it altogether, rather than put them to such infinite pain. As for you, ladies, I beg that, for the maintenance of your dignity, you will either not love at all, or love as perfectly as this demoiselle. Do not say that she exposed her honor, since by her firmness she has been the means of so augmenting ours.

"It is true, Oisille," said Parlamente, "that your heroine was a woman of a very lofty spirit, and the more commendable for her steadfastness, as she had to do with an unfaithful husband, who wished to quit her for another."

"That, I think," said Longarine, "must have been the hardest thing for her to bear; for there is no burden so heavy which the love of two persons who are truly united may not bear with ease and comfort; but when one of the two deserts his duty, and leaves the whole burden to the other, the weight becomes insupportable."

"You ought then to have pity on us," said Geburon, "since we have to bear the whole weight of love, and you will not so much as help with a finger-end to ease the burden."

"The burdens of the man and of the woman are often different," observed Parlamente. "The wife's love, founded on piety and virtue, is so just and reasonable, that he who is untrue to the duties of such a friendship ought to be regarded as a dastard, and wicked in the sight of God and man. But as men love only with a view to pleasure, women, who in their ignorance are always the dupes of wicked men, often engage themselves too deeply in a commerce of tenderness; but when God makes known to them the criminal intentions of those whom they supposed to entertain none but good ones, they may break off with honor, and without damage to their reputation, for the shortest follies are always the best."

"That is a mere whim of your own," said Hircan, "to assert that virtuous women may honorably cease to love men, whilst the latter may not in like manner cease to love women; as if the heart of one sex was different from that of the other. For my part, I am persuaded that, in spite of the diversity in faces and dresses, the inclinations of both are the same; the only difference is, that the more hidden guilt is the worse."

"I am very well aware," said Parlamente, with some anger, "that in your opinion the least guilty women are those whose guilt is known."

"Let us change the subject," interrupted Simontault, "and dismiss that of the heart of man and of woman by saying that the best of them is good for nothing. Let us see to whom Parlamente will give her voice."

"To Geburon," she said.

"Since I have begun with mentioning the Cordeliers," said he, "I must not forget the monks of St. Benedict, and cannot forbear relating what happened in my time to two of these good fathers; at the same time, let not what I am going to tell you of a wicked monk hinder you from having a good opinion of those that deserve it. But as the Psalmist says that all men are liars, and that there is none that worketh righteousness, no not one, it seems to me that one cannot fail to esteem a man such as he is. In fact, if there is good in him, it is to be attributed, not to the creature, but to Him who is the principle and the source of all good. Most people deceive themselves in giving too much to the creature, or in too much esteeming themselves. And that you may not suppose it impossible to find extreme concupiscence under an extreme austerity, I will relate to you a fact which happened in the time of King Francis I."

Novel XXII.

A hypocritical Prior tries every means to seduce a Nun, but at last his villainy is discovered.

There was at St. Martin-des-Champs, at Paris, a prior, whose name I will not mention, because of the friendship I once bore him. He led so austere a life until the age of fifty, and the fame of his sanctity was so strong throughout the kingdom, that there was no prince or princess who did not receive him with veneration when he paid them a visit. No monastic reform was effected in which he had not part; and he received the name of the "Father of true monasticism." He was elected visitor of the celebrated society of the Ladies of Fontevrault, who were in so much awe of him, that when he came to any of their convents the nuns trembled with fear, and treated him just as they might have treated the king, hoping thereby to soften his rigor towards them. At first, he did not wish that such deference should be paid him; but as he approached his fifty-fifth year, he at last came to like the honors he had refused in the beginning; and coming by degrees to regard himself as the public property of the religious societies, he was more careful to preserve his health than he had been. Though he was bound by the rules of his order never to eat meat, he granted himself a dispensation in that respect, a thing he would never do for any one else, alleging as his reason, that the whole burden of the brethren's spiritual interests rested upon him. Accordingly, he pampered himself, and to such good purpose, that from being a very lean monk he became a very fat one.

With the change in his manner of living a change took place in his heart also, and he began to look at faces on which he had before made it a matter of conscience to cast his eyes casually. By dint of looking at beauties, rendered more desirable by their veils, he began to lust after them. In order to satisfy his unholy passion he changed from a shepherd into a wolf; and if he found an Agnes in any of the convents under his jurisdiction, he failed not to corrupt her. After he had long led this wicked life, Divine goodness taking pity on the poor misused sheep, was pleased to unmask the villain, as you shall hear.

He had gone one day to visit a convent near Paris named Gif, and while he was confessing the nuns there came before him one named Sister Marie Herouet, whose sweet and pleasing voice indicated that her face and heart were not less so. The mere sound inspired the good father with a passion exceeding all he had ever felt for other nuns. In speaking to her he stooped down to look at her, and seeing her mouth so rosy and charming, he could not help lifting up her veil to satisfy himself if her eyes corresponded to the beauty of her lips. He found what he sought, and noted it so well that his heart became filled with a most vehement ardor; he lost his appetite for food and drink, and even all countenance, in spite of his efforts to dissemble. On his return to his priory there was no rest for him. He passed his days and nights in extreme disquietude, his mind continually occupied in devising means to gratify his passion, and make of this nun what he had made of so many others. As he had observed that she possessed steadiness of character and quickness of perception, the thing appeared to him hard to accomplish. Conscious, moreover, that he was ugly and old-looking, he resolved not to attempt to win her by soft words, but extort from her by fear what he could not hope to obtain for love.

With this intention, he returned a few days after to the convent of Gif, and displayed more austerity there than ever he had done before, angrily rating all the nuns. One did not wear her veil low enough; another carried her head too high; another did not make obeisance properly like a nun. So severe was he with regard to all these trifles, that he seemed as terrible as the picture of God on the day of judgment. Being gouty, he was much fatigued in visiting all the parts of the convent, and it was about the hour of vespers (an hour assigned by himself) that he reached the dormitory. The abbess told him it was time to say vespers. "Have them said, mother," replied the prior, "for I am so tired that I will remain here, not to repose, but to speak to Sister Marie about a scandalous thing I heard of her; for I am told that she babbles like a worldling." The prioress, who was aunt to Sister Marie's mother, begged that he would chapter her soundly, and left her in the hands of the prior, quite alone, except that a young monk was with him.

Left alone with Sister Marie, he began by lifting up her veil, and bidding her look in his face. Sister Marie replied, that her rule forbade her to look at men. "That is well said, my daughter," said the prior, "but you are not to believe that monks are men."

For fear, then, of being guilty of disobedience, Sister Marie looked at him, and thought him so ugly, that it seemed to her more a penance than a sin to look at him. The reverend father, after talking of the love he bore her, wanted to put his hands on her breasts. She repulsed him as she ought; and the reverend father, vexed at so untoward a beginning, exclaimed in great anger, "What business has a nun to know that she has breasts?"

"I know that I have," replied Sister Marie; "and I am very certain that neither you nor any one else shall ever touch them. I am neither young enough nor ignorant enough not to know what is a sin and what is not so."

Seeing, then, that he could not compass his designs in that way, he had recourse to another expedient, and said, "I must declare my infirmity to you, my daughter; I have a malady which all physicians deem incurable, unless I delight myself with a women whom I passionately love. I would not for my life commit a mortal sin; but even should it come to that, I know that simple fornication is not to be compared to the sin of homicide. So, if you love my life, you will hinder me from dying, and save your own conscience."

She asked him what sort of diversion it was that he contemplated; to which he replied, that she might rest her conscience on his, and he assured her that he would do nothing which would leave any weight on either. To let her judge by the preliminaries what sort of pastime it was he asked of her, he embraced her and tried to throw her on a bed. Making no doubt then of his wicked intention, she cried out, and defended herself so well that he could only touch her clothes. Seeing, then, that all his devices and efforts were fruitless, like—I will not say a madman, but like a man without conscience or reason, he put his hand under her robe, and scratched all that came under his nails with such fury, that the poor girl, shrieking with all her might, fell in a faint. The abbess, hearing her cries, ran to the dormitory, reproaching herself for having left her relation alone with the reverend father. She stood for a moment at the door to listen, but, hearing her niece's voice, she pushed open the door, which was held by the young monk. When she entered the dormitory, the prior, pointing to her niece, said, "You did wrong, mother, not to acquaint me with Sister Marie's constitution; for, not knowing her weakness, I made her stand before me, and while I was reprimanding her, she fainted away, as you see."

Vinegar and other remedies being applied, Sister Marie recovered from her faint; and the prior, fearing lest she should tell her aunt the cause of it, found means to whisper in her ear, "I command you, my daughter, on pain of disobedience and eternal damnation, never to speak of what I have done to you. It was my great love for you that made me do it; but since I see that you will not respond to my passion, I will never mention it to you while I live. I may, however, assure you for the last time, that if you will love me I will have you chosen abbess of one of the best abbeys in this kingdom."

She replied that she would rather die in perpetual imprisonment than ever have any other friend than Him who had died for her on the cross; deeming herself happier in suffering all ills with Him, than enjoying without Him all the pleasures the world can afford. She warned him once for all not to speak to her any more in that manner, if he did not wish her to complain of it to the abbess; but if he desisted, she would say nothing of what was past. Before this bad shepherd withdrew, in order to appear quite different from what he was in reality, and to have the pleasure of again gazing on her he loved, he turned to the abbess and said, "I beg, mother, that you will make all your daughters sing a *Salve Regina* in honor of the Virgin, in whom I rest my hope." The *Salve*

Regina was sung; and all the while the fox did nothing but weep, not with devotion, but with regret at having so ill succeeded. The nuns, who attributed his emotion to the love he felt for the Virgin Mary, regarded him as a saint; but Sister Marie, who knew his hypocrisy, prayed to God in her heart to confound a villain who had such contempt for virginity.

The hypocrite returned to St. Martin's, carrying with him the criminal fire which consumed him day and night, and occupied his mind only in trying to find means for accomplishing his unrighteous end. Being afraid of the abbess, whose virtue he was aware of, he thought he could not do better than to remove her from that convent. With that view, he went to Madame de Vendôme, who was then residing at La Fère, where she had built and endowed a convent of the order of St. Benedict, named Mont d'Olivet. In his professed character of a sovereign reformer, he represented to her that the abbess of Mont d'Olivet was not capable of governing such a community. The good lady begged him to name one who should be worthy to fill that office. This was just what he wanted, and he at once recommended her to take the abbess of Gif, whom he depicted to her as the abbess of the greatest capacity in France. Madame de Vendôme sent for her forthwith, and gave her the government of her convent of Mont d'Olivet; whilst the prior, who commanded the suffrages of all the communities, had one who was devoted to him elected abbess of Gif.

This being done, he went to the convent to try once more if by prayers or promises he could prevail over Sister Marie. He succeeded no better than the first time, and returning in despair to St. Martin's, he there contrived more villainy. As much with a view to accomplish his original purpose as to be revenged on the uncomplying nun, and for fear the affair should obtain publicity, he had the relics stolen from the convent of Gif by night, accused the confessor of the convent, an aged and worthy monk, of having committed the theft, and imprisoned him at St. Martin's. Whilst he kept him there he suborned two witnesses, who deposed that they had seen the confessor and Sister Marie committing an infamous and indecent act in a garden: and this he wanted to make the old monk confess. The good man, who knew all the prior's tricks, begged him to assemble the chapter, and said he would state truly all he knew in presence of the monks. This demand he took care not to grant, fearing lest the confessor's justification should condemn himself; but finding the latter so invincibly steadfast, he treated him so ill that some say he died in prison; others say that the prior forced him to unfrock and quit the realm. Be that as it may, he was never seen afterwards.

The prior, having, as he thought, such a great hold on Sister Marie, went to Gif, where the abbess his creature never disputed a word that fell from his lips. He began by exercising his authority as visitor, and summoned all the nuns one by one, that he might hear them in chamber in form of confession and visitation. Sister Marie, who had lost her good aunt, having at last appeared in her turn, he began by saying to her, "You know, Sister Marie, of what a crime you are accused; and consequently you know that the great chastity you affect has availed you nothing, for it is well known that you are anything but chaste."

"Produce my accuser," replied Sister Marie, undauntedly, "and you will see how he will maintain such a statement in my presence."

"The confessor himself has been convicted of the fact, and that must be proof enough for you," returned the prior.

"I believe him to be such a good man," said Sister Marie, "that he is incapable of confessing such a falsehood. But even should he have done so, set him before me and I will prove the contrary."

The prior, seeing she was not daunted, said, "I am your father, and as such I wish to be tender with your honor; I leave the matter between you and your conscience, and will believe what you shall tell me. I conjure you, then, on pain of mortal sin, to tell me the truth. Were you a virgin when you entered this house?"

"My age at that time, father, is warrant for my virginity. I was then but five years old."

"And since then, my daughter, have you not lost that fair flower?"

She swore she had not, and that she had never undergone any temptation except from him.

"I cannot believe it," the hypocrite replied: "it remains to be proved."

"What proof do you require?"

"That which I exact from other nuns. As I am the visitor of souls, so am I also of bodies. Your abbess and prioresses have all passed through my hands, and you must not scruple to let me examine your virginity. Lay yourself on that bed, and turn the front of your robe over your face."

"You have told me so much of your criminal love for me," replied Sister Marie, indignantly, "that I have reason to believe your intention is not so much to examine my virginity as to despoil me of it. So be assured I will never consent."

"You are excommunicated," returned the prior, "to refuse obedience; and unless you do as I bid you, I will dishonor you in full chapter, and will state all I know of you and the confessor."

Sister Marie, without suffering herself to be dismayed, replied that He who knew the hearts of His servants would be her stay. "And since you carry your malevolence so far," she said, "I would rather be the victim of your cruelty than the accomplice of your criminal desires; because I know that God is a just judge."

In a rage that may be more easily imagined than described, the prior hurried off to assemble the chapter. Summoning Sister Marie before him, he made her kneel, and thus addressed her: "It is with extreme grief, Sister Marie, that I see how the wholesome remonstrances which I have addressed to you on so capital a fault have been of no avail, and I am compelled with regret to impose a penance on you contrary to my custom. I have examined your confessor touching certain crimes of which he was accused, and he has confessed to me that he has abused you, and that in a place where two witnesses depose to having seen you. Instead, then, of the honorable post of mistress of the novices in which I had placed you, I ordain that you be the lowest of all, and also that you eat your diet of bread and water on the ground in the presence of all the sisters, until you shall have merited pardon by your repentance."

Sister Marie, having been warned beforehand, by one of her companions who knew her whole affair, that if she made any reply which was displeasing to the prior he would put her *in pace*, that is, immure her forever in a cell, heard her sentence without saying a word, raising her eyes to heaven, and praying that He who had given her the grace to resist sin, would give her the patience necessary to endure her sufferings. This was not all. The venerable prior further prohibited her speaking for three years to her mother or her relations, or writing any letters excepting in community.

After this the wretch went away and returned no more. The poor girl remained a long time in the condition prescribed by her sentence; but her mother, who had a more tender affection for her than for her other children, was surprised at not hearing from her, and said to one of her sons that she believed her daughter was dead, and that the nuns concealed her death in order the longer to enjoy the annual payment made for her maintenance. She begged him to inquire into the matter and see his sister if it were possible. The brother went of at once to the convent, was answered with the usual excuses, and was told that for three years his sister had not quitted her bed. The young man would not be put off with that reply, and swore that unless she were shown to him he would scale the walls and break into the convent. This threat so alarmed the nuns that they brought his sister to the grating: but the abbess followed her so closely, that she could not speak to her brother without being heard by the good mother. But Sister Marie, having her wits about her, had taken the precaution beforehand to write down all the facts I have related, together with the details of a thousand other stratagems which the prior had employed to seduce her, and which, for the sake of brevity, I omit.

I must not, however, forget to mention that, whilst her aunt was abbess, the prior, fancying that it was on account of his ugliness he was repulsed, caused Sister Marie to be tempted by a young and handsome monk, hoping that, if she yielded to the latter for love, he himself might afterwards have his will of her through fear. But the young monk having accosted her in a garden, with words and gestures so infamous that I should be ashamed to repeat them, the poor girl ran to the abbess, who was talking with the prior, and cried to her, "Mother, they are demons, and not monks, who come to visit us." Upon this the prior, afraid of being discovered, said to the abbess, with a laugh, "Certainly, mother, Sister Marie is right." He then took her hand, and said, in presence of the abbess, "I had heard that Sister Marie spoke very well, and with such facility as led people to believe that she was mundane. For this reason I have done violence to my nature, and have spoken to her as worldlings speak to women, so far as I know that language from books: for in point of personal experience I am as ignorant as I was the day I was born. And as I attributed her virtue to my age and ugliness, I ordered my young monk to speak to her in the same tone. She has made, as you see, a sage and virtuous resistance. I am pleased with her for it, and esteem her so highly, that henceforth I desire that she be the first after you, and the mistress of the novices, in order that her virtue may be fortified more and more." The venerable prior did many feats of the same sort during the three years he was in love with the nun, who, as I have said, gave her brother a full written narrative of her sad adventures through the grating.

The brother carried the paper to his mother, who hurried distractedly to Paris, where she found the Queen of Navarre, only sister to the king, and laid this piteous tale before her, saying, "Put no more trust, madam, in these hypocrites. I thought I had placed my daughter on the outskirts of heaven, or at least on the way to it; but I find I have placed her in hell, and in the hands of people worse than all the devils there; for the devils tempt us only so far as we are ourselves consenting parties, but these wretches try to prevail over us by violence when they cannot do so by love." The Queen of Navarre was greatly perplexed. She had implicit confidence in the prior of St. Martin's, and had committed to his charge the abbesses of Montivilliers and of Caen, her sisters-in-law. On the other hand, the crime appeared to her so black and horrible, that she longed to avenge the poor innocent girl, and communicated the matter to the king's chancellor, who was then legate in France.[3] The legate made the prior appear before him, and all that the latter could allege in excuse for himself was that he was seventy years of age. He appealed to the Queen of Navarre, beseeching, by all the pleasures she could ever wish to do him, and as the sole recompense of his past services, that she would have the goodness to put a stop to these proceeding, assuring her he would avow that Sister Marie Herouet was a pearl of honor and chastity. The queen was so astounded at this speech, that, not knowing how to reply to it, she turned her back upon him, and left him there. The poor monk, overwhelmed with confusion, retired to his monastery, where he never more would let himself be seen by anybody, and died a year afterwards. Sister Marie Herouet, esteemed as the virtues God had given her deserved, was taken from the abbey of Gif, where she had suffered so much, and was made by the king abbess of the abbey of Giy, near Montargis. She reformed the abbey which his majesty had given her, and lived like a saint, animated by the spirit of God whom she praised all her life long for the repose He had procured her, and the dignity with which he had in vested her.[4]

There, ladies, is a story which well confirms what St. Paul says to the Corinthians, that God makes use of weak things to confound the strong, and of those who seem useless in men's eyes to overthrow the glory and splendor of those who, thinking themselves something, are yet in reality nothing. There is no good in any man but what God put into him by His grace; and there is no temptation out of which one does not come victorious, when God grants us aid. You see this by the confession of a monk, who was believed to be a good man, and by the elevation of a girl whom he wished to exhibit as criminal and wicked. In this we see the truth of our Lord's saying, that "He that exalteth himself shall be humbled, and he that humbleth himself shall be exalted."

"How many worthy people this monk deceived!" said Oisille; "for I have seen how they trusted in him more than in God."

"I should not have been one of those he deceived," said Nomerfide, "for I have such a horror of the very sight of a monk that I could not even confess to them, believing them to be worse than all other men, and never to frequent any house without leaving in it some shame or dissension."

"There are some good men amongst them," said Oisille; "and the wickedness of an individual ought not to be imputed to the whole body; but the best are those who least frequent secular houses and women."

"That is very well said," observed Ennasuite, "for the less one sees and knows them the better one esteems them; for upon more experience one comes to know their real nature."

"Let us leave the monastery where it is," said Nomerfide, "and see to whom Geburon will give his voice."

"To Madame Oisille," replied Geburon, "in order that she may tell us something in honor of the regular clergy."

"We have pledged ourselves so strongly to speak the truth," replied Oisille, "that I could not undertake that task. Besides, your tale reminded me of a piteous one, which I must relate to you, as I come from the neighborhood of the country where the thing occurred in my own time. I choose this story of recent date, ladies, in order that the hypocrisy of those who believe themselves more religious than others may not so beguile you as to make your faith quit the right path, and induce

you to hope for salvation in any other than Him who will have no companion in the work of our creation and redemption. He alone is almighty to save us in eternity, and to comfort us in this life, and deliver us out of all our afflictions. You know that Satan often assumes the appearance of an angel of light, in order that the eye, deceived by the semblance of sanctity and devotion, may attach itself to the things it ought to shun."

• • •

From the Fourth Day:

Madame Oiselle rose earlier than the rest, according to her good custom, and meditated on Holy Writ whilst awaiting the gradual assemblage of the company. The laziest excused themselves with the words of Scripture, "I have a wife and I cannot come so soon." Thus it was, that when Hircan and his wife made their appearance, Madame Oisille had already begun her reading; but she knew how to pick out the passages in which those are censured who neglect the hearing of the Word. She not only read the text, but she made them such good and holy exhortations, that it was impossible for them to take offence at them. When these devotional exercises were ended, Parlamente said to her, "I was vexed when I came in at having been lazy, but I now congratulate myself on my laziness, since it has made you speak so well. I derive a double advantage from it—repose of body, and satisfaction of mind."

"For penance, then, let us go to mass," said Oisille, "to pray to our Lord for the will and the strength to do His commands; and then let Him command what he pleases."

As she said these words they entered the church, and after having heard mass with much devotion, they sat down to table, where Hircan did not fail to banter his wife for her laziness. After dinner every one retired to study his part, and at the appointed hour they all repaired punctually to the usual rendezvous. Oisille asked Hircan who should begin the day. "If my wife had not been the first speaker yesterday," he said. "I would give my voice for her; for though I have always believed that she loved me better than any man in the world, she has shown me to-day that she loves me a great deal better than God and his Word, since she has preferred my company to your reading." . . .

"If new things are good," replied Oisille, "I will tell you one which cannot be bad, since the event happened in my time, and I have it from an eye-witness. You are, doubtless, not ignorant that death being the end of all our woes, it may, consequently, be called the beginning of our felicity and our repose. Thus man's greatest misery is to wish for death and not be able to obtain it. The greatest ill which can befall a criminal is not to be put to death, but to be made to suffer so much that

he longs for death, while his sufferings, though continual, are of such a nature as not to be capable of abridging his life. It was in this way that a gentleman treated his wife, as you shall hear."

Novel XXXII.

A husband surprises his wife in flagrante delicto, and subjects her to a punishment more terrible than death itself.

King Charles VIII sent to Germany a gentleman named Bernage, Lord of Sivray, near Amboise. This gentleman, traveling day and night, arrived very late one evening at the house of a gentleman, where he asked for a night's lodging; and obtained it, but with difficulty. The owner of the house, nevertheless, learning in whose service he was, came to him and begged he would excuse the incivility of his servants, stating that certain of his wife's relations, who meant him mischief, obliged him to keep his doors thus closed. Bernage told him on what business he was travelling, and his host expressing his readiness to render the king his master all possible services, received his ambassador into his house, and lodged and treated him honorably. Supper-time being come, he showed him into a richly-tapestried hall, where, entering from behind the hangings, there appeared the most beautiful woman that ever was seen; but her hair was cropped close, and she was dressed in black garments of German cut. After the gentleman had washed with Bernage, water was set before this lady, who washed also, and took her seat at the end of the table without speaking to anyone, or anyone to her. Bernage often looked at her, and thought her one of the handsomest women he had ever seen, except that her face was very pale, and her air extremely sad. After she had eaten a little, she asked for drink, which was given to her by a domestic in a very singular vessel. This was a death's head, the holes of which were stopped with silver; and out of this vessel she drank two or three times. After she had supped and washed, she made a reverence to the master of the house, and retired again behind the tapestry without speaking to anyone.

Bernage was so surprised at this extraordinary spectacle that he became quite sombre and pensive. His host perceived this, and said to him, "You are surprised, I see, at what you have beheld at table. Now, the courteous demeanor I have marked in you does not permit me to make a secret of the matter to you, but to explain it, in order that you may not suppose me capable of acting so cruelly without great reason. That lady whom you have seen is my wife, whom I loved more than man ever loved woman. I risked everything to marry her, and I brought her hither in spite of her relations. She, too, evinced so much love for me, that I would have hazarded a thousand lives to obtain her. We lived long in such concord and pleasure that I esteemed myself the happiest gentleman in Christendom; but honor having obliged me to make a journey, she forgot hers and the love she had for me, and conceived a passion for a young gentleman I had brought up in this house. I was near discovering the fact on my return home, but I loved her so ardently that I could not bring myself to doubt her. At last, however, experience opened my eyes, and I saw what I feared more than death. The love I had felt for her changed into fury and despair. Feigning one day to go into the country, I hid myself in the chamber which she at present occupies. Soon after my pretended departure, she retired to it, and sent for the young gentleman. I saw him enter the room and take liberties with her which should have been reserved for me alone. When I saw him about to enter the bed with her, I issued from my hiding-place, seized him in her arms, and slew him. But as my wife's crime seemed to me so great that it would not have been a sufficient punishment for it had I killed her as I had killed her gallant, I imposed upon her one which I believe is more insupportable than death; which was, to shut her up in the chamber in which she used to enjoy her stolen pleasures. I have hung there in a press all the bones of her gallant as one hangs up something precious in a cabinet; and that she may not forget them at her meals, I have her served, as she sits opposite to me at table, with the skull of that ingrate instead of a cup, in order that she may see living him whom she has made her mortal enemy by her crime, and dead, for her sake, him whose love she preferred to mine. In this way, when she dines and when she sups, she sees the two things which must afflict her most, namely, the living enemy and the dead friend; and all this through her guilt. In other respects, I treat her as I do myself, except that her hair is cropped; for the hair is an ornament no more appropriate to the adulteress than the veil to a harlot; therefore, her cropped head denotes that she has lost honor and chastity. If you please to take the trouble to see her, I will take you into her room."

Bernage willingly accepted the offer, and going down stairs with his host, found the lady seated alone by an excellent fire in a very handsome chamber. The gentleman drew back a curtain which concealed a great press, and there he saw all the bones of a man suspended. Bernage had a great wish to speak to the lady, but durst not for fear of the husband, until the latter, guessing his thoughts, said to him, "If you like to say anything to her, you will see how she expresses herself."

"Your patience, madam," said Bernage, turning to her, "is equal to your torture; I regard you as the most unhappy woman in the world."

The lady, with eyes filled with tears, and with incomparable grace and humility, replied, "I confess, sir, that my fault is so great, that all the ills which the master of this house, whom I am not worthy to call husband, could inflict upon me, are nothing in comparison to the grief I feel for having offended him." So saying, she wept profusely.

The gentleman took Bernage by the arm and led him away. Next morning he continued his journey upon the king's service; but on taking leave of the gentleman he could not help saying to him, "The esteem I entertain for you, sir, and the courtesies you have shown me in your house, oblige me to tell you, that, in my opinion, considering the great repentance of your poor wife, you ought to forgive her; the more so as you are young and have no children. It would be a pity that a house like yours should fall, and that those who perhaps do not love you should become inheritors of your substance."

The gentleman, who had resolved never to forgive his wife, pondered long over what Bernage had said to him, and at last, owning that he had spoken the truth, promised that if she persevered in her present humility, he would forgive her after some time. Bernage, on his return to the court, related the whole story to the king, who directed inquiries to be made into the matter, and found that it was all just as Bernage had reported. The description he gave of the lady's beauty so pleased the king, that he sent his painter, Jean de Paris, to take her portrait exactly as she was, which he did with the husband's consent. After she had undergone a long penance, and always with the same humility, the gentleman, who longed much for children, took pity on his wife, reinstated her, and had by her several fine children.

If all those wives who have done the same sort of thing had to drink out of similar vessels, I am greatly afraid, ladies, that many a gilt cup would be turned into a death's-head. God keep us from the like, for, if His goodness does not restrain, there is not one of us but may do worse; but if we trust in Him, He will guard those who own that they cannot guard themselves. Those who rely on their own strength run great risk of being tempted, and of being constrained by experience to acknowledge their infirmity. I can assure you that there are many who have stumbled through pride in this way, whilst others, who were reputed less discreet, have been saved through their humility. The old proverb says truly, What God keeps is well kept.

"I look upon the punishment inflicted in this case as quite reasonable," said Parlamente; "for, as the offence was worse than death, so also ought the penalty to be."

"I am not of your opinion," said Ennasuite. "I would rather see the bones of all my lovers hung up in my cabinet all my life long than die for them. There is no misdeed that cannot be repaired, but from death there is no return."

"How can infamy be repaired?" asked Longarine. *"Do what she may, you know that a woman cannot retrieve her honor after a crime of this nature."*

"I should like to know," returned Ennasuite, *"if the Magdalen is not now in more honor among men than her sister who was a virgin?"*

"I admit," replied Longarine, *"that we praise her for her love for Jesus Christ, and for her great penitence; nevertheless, the name of sinner clings to her always."*

"Much I care what name men give me," said Ennasuite; *"only let me have God's pardon and my husband's too, there is no reason why I should wish to die."*

"If this lady loved her husband as she ought," said Dagoucin, *"I am surprised she did not die of grief at looking upon the bones of him whom her crime had brought to death."*

"Why, Dagoucin," said Simontault, *"have you yet to learn that women know neither love nor regret?"*

"Yes," he replied, *"for I have never ventured to prove their love for fear of finding it less than I should have wished."*

"You live, then, on faith and hope," said Nomerfide, *"as the plover lives on wind. You are easily kept."*

"I content myself with the love I feel in my own heart," he replied, *"and with the hope that there is the same in the hearts of ladies. But if I was quite sure that that love corresponded to my hope, I should feel a pleasure so extreme, that I could not sustain it and live."*

Notes

[1] The King who figures in this novel appears to be Alfonso V., King of Aragon and Sicily, who supplanted King René on the throne of Naples in 1443, and remained in possession of it until his death in 1458. He married, in 1415, Maria, daughter of Henry III., King of Castile, and lived on very bad terms with that princess, who, according to the authors of *l'Art de vérifier les Dates*, never set foot in Italy. Queen Mary, who was married in 1415, must have been long past her bloom in 1443. For this reason the Bibliophiles Français are inclined to believe that the Queen of Navarre has here related under borrowed names a true story of her own times.

[2] The Bibliophiles Français have clearly enough identified the persons in this story. The Queen of France is the celebrated Anne of Bretagne, wife of Charles VIII, and of Louis XII. Rolandine is Anne de Rohan, third child and eldest daughter of Jean II., Viscount of Rohan, Count of Porhoet, Leon, and La Garnache. She married in 1517 Pierre de Rohan, Baron of Frontenay, by whom she had two sons. The bastard appears to be Jean, Bastard of Angoulême, legitimized in 1458 by Charles VII.; and the lady, the mother of the young prince, who forbade the bastard to continue his interviews with Rolandine at the window, and who must, therefore, have had a certain right to command him, was probably Louise of Savoy.

[3] Antoine Duprat, cardinal-legate, chancellor of France, was appointed legate in 1530, and died 1535. The events related in this novel must have occurred between those years.

[4] The prior who figures in this novel was Etienne Gentil, who became prior in 1508, and died in 1536. The abbey of St. Martin-des-Champs stood on the site now occupied by the Conservatoire des Arts et Métiers. The church and the refectory are still standing.

from *Discourse on the Method for Conducting One's Reason Well and for Seeking the Truth in the Sciences*

René Descartes
Translated by Donald A. Cress

Part One

Good sense is the best distributed thing in the world, for everyone thinks himself to be so well endowed with it that even those who are the most difficult to please in everything else are not at all wont to desire more of it than they have. It is not likely that everyone is mistaken in this. Rather, it provides evidence that the power of judging well and of distinguishing the true from the false (which is, properly speaking, what people call "good sense" or "reason") is naturally equal in all men, and that the diversity of our opinions does not arise from the fact that some people are more reasonable than others, but solely from the fact that we lead our thoughts along different paths and do not take the same things into consideration. For it is not enough to have a good mind; the main thing is to apply it well. The greatest souls are capable of the greatest vices as well as of the greatest virtues. And those who proceed only very slowly can make much greater progress, provided they always follow the right path, than do those who hurry and stray from it.

For myself, I have never presumed that my mind was in any respect more perfect than that of ordinary men. In fact, I have often desired to have as quick a wit, or as keen and distinct an imagination, or as full and responsive a memory as some other people. And other than these I know of no qualities that serve in the perfecting of the mind, for as to reason or sense, inasmuch as it alone makes us men and distinguishes us from the beasts, I prefer to believe that it exists whole and entire in each of us, and in this to follow the opinion commonly held by the philosophers, who say that there are differences of degree only between accidents, but not at all between forms or natures of individuals of the same species.

But I shall have no fear of saying that I think I have been rather fortunate to have, since my youth, found myself on certain paths that have led me to considerations and maxims from which I have formed a method by which, it seems to me, I have the means to increase my knowledge by degrees and to raise it little by little to the highest point which the mediocrity of my mind and the short duration of my life will be able to allow it to attain. For I have already reaped from it such a harvest that, although I try, in judgments I make of myself, always to lean more on the side of diffidence than of presumption, and although, looking with a philosopher's eye at the various actions and enterprises of all men, there is hardly one of them that does not seem to me vain and useless, I cannot but take immense satisfaction in the progress that I think I have already made in the search for truth, and I cannot but envisage such hopes for the future that if, among the occupations of men purely as men, there is one that is solidly good and important, I dare to believe that it is the one I have chosen.

All the same, it could be that I am mistaken, and what I take for gold and diamonds is perhaps nothing but a bit of copper and glass. I know how much we are prone to err in what affects us, and also how much the judgments made by our friends should be distrusted when these judgments are in our favor. But I will be very happy to show in this discourse what paths I have followed and to represent my life in it as if in a picture, so that everyone may judge it for himself; and thus, that, learning from the common response the opinions one will have of it, this may be a new means of teaching myself, which I shall add to those that I am accustomed to using.

Thus my purpose here is not to teach the method that everyone ought to follow in order to conduct his reason well, but merely to show how I have tried to conduct my own. Those who take it upon themselves to give precepts must regard themselves as more competent than those to whom they give them; and if they are found wanting in the least detail, they are to blame. But putting forward this essay merely as a story or, if you prefer, as a fable in which, among some examples one can imitate, one will perhaps also find many others which one will have reason not to follow, I hope that it will be useful to some without being harmful to anyone, and that everyone will be grateful to me for my frankness.

I have been nourished on letters since my childhood, and because I was convinced that by means of them one could acquire a clear and assured knowledge of everything that is useful in life, I had a tremendous desire to master them. But as soon as I had completed this entire course of study, at the end of which one is ordinarily received into the ranks of the learned, I completely changed my mind. For I found myself confounded by so many doubts and errors that it seemed to me that I had not gained any profit from my attempt to teach myself, except that more and more I had discovered my ignorance. And yet I was at one of the most renowned schools of Europe, where I thought there must be learned men, if in fact any such men existed anywhere on earth. There I had learned everything the others were learning; and, not content with the disciplines we were taught there, I had gone through all the books I could lay my hands on that treated those disciplines considered the most curious and most unusual. Moreover, I knew what judgments the others were making about me; and I did not at all see that I was rated inferior to my fellow students, even though there already were some among them who were destined to take the place of our teachers. And finally our age seemed to me to be just as flourishing and as fertile in good minds as any of the preceding ones. This made me feel free to judge all others by myself, and to think that there was no doctrine in the world that was of the sort that I had previously been led to hope for.

I did not, however, cease to hold in high regard the academic exercises with which we occupy ourselves in the schools. I knew that the languages learned there are necessary for the understanding of classical texts; that the charm of fables awakens the mind; that the memorable deeds recounted in histories uplift it, and, if read with discretion, aid in forming one's judgment; that the reading of all good books is like a conversation with the most honorable people of past ages, who were their authors, indeed, even like a set conversation in which they reveal to us only the best of their thoughts; that oratory has incomparable power and beauty; that poetry has quite ravishing delicacy and sweetness; that mathematics has some very subtle stratagems that can serve as much to satisfy the curious as to facilitate all the arts and to lessen men's labor; that writings dealing with morals contain many lessons and many exhortations to virtue that are very useful; that theology teaches one how to reach heaven; that philosophy provides the means of speaking plausibly about all things and of making oneself admired by the less learned; that jurisprudence, medicine, and the other sciences bring honors and riches to those who cultivate them; and, finally, that it is good to have examined all these disciplines, even the most superstition-ridden and the most false of them, in order to know their true worth and to guard against being deceived by them. But I believed I had already given enough time to languages, and also to the reading of classical texts, both to their histories and to their fables. For conversing with those of other ages is about the same thing as traveling. It is good to know something of the customs of various peoples, so as to judge our own more soundly and so as not to think that everything that is contrary to our ways is ridiculous and against reason, as those who have seen nothing have a habit of doing. But when one takes too much time traveling, one eventually becomes a stranger in one's own country; and when one is too curious about what commonly took place in past ages, one usually remains quite ignorant of what is taking place in one's own country. Moreover, fables make one imagine many events to be possible which are not so at all. And even the most accurate histories, if they neither alter nor exaggerate the significance of things in order to render them more worthy of being read, almost always at least omit the baser and less note-worthy details. Consequently the rest do not appear as they really are, and those who govern their own conduct by means of examples drawn from these texts are liable to fall into the extravagances of the knights of our romances and to conceive plans that are beyond their powers.

I held oratory in high regard and was enamored of poetry, but I thought both were gifts of the mind, rather than fruits of study. Those who possess the strongest reasoning and who best order their thoughts in order to make them clear and intelligible can always best persuade others of what they are propos-ing, even if they were to speak only Low Breton[1] and had never learned rheto-ric. And those who have the most pleasing rhetorical devices and who know how to express themselves with the most embellishment and sweetness would not fail to be the greatest poets, even if the art of poetry were unknown to them.

I delighted most of all in mathematics because of the certainty and the evidence of its reasonings. But I did not yet notice its true use, and, thinking that it was of service merely to the mechanical arts, I was astonished by the fact that no one had built anything more noble upon its foundations, given that they were so solid and firm. On the other hand, I compared the writings of the ancient pagans that deal with morals to very proud and very magnificent palaces that were built on nothing but sand and I mud. They place virtues on a high plateau and make them appear to be valued more than anything else in the world, but they do not sufficiently instruct us about how to recognize them; and often what they call by so fine-sounding a name is nothing more than a kind of insensibility, pride, desperation, or parricide.

I revered our theology, and I desired as much as anyone else to reach heaven; but having learned as something very certain that the road to heaven is open no less to the most ignorant than to the most learned, and that the revealed truths guiding us there are beyond our understanding, I would not have dared to submit them to the frailty of my reasonings. And I thought that, in order to undertake an examination of these truths and to succeed in doing so, it would be necessary to have some extraordinary assistance from heaven and to be more than a man.

Concerning philosophy I shall say only that, seeing that it has been cultivated for many centuries by the most excellent minds that have ever lived and that, nevertheless, there still is nothing in it about which there is not some dispute, and consequently nothing that is not doubtful, I was not at all so presumptuous as to hope to fare any better there than the others; and that, considering how many opinions there can be about the very same matter that are held by learned people without there ever being the possibility of more than one opinion being true, I deemed everything that was merely probable to be well-nigh false.

Then, as for the other sciences, I judged that, insofar as they borrow their principles from philosophy, one could not have built anything solid upon such unstable foundations. And neither the honor nor the monetary gain they promised was sufficient to induce me to master them, for I did not perceive myself, thank God, to be in a condition that obliged me to make a career out of science in order to enhance my fortune. And although I did not make a point of rejecting glory after the manner of a Cynic, nevertheless I placed very little value on the glory that I could not hope to acquire except through false pretenses. And finally, as to the false doctrines, I thought I already knew well enough what they were worth, so as not to be liable to be deceived either by the promises of an alchemist, the predictions of an astrologer, the tricks of a magician, or the ruses or boasts of any of those who profess to know more than they do.

That is why, as soon as age permitted me to emerge from the supervision of my teachers, I completely abandoned the study of letters. And resolving to search for no knowledge other than what could be found within myself, or else in the great book of the world, I spent the rest of my youth traveling, seeing courts and armies, mingling with people of diverse temperaments and circumstances, gathering various experiences, testing myself in the encounters that fortune offered me, and everywhere engaging in such reflection upon the things that presented themselves that I was able to derive some profit from them. For it seemed to me that I could find much more truth in the reasonings that each person makes concerning matters that are important to him, and whose outcome ought to cost him dearly later on if he has judged badly, than in those reasonings engaged in by a man of letters in his study, which touch on speculations that produce no effect and are of no other consequence to him except perhaps that, the more they are removed from common sense, the more pride he will take in them, for he will have to employ that much more wit and ingenuity in attempting to render them plausible. And I have always had an especially great desire to learn to distinguish the true from the false, in order to see my way clearly in my actions, and to go forward with confidence in this life.

It is true that, so long as I merely considered the customs of other men, I found hardly anything there about which to be confident, and that I noticed there was about as much diversity as I had previously found among the opinions of philosophers. Thus the greatest profit I derived from this was that, on seeing many things that, although they seem to us very extravagant and ridiculous, do not cease to be commonly accepted and approved among other great peoples, I learned not to believe anything too firmly of which I had been persuaded only by example and custom; and thus I little by little freed myself from many errors that can darken our natural light and render us less able to listen to reason. But after I had spent some years thus studying in the book of the world and in trying to gain some experience, I resolved one day to study within myself too and to spend all the powers of my mind in choosing the paths that I should follow. In this I had much more success, it seems to me, than had I never left either my country or my books.

Part Two

I was then in Germany, where the occasion of the wars which are not yet over there[2] had called me; and as I was returning to the army from the coronation of the emperor, the onset of winter detained me in quarters where, finding no conversation to divert me and fortunately having no worries or passions to trouble me, I remained for an entire day shut up by myself in a stove-heated room,[3] where I was completely free to converse with myself about my thoughts. Among them, one of the first was that it occurred to me to consider that there is often not so much perfection in works composed of many pieces and made by the hands of various master craftsmen as there is in those works on which but a single individual has worked. Thus one sees that buildings undertaken and completed by a single architect are usually more attractive and better ordered than those which many architects have tried to patch up by using old walls that had been built for other purposes. Thus those ancient cities that were once mere villages and in the course of time have become large towns are usually so poorly laid out, compared to those well-ordered places that an engineer traces out on a vacant plain as it suits his fancy, that even though, upon considering each building one by one in the former sort, one often finds as much, if not more, art than one finds in those of the latter sort, still, upon seeing how the buildings are arranged—here a large one, there a small one—and how they make the streets crooked and uneven, one would say that it is chance rather than the will of some men using reason that has arranged them thus. And if one considers that there have nevertheless always been officials responsible for seeing that private buildings contribute to the attractiveness of public areas, one will well understand that it is difficult to make things that are very finely crafted by laboring only on the works of others. Thus I imagined that peoples who, having once been half savages and having been civilized only little by little, have made their laws only to the extent that the inconvenience due to crimes and quarrels have forced them to do so, could not be as well ordered as those who, from the very beginning of their coming together, have followed the fundamental precepts of some prudent legislator. Likewise, it is quite certain that the state of the true religion, whose ordinances were made by God alone, must be incomparably better ordered than all the others. And, speaking of things human, I believe that if Sparta was at one time very flourishing, this was not because of the goodness of each one of its laws taken by itself, seeing that many of them were very strange and even contrary to good morals, but because, having been devised by a single individual, they all tended toward the same end. And thus I thought that book learning, at least the kind whose reasonings are merely probable and that do not have any demonstrations, having been composed and enlarged little by little from the opinions of many different persons, does not draw nearly so close to the truth as the simple reasonings that a man of good sense can naturally make about the things he encounters. And thus, too, I thought that, because we were all children before being men and because for a long time it was necessary for us to be governed by our appetites and our teachers (which were frequently in conflict with one another, and of which perhaps neither always gave us the best advice), it is nearly impossible for our judgments to be as pure or as solid as they would have been if we had had the full use of our reason from the moment of our birth and if we had always been guided by it alone.

It is true that we never see anyone pulling down all the houses in a city for the sole purpose of rebuilding them in a different style and of making the streets more attractive; but one does see very well that many people tear down their own houses in order to rebuild them, and that in some cases they are even forced to do so when their houses are in danger of collapsing and when the foundations are not very secure. This example persuaded me that it would not really be at all reasonable for a single individual to plan to reform a state by changing everything in it from the foundations up and by toppling it in order to set it up again, nor even also to reform the body of the sciences or the order established in the schools for teaching them; but that, as regards all the opinions to which I had until now given credence, I could not do better than to try to get rid of them once and for all, in order to replace them later on, either with other ones that are better, or even with the same ones once I had reconciled them to the norms of reason. And I firmly believed that by this means I would succeed in conducting my life much better than if I were to build only upon old foundations and if I were to rely only on the principles of which I had allowed myself to be persuaded in my youth without ever having examined whether they were true. For although I noticed various difficulties in this undertaking, still they were not irremediable, nor were they comparable to those difficulties occurring in the reform of the least things that affect the public. These great bodies are too difficult to raise up once they have been knocked down, or even to hold up once they have been shaken; and their fall can only be very violent. Moreover, as to their imperfections, if they have any (and the mere fact of the diversity that exists among them suffices to assure one that many do have imperfections), custom has doubtless greatly mitigated them and has even prevented or imperceptibly corrected many of them, against which prudence could not provide so well. And finally, these imperfections are almost always more tolerable than changing them would be; similarly, the great roads that wind through mountains little by little become so smooth and so convenient by dint of being frequently used, that it is much better to follow them than to try to take a more direct route by climbing over rocks and descending to the bottom of precipices.

That is why I could in no way approve of those troublemaking and restless personalities who, called neither by their birth nor by their fortune to manage public affairs, are forever coming up with an idea for some new reform in this matter. And if I thought there were in this writing the slightest thing by means of which one might suspect me of such folly, I would be very sorry to permit its publication. My plan has never gone beyond trying to reform my own thoughts and building upon a foundation which is completely my own. And if, my work having pleased me sufficiently, I here show you a model of it, it is not for the reason that I would wish to advise anyone to imitate it. Perhaps those with whom God has better shared his graces will have more lofty plans; but I fear that even this one here may already be too daring for many. The single resolution to rid oneself of all the opinions to which one has heretofore given credence is not an example that everyone ought to follow; and the world consists almost exclusively of two kinds of minds for whom it is not at all suitable. First, there are those who, believing themselves more capable than they are, are unable to avoid being hasty in their judgments or to have enough patience to conduct all their thoughts in an orderly manner; as a result, if they have once taken the liberty of doubting the principles they had accepted and of straying from the common path, they could never keep to the path one must take in order to go in a more straightforward direction, and they would remain lost all their lives. Second, there are those who have enough reason or modesty to judge that they are less capable of distinguishing the true from the false than certain others by whom they can be instructed; they should content themselves more with following the opinions of these others than with looking for better ones themselves. And as for myself, I would unquestionably have been counted among these latter persons if I had always had only one master or if I had not known at all the differences that have always existed among the opinions of the most learned. But I had learned in my college days that one cannot imagine anything so strange or so little believable that it had not been said by one of the philosophers, and since then, I had recognized in my travels that all those who have sentiments quite contrary to our own are not for that reason barbarians or savages, but that many of them use their reason as much as or more than we do. And I considered how one and the same man with the very same mind, were he brought up from infancy among the French or the Germans, would become different from what he would be had he always lived among the Chinese or the cannibals, and how, even down to the styles of our clothing, the same thing that pleased us ten years ago, and that perhaps will again please us ten years hence, now seems to us extravagant and ridiculous. Thus it is more custom and example that persuades us than any certain knowledge; and yet the majority opinion is worthless as a proof of truths that are at all difficult to discover, since it is much more likely that one man would have found them than a whole multitude of people. Hence I could not choose anyone whose opinions seemed to me should be preferred over those of the others, and I found myself, as it were, constrained to try to guide myself on my own.

But, like a man who walks alone and in the dark, I resolved to go so slowly and to use so much circumspection in all things that, if I advanced only very slightly, at least I would effectively keep myself from falling. Nor did I want to begin to reject totally any of the opinions that had once been able to slip into my head without having been introduced there by reason, until I had first spent sufficient time planning the work I was undertaking and seeking the true method for arriving at the knowledge of everything of which my mind would be capable.

When I was younger, I had studied, among the parts of philosophy, a little logic, and among those of mathematics, a bit of geometrical analysis and algebra—three arts or sciences that, it seemed, ought to contribute something to my plan. But in examining them, I noticed that, in the case of logic, its syllogisms and the greater part of its other lessons served more to explain "to someone else the things one knows, or even, like the art of Lully,[4] to speak without judgment concerning matters about which one is ignorant, than to learn them. And although, in effect, it might well contain many very true and very good precepts, nevertheless there are so many others mixed up with them that are either harmful or superfluous, that it is almost as difficult to separate the latter precepts from the former as it is to draw a Diana or a Minerva from a block of marble that has not yet been hewn. Then, as to the analysis of the ancients and the algebra of the moderns, apart from the fact that they apply only to very abstract matters and seem to be of no use, the former is always so closely tied to the consideration of figures that it cannot exercise the understanding without greatly fatiguing the imagination; and in the case of the latter, one is so subjected to certain rules and to certain symbols, that out of it there results a confused and obscure art that encumbers the mind, rather than a science that cultivates it. That is why I thought it necessary to search for some other method embracing the advantages of these three yet free from their defects. And since the multiplicity of laws often provides excuses for vices, so that a state is much better ruled when it has but very few laws and when these are very strictly observed; likewise, in place of the large number of precepts of which logic is composed, I believed that the following four rules would be sufficient for me, provided I made a firm and constant resolution not even once to fail to observe them:

The first was never to accept anything as true that I did not plainly know to be such; that is to say, carefully to avoid hasty judgment and prejudice; and to include nothing more in my judgments than what presented itself to my mind so clearly and so distinctly that I had no occasion to call it in doubt.

The second, to divide each of the difficulties I would examine into as many parts as possible and as was required in order better to resolve them.

The third, to conduct my thoughts in an orderly fashion, by commencing with those objects that are simplest and easiest to know, in order to ascend little by little, as by degrees, to the knowledge of the most composite things, and by supposing an order even among those things that do not naturally precede one another.

And the last, everywhere to make enumerations so complete and reviews so general that I was assured of having omitted nothing.

Those long chains of utterly simple and easy reasonings that geometers commonly use to arrive at their most difficult demonstrations had given me occasion to imagine that all the things that can fall within human knowledge follow from one another in the same way, and that, provided only that one abstain from accepting any of them as true that is not true, and that one always adheres to the order one must follow in deducing the ones from the others, there cannot be any that are so remote that they are not eventually reached nor so hidden that they are not discovered. And I was not very worried about trying to find out which of them it would be necessary to begin with; for I already knew that it was with the simplest and easiest to know. And considering that, of all those who have hitherto searched for the truth in the sciences, only mathematicians have been able to find any demonstrations, that is to say, certain and evident reasonings, I did not at all doubt that it was with these same things that they had examined [that I should begin]; although I expected from them no other utility but that they would accustom my mind to nourish itself on truths and not to be content with false reasonings. But it was not my plan on that account to try to learn all those particular sciences commonly called "mathematical"; and seeing that, even though their objects differed, these sciences did not cease to be all in accord with one another in considering nothing but the various relations or proportions which are found in their objects, I thought it would be more worthwhile for me to examine only these proportions in general, and to suppose them to be only in subjects that would help me make the knowledge of them easier, and without at the same time in any way restricting them to those subjects, so that later I could apply them all the better to everything else to which they might pertain. Then, having noted that, in order to know these proportions, I would sometimes need to consider each of them individually, and sometimes only to keep them in mind, or to grasp many of them together, I thought that, in order better to consider them in particular, I ought to suppose them to be relations between lines, since I found nothing more simple, or nothing that I could represent more distinctly to my imagination and to my senses; but that, in order to keep them in mind or to grasp many of them together, I would have to explicate them by means of certain symbols, the briefest ones possible; and that by this means I would be borrowing all that is best in geometrical analysis and algebra, and correcting all the defects of the one by means of the other.

In fact, I dare say the strict adherence to these few precepts I had chosen gave me such facility for disentangling all the questions to which these two sciences extend, that, in the two or three months I spent examining them, having begun with the simplest and most general, and each truth that I found being a rule that later helped me to find others, not only did I arrive at a solution of many problems that I had previously judged very difficult, but also it seemed to me toward the end that, even in those instances where I was ignorant, I could determine by what means and how far it was possible to resolve them. In this perhaps I shall not seem to you to be too vain, if you will consider that, there being but one truth with respect to each thing, whoever finds this truth knows as much about a thing as can be known; and that, for example, if a child who has been instructed in arithmetic has made an addition following its rules, he can be assured of having found everything regarding the sum he was examining that the human mind would know how to find. For ultimately, the method that teaches one to follow the true order and to enumerate exactly all the circumstances of what one is seeking contains everything that gives certainty to the rules of arithmetic.

But what pleased me most about this method was that by means of it I was assured of using my reason in everything, if not perfectly, at least as well as was in my power; and in addition that I felt that in practicing this method my mind was little by little getting into the habit of conceiving its objects more rigorously and more distinctly and that, not having restricted the method to any particular subject matter, I promised myself to apply it as usefully to the problems of the other sciences as I had to those of algebra. Not that, on this account, I would have dared at the outset to undertake an examination of all the problems that presented themselves, for that would itself have been contrary to the order prescribed by the method. But having noted that the principles of these sciences must all be derived from philosophy, in which I did not yet find any that were certain, I thought that it was necessary for me first of all to try to establish some there and that, this being the most important thing in the world, and the thing in which hasty judgment and prejudice were most to feared, I should not try to accomplish that objective until I had reached a much more mature age than that of merely twenty-three, which I was then, and until I had first spent a great deal of time preparing myself for it, as much in rooting out from my mind all the wrong opinions that I had accepted before that time as in accumulating many experiences, in order for them later to be the subject matter of my reasonings, and in always practicing the method I had prescribed for myself so as to strengthen myself more and more in its use.

Part Three

And finally, just as it is not enough, before beginning to rebuild the house where one is living, simply to pull it down, and to make provision for materials and architects or to train oneself in architecture, and also to have carefully drawn up the building plans for it; but it is also necessary to be provided with someplace else where one can live comfortably while working on it; so too, in order not to remain irresolute in my actions while reason required me to be so in my judgments, and in order not to cease to live as happily as possible during this time, I formulated a provisional code of morals, which consisted of but three of four maxims, which I very much want to share with you.

The first was to obey the laws and the customs of my country, constantly holding on to the religion in which, by God's grace, I had been instructed from my childhood, and governing myself in everything else according to the most moderate opinions and those furthest from excess—opinions that were commonly accepted in practice by the most judicious of those with whom I would have to live. For, beginning from then on to count my own opinions as nothing because I wished to submit them all to examination, I was assured that I could not do better than to follow those of the most judicious. And although there may perhaps be people among the Persians or the Chinese just as judicious as there are among ourselves, it seemed to me that the most useful thing was to rule myself in accordance with those with whom I had to live, and that, in order to know what their opinions truly were, I ought to pay attention to what they did rather than to what they said, not only because in the corruption of our morals there are few people who are willing to say everything they believe, but also because many do not know what they believe, for, given that the action of thought by which one believes something is different from that by which one knows that one believes it, the one often occurs without the other. And among many opinions that are equally accepted, I would choose only the most moderate, not only because they are always the most suitable for practical affairs and probably the best (every excess usually being bad), but also so as to stray less from the true path, in case I should be mistaken, than if I had chosen one of the two extremes when it was the other one I should have followed. And in particular I counted among the excesses all the promises by which one curtails something of one's freedom. Not that I disapproved of laws that, to remedy the inconstancy of weak minds, permit someone, when he has a good plan or even, for the security of commerce, some plan that is merely indifferent, to make vows or contracts that oblige him to persevere in it, but because I saw nothing in the world that always remained in the same state, and because, for my part, I promised myself to improve my judgments more and more, and never to make them worse, I would have thought I committed a grave indiscretion against good sense if, having once approved of something, I had obliged myself to take it as good again later, when perhaps it might have stopped being so or when I might have stopped considering it as such.

My second maxim was to be as firm and resolute in my actions as I could, and to follow the most doubtful opinions, once I had decided on them, with no less constancy than if they had been very well assured. In this I would be imitating travelers who, finding themselves lost in some forest, should not wander about turning this way and that, nor, worse still, stop in one place, but should always walk in as straight a line as they can in one direction and never change it for feeble reasons, even if at the outset it had perhaps been only chance that made them choose it, for by this means, even if they are not going exactly where they wish, at least they will eventually arrive somewhere where they will probably be better off than in the middle of a forest. And thus the actions of life often tolerating no delay, it is a very certain truth that, when it is not in our power to discern the truest opinions, we must follow the most probable, and even if we notice no more probability in some than in others, nevertheless we must settle on some, and afterwards no longer regard them as doubtful, insofar as they relate to practical matters, but as very true and very certain, because the reason that made us decide on them appears so. And from then on this was able to free me from all the regret and remorse that usually agitate the consciences of those frail and irresolute minds that allow themselves inconstantly to go about treating as if good things they later judge to be bad.

My third maxim was always to try to conquer myself rather than fortune, and to change my desires rather than the order of the world, and generally to accustom myself to believing that there is nothing that is completely within our power except our thoughts, so that, after we have done our best regarding things external to us, everything that is lacking for us to succeed is, from our point of view, absolutely impossible. And this alone seemed to me sufficient to prevent me in the future from desiring anything but what I was to acquire, and thus to make me contented. For, our will tending by nature to desire only what our understanding represents to it as somehow possible, it is certain that, if we consider all the goods that are outside us as equally beyond our power, we will have no more regrets about lacking those that seem owed to us as our birthright when we are deprived of them through no fault of our own, than we have in not possessing the kingdoms of China or Mexico, and that, making a virtue of necessity, as they say, we shall no more desire to be healthy if we are sick, or to be free if we are in prison, than we now do to have a body made of a material as incorruptible as diamonds, or wings to fly like birds. But I admit that long exercise is needed as well as frequently repeated meditation, in order to become accustomed to looking at everything from this point of view; and I believe that it is principally in this that the secret of those philosophers consists, who in earlier times were able to free themselves from fortune's domination and who, despite sorrows and poverty, could rival their gods in happiness. For occupying themselves ceaselessly with considering the limits prescribed to them by nature, they so perfectly persuaded themselves that nothing was in their power but their thoughts, that this alone was sufficient to prevent them from having any affection for other things, and they controlled their thoughts so absolutely that in this they had some reason for reckoning themselves richer, more powerful, freer, and happier than any other men who, not having this philosophy, never thus controlled everything they wished to control, however favored by nature and fortune they might be.

Finally, to conclude this code of morals, I took it upon myself to review the various occupations that men have in this life, in order to try to choose the best one, and, not wanting to say anything about the occupations of others, I thought I could not do better than to continue in that very one in which I found myself, that is to say, spending my whole life cultivating my reason and advancing, as far as I could, in the knowledge of the truth, following the method I had prescribed to myself, I had met with such extreme contentment since the time I had begun to make use of this method, that I did not believe one could obtain any sweeter or more innocent contentment in this life, and, discovering every day by its means some truths that to me seemed quite important and commonly ignored by other men, the satisfaction I had from them so filled my mind that nothing else was of any consequence to me. In addition, the three preceding maxims were founded solely on the plan I had of continuing to instruct myself, for since God has given each of us some light to distinguish the true from the false, I would not have believed I ought to rest content for a single moment with the opinions of others, had I not proposed to use my own judgment to examine them when there would be time; and I would not have been able to free myself of scruples in following these opinions, had I not hoped that I would not, on that account, lose any opportunity of finding better ones, in case there were any. And finally, I could not have limited my desires or have been content, had I not followed a path by which, thinking I was assured of acquiring all the knowledge of which I was capable, I thought I was assured by the same means of the knowledge of all the true goods that would ever be in my power. For, given that our will tends not to pursue or flee anything unless our understanding represents it to the will as either good or bad, it suffices to judge well in order to do well, and to judge as best one can, in order also to do one's very best, that is to say, to acquire all the virtues and in general all the other goods that one could acquire, and, when one is certain that this is the case, one could not fail to be contented.

When I had thus assured myself of these maxims and put them to one side along with the truths of the faith, which have always held first place among my beliefs, I judged that, as for the rest of my opinions, I could freely undertake to rid myself of them. And inasmuch as I hoped to be able to reach my goal better by conversing with men than by staying shut up any longer in the stove-heated room[5] where I had had all these thoughts, the winter was not yet over when I set out again on my travels. And in all the nine years that followed I did nothing but wander here and there in the world, trying to be more a spectator than an actor in all the comedies that are played out there; and reflecting particularly in each matter on what might render it suspect and give us occasion for erring, I meanwhile rooted out from my mind all the errors that had previously been able to slip into it. Not that, in order to do this, I was imitating the skeptics who doubt merely for the sake of doubting and put on the affectation of being perpetually undecided, for, on the contrary, my entire plan tended simply to give me assurance and to cast aside the shifting earth and sand in order to find rock or clay. In this I was quite successful, it seems to me, inasmuch as, trying to discover the falsity or the uncertainty of the propositions I was examining, not by feeble conjectures but by clear and certain reasonings, I never found any that was so doubtful that I could not draw from it some quite certain conclusion, even if it had been merely that it contained nothing certain. And just as in tearing down an old house, one usually saves the wreckage for use in building a new one, similarly, in destroying all those opinions of mine that I judged to be poorly founded, I made various observations and acquired many experiences that have since served me in establishing more certain opinions. Moreover, I continued to practice the method I had prescribed for myself, for, besides taking care generally to conduct all my thoughts according to its rules, from time to time I set aside some hours that I spent particularly in applying it to mathematical problems, or even also to some other problems that I could make as it were similar to those of mathematics, by detaching them from all the principles of the other sciences, which I did not find to be sufficiently firm, as you will see I have done in many problems that are explained in this volume.[6] And thus, without living any differently in outward appearance than do those who, having no task but to live a sweet and innocent life, make a point of separating pleasures from vices, and who, in order to enjoy their leisure without becoming bored, involve themselves in all sorts of honest diversions, I did not cease to carry out my plan and to progress in the knowledge of the truth, perhaps more than if I had done nothing but read books or keep company with men of letters.

Nevertheless, those nine years slipped by before I had as yet taken any stand regarding the difficulties commonly debated among learned men, or had begun to seek the foundations of any philosophy that was more certain than the commonly accepted one. And the example of many excellent minds, who had previously had this plan and had not, it seemed to me, succeeded in it, made me imagine so much difficulty in it that perhaps I would not have dared to undertake it so soon again, if I had not seen that some had already spread the rumor that I had achieved my goal. I cannot say on what they based this opinion, and if I have contributed something to it by my conversation, this must have been because I confessed that of which I was ignorant more ingenuously than those who have studied only a little are in the habit of doing, and perhaps also because I showed the reasons I had for doubting many things that other people regard as certain, rather than because I was boasting of any learning. But having a good enough heart not to want someone to take me for something other than I was, I thought it necessary to try by every means to render myself worthy of the reputation that was bestowed on me. And it is exactly eight years ago that this desire made me resolve to take my leave of all those places where I might have acquaintances, and to retire here, to a country where the long duration of the war has led to the establishment of such well-ordered discipline that the armies quartered here seem to serve only to make one enjoy the fruits of peace with even greater security, and where, in the midst of the crowd of a great and very busy people who are more concerned with their own affairs than they are curious about those of others, I have been able, without lacking any of the amenities to be found in the most bustling cities, to live as solitary and as withdrawn a life as I could in the remotest deserts.

Part Four

I do not know whether I ought to tell you about the first meditations I engaged in there, for they are so metaphysical and so out of the ordinary that perhaps they will not be to everyone's liking. And yet, in order that it should be possible to judge whether the foundations I have laid are sufficiently firm, I find myself in some sense forced to talk about them. For a long time I had noticed that in matters of morality one must sometimes follow opinions that one knows to be quite uncertain, just as if they were indubitable, as has been said above, but because I then desired to devote myself exclusively to the search for the truth, I thought it necessary that I do exactly the opposite, and that I reject as absolutely false everything in which I could imagine the least doubt, in order to see whether, after this process, something in my beliefs remained that was entirely indubitable. Thus, because our senses sometimes deceive us, I wanted to suppose that nothing was exactly as they led us to imagine. And because there are men who make mistakes in reasoning, even in the simplest matters in geometry, and who commit paralogisms, judging that I was just as prone to err as any other, I rejected as false all the reasonings that I had previously taken for demonstrations. And finally, considering the fact that all the same thoughts we have when we are awake can also come to us when we are asleep, without any of them being true, I resolved to pretend that all the things that had ever entered my mind were no more true than the illusions of my dreams. But immediately afterward I noticed that, while I wanted thus to think that everything was false, it necessarily had to be the case that I, who was thinking this, was something. And noticing that this truth—*I think, therefore I am*—was so firm and so assured that all the most extravagant suppositions of the skeptics were incapable of shaking it, I judged that I could accept it without scruple as the first principle of the philosophy I was seeking.

Then, examining with attention what I was, and seeing that I could pretend that I had no body and that there was no world nor any place where I was, I could not pretend, on that account, that I did not exist at all, and that, on the contrary, from the very fact that I thought of doubting the truth of other things, it followed very evidently and very certainly that I existed; whereas, on the other hand, had I simply stopped thinking, even if all the rest of what I had ever imagined had been true, I would have had no reason to believe that I had existed. From this I knew that I was a substance the whole essence or nature of which is simply to think, and which, in order to exist, has no need of any place nor depends on any material thing. Thus this "I," that is to say, the soul through which I am what I am, is entirely distinct from the body and is even easier to know than the body, and even if there were no body at all, it would not cease to be all that it is.

After this, I considered in general what is needed for a proposition to be true and certain, for since I had just found one of them that I knew to be such, I thought I ought also to know in what this certitude consists. And having noticed that there is nothing at all in this *I think, therefore I am* that assures me that I am speaking the truth, except that I see very clearly that, in order to think, it is necessary to exist, I judged that I could take as a general rule that the things we conceive very clearly and very distinctly are all true, but that there is merely some difficulty in properly discerning which are those that we distinctly conceive.

Following this, reflecting upon the fact that I doubted and that, as a consequence, my being was not utterly perfect (for I saw clearly that it is a greater perfection to know than to doubt), I decided to search for the source from which I had learned to think of something more perfect than I was, and I plainly knew that this had to be from some nature that was in fact more perfect. As to those thoughts I had of many other things outside me, such as the heavens, the earth, light, heat, and a thousand others, I had no trouble at all knowing where they came from, because, noticing nothing in them that seemed to me to make them superior to me, I could believe that, if they were true, they were dependencies of my nature, insofar as it had some perfection, and that, if they were not true, I obtained them from nothing, that is to say, they were in me because I had some defect. But the same could not hold for the idea of a being more perfect than my own, for it is a manifest contradiction to receive this idea from nothing, and because it is no less a contradiction that something more perfect should follow from and depend upon something less perfect than that something should come from nothing, I could not obtain it from myself. It thus remained that this idea had been placed in me by a nature truly more perfect than I was and that it even had within itself all the perfections of which I could have any idea, that is to say, to explain myself in a single word, that it was God. To this I added that, since I knew of some perfections that I did not at all possess, I was not the only being that existed (here, if you please, I shall freely use the terminology of the School), but that of necessity there must be something else more perfect, upon which I depended, and from which I had acquired all that I had. For, had I been alone and independent of everything else, so that I had had from myself all that small amount of perfection in which I participated in the perfect being, I would have been able, for the same reason, to have from myself everything else I knew I lacked, and thus to be myself infinite, eternal, unchanging, all-knowing, all-powerful; in short, to have all the perfections I could observe to be in God. For, following the reasonings I have just gone through, in order to know the nature of God, so far as my own nature was capable of doing so, I had only to consider, regarding all the things of which I found in myself some idea, whether or not it was a perfection to possess them, and I was assured that none of those that indicated any imperfection were in God, but that all others were in him. Thus I saw that doubt, inconstancy, sadness, and the like could not be in God, since I myself would have been happy to be exempt from them. Then, besides this, I had ideas of a number of sensible and corporeal things, for even if I were to suppose that I was dreaming and that everything I saw or imagined was false, I still could not deny that the ideas of these things were not truly in my thought. But since I had already recognized very clearly in myself that intelligent nature is distinct from corporeal nature, taking into consideration that all composition attests to dependence and that dependence is manifestly a defect, I judged from this that being composed of these two natures could not be a perfection in God and that, as a consequence, God was not thus composed, but that, if there are bodies in the world, or even intelligences, or other natures that were not at all entirely perfect, their being had to depend on God's power in such wise that they could not subsist without God for a single moment.

After this, I wanted to search for other truths, and, having set before myself the object dealt with by geometers, which I conceived of as a continuous body or a space indefinitely extended in length, breadth, and height or depth, divisible into various parts which could have various shapes and sizes and which may be moved or transposed in all sorts of ways—for the geometers assume all this in their object—I went through some of their simplest demonstrations. And, having noted that the great certitude that everyone attributes to these demonstrations is founded exclusively on the fact that they are plainly conceived, following the rule that I mentioned earlier, I also noted that there was nothing at all in them that assured me of the existence of their object. For I saw very well that if one supposed, for example, a triangle, it was necessary for its three angles to be equal to two right angles, but I did not see anything in all this to assure me that there was any triangle existing in the world. On the other hand, returning to examine the idea I had of a perfect being, I found that existence was contained in it in the same way in which the equality of its three angles to two right angles is contained in the idea of a triangle, or that the equidistance of all its parts from its center is contained in the idea of a sphere, or even more plainly still, and that, consequently, it is, at the very least, just as certain that God, who is this perfect being, is or exists, as any demonstration in geometry could be.

But what brings it about that there are many people who are persuaded that it is difficult to know this and also even to know what their soul is is that they never lift their minds above sensible things and that they are so accustomed to consider nothing except by imagining it (which is a way of thinking appropriate for material things), that everything unimaginable seems to them unintelligible. This is obvious enough from the fact that even philosophers take it as a maxim in the schools that there is nothing in the understanding that has not first been in the senses, where it is nevertheless certain that the ideas of God and the soul have never been. And it seems to me that those who want to use their imagination in order to grasp these ideas are doing the very same thing as if, in order to hear sounds or to smell odors, they wanted to use their eyes. There is just this difference: the sense of sight assures us no less of the truth of its objects than do the senses of smell or hearing, whereas neither our imagination nor our senses could ever assure us of anything if our understanding did not intervene.

Finally, if there still are men who have not been sufficiently persuaded of the existence of God and of their soul by means of the reasons I have brought forward, I very much want them to know that all the other things of which they think themselves perhaps more assured, such as having a body, that there are stars and an earth, and the like, are less certain. For although one might have a moral assurance about these things, which is such that it seems one cannot doubt them without being extravagant, still when it is a question of metaphysical certitude, it seems unreasonable for anyone to deny that there is not a sufficient basis for one's being completely assured about them, when one observes that while asleep one can, in the same fashion, imagine that one has a different body and that one sees different stars and a different earth, without any of these things being the case. For how does one know that the thoughts that come to us in dreams are any more false than the others, given that they are often no less vivid and explicit? And even if the best minds study this as much as they please, I do not believe they can give any reason sufficient to remove this doubt, unless they presuppose the existence of God. For first of all, even what I have already taken for a rule, namely that the things we very clearly and very distinctly conceive are all true, is assured only for the reason that God is or exists, and that he is a perfect being, and that all that is in us comes from him. It follows from this that our ideas or notions, being real things and coming from God, cannot, in all that is clear and distinct in them, be anything but true. Thus, if we quite often have ideas that contain some falsity, this can only be the case with respect to things that have something confused or obscure about them, because in this respect they participate in nothing; that is, they are thus confused in us only because we are not perfect. And it is evident that it is no less a contradiction that falsity or imperfection as such proceeds from God, than that truth or perfection proceeds from nothing. But if we did not know that all that is real and true in us comes from a perfect and infinite being, however clear and distinct our ideas were, we would have no reason that assured us that they had the perfection of being true.

But once the knowledge of God and the soul has thus made us certain of this rule, it is very easy to know that the dreams we imagine while asleep ought in no way to make us doubt the truth of the thoughts we have while awake. For if it did happen, even while asleep, that one had a very distinct idea (as, for example, if a geometer found some new demonstration), one's being asleep would not prevent its being true. And as to the most common error of our dreams, which consists in the fact that they represent to us various objects in the same way as our external senses do, it does not matter that it gives us occasion to question the truth of such ideas, since they can also deceive us quite often without our being asleep, such as when those with jaundice see everything as yellow, or when the stars or other very distant bodies appear to us much smaller than they are. For finally, whether awake or asleep, we should never allow ourselves to be persuaded except by the evidence of our reason. And it is to be observed that I say "of our reason," and not "of our imagination" or "of our senses." Even though we see the sun very clearly, we should not on that account judge that it is only as large as we see it, and we can well imagine distinctly the head of a lion grafted onto the body of a goat, without having to conclude for that reason that there is a chimera in the world, for reason does not at all dictate to us that what we thus see or imagine is true. But it does dictate to us that all our ideas or notions must have some foundation of truth, for it would not be possible that God, who is all-perfect and all-truthful, would have put them in us without that. And because our reasonings are never so evident nor so complete while we are asleep as they are while we are awake, even though our imaginings while we are asleep are sometimes just as vivid and explicit as those we have while we are awake, or even more so, reason also dictates to us that our thoughts cannot all be true, since we are not all-perfect; what truth there is in them must infallibly be encountered in those we have when we are awake rather than in those we have in our dreams.

Notes

1. This dialect was considered rather barbarous and hardly suitable for sophisticated literary endeavors.

2. The Thirty Years' War (1618–48).

3. There is no need to allege that Descartes sat in or on a stove. A *poêle* is simply a room heated by an earthenware stove. Cf. E. Gilson, *Discours de la méthode: texte et commentaire*, 4th edition (Paris: Vrin, 1967), p. 157.

4. Ramon Llull (ca. 1236–1315), Catalan philosopher and Franciscan who wrote in defense of Christianity against the Moors by attempting to demonstrate the articles of faith by means of logic. Descartes seems to have encountered a Lullist in Dordrecht who could hold forth on any subject whatever for long periods of time. This encounter, more than any direct contact with the writings of Lull, seems to have colored Descartes' understanding of the "art of Lully." Cf. E. Gilson, *Discours de la méthode: texte et commentaire*, pp. 185–86.

5. See f.n. 3.

6. Descartes also published treatises on optics, geometry, and meteorology in this same volume.

from *Leviathan*

Thomas Hobbes

Chapter XIII.
Of the Natural Condition of Mankind as Concerning
Their Felicity, and Misery.

Part I.

Part I.
13.
Men by nature
equal.

NATURE hath made men so equal, in the faculties of the body, and mind; as that though there be found one man sometimes manifestly stronger in body, or of quicker mind than another; yet when all is reckoned together, the difference between man, and man, is not so considerable, as that one man can thereupon claim to himself any benefit, to which another may not pretend, as well as he. For as to the strength of body, the weakest has strength enough to kill the strongest, either by secret machination, or by confederacy with others, that are in the same danger with himself.

And as to the faculties of the mind, setting aside the arts grounded upon words, and especially that skill of proceeding upon general, and infallible rules, called science; which very few have, but in few things; as being not a native faculty, born with us; nor attained, as prudence, while we look after somewhat else, I find yet a greater equality amongst men, than that of strength. For prudence, is but experience; which equal time, equally bestows on all men, in those things they equally apply themselves unto. That which may perhaps make such equality incredible, is but a vain conceit of one's own wisdom, which almost all men think they have in a greater degree, than the vulgar; that is, than all men but themselves, and a few others, whom by fame, or for concurring with themselves, they approve. For such is the nature of men, that howsoever they may acknowledge many others to be more witty, or more eloquent, or more learned; yet they will hardly believe there may be so wise as themselves; for they see their own wit at hand, and other men's at a distance. But this proveth rather that men are in that point equal, than unequal. For there is not ordinarily a greater sign of the equal distribution of any thing, than that every man is contented with his share.

From this equality of ability, ariseth equality of hope in the attaining of our ends. And therefore if any two men desire the same thing, which nevertheless they cannot both enjoy, they become enemies; and in the way to their end, which is principally their own conservation, and sometimes their delectation only, endeavour to destroy, or subdue one another. And from hence it comes to pass, that where an invader hath no more to fear, than another man's single power; if one plant, sow, build, or possess a convenient seat, others may probably be expected to come prepared with forces united, to dispossess, and deprive him, not only of the fruit of his labour, but also of his life, or liberty. And the invader again is in the like danger of another.

And from this diffidence of one another, there is no way for any man to secure himself, so reasonable, as anticipation; that is, by force, or wiles, to master the persons of all men he can, so long, till he see no other power great enough to endanger him: and this is no more than his own conservation requireth, and is generally allowed. Also because there be some, that taking pleasure in contemplating their own power in the acts of conquest, which they pursue farther than their security requires; if others, that otherwise would be glad to be at ease within modest bounds, should not by invasion increase their power, they would not be able, long time, by standing only on their defence, to subsist. And by consequence, such augmentation of dominion over men being necessary to a man's conservation, it ought to be allowed him.

Again, men have no pleasure, but on the contrary a great deal of grief, in keeping company, where there is no power able to overawe them all. For every man looketh that his companion should value him, at the same rate he sets upon himself: and upon all signs of contempt, or undervaluing, naturally endeavours, as far as he dares, (which amongst them that have no common power to keep them in quiet, is far enough to make them destroy each other), to extort a greater value from his contemners, by damage; and from others, by the example.

So that in the nature of man, we find three principal causes of quarrel. First, competition; secondly, diffidence; thirdly, glory.

The first, maketh men invade for gain; the second, for safety; and the third, for reputation. The first use violence, to make themselves

Part I.
13.

masters of other men's persons, wives, children, and cattle; the second, to defend them; the third, for trifles, as a word, a smile, a different opinion, and any other sign of undervalue, either direct in their persons, or by reflection in their kindred, their friends, their nation, their profession, or their name.

Out of civil states, there is always war of every one against every one.

Hereby it is manifest; that during the time men live without a common power to keep them all in awe, they are in that condition which is called war; and such a war, as is of every man, against every man. For WAR, consisteth not in battle only, or the act of fighting; but in a tract of time, wherein the will to contend by battle is sufficiently known: and therefore the notion of *time*, is to be considered in the nature of war; as it is in the nature of weather. For as the nature of foul weather, lieth not in a shower or two of rain; but in an inclination thereto of many days together: so the nature of war, consisteth not in actual fighting; but in the known disposition thereto, during all the time there is no assurance to the contrary. All other time is PEACE.

The incommodities of such a war.

Whatsoever therefore is consequent to a time of war, where every man is enemy to every man; the same is consequent to the time, wherein men live without other security, than what their own strength, and their own invention shall furnish them withal. In such condition, there is no place for industry; because the fruit thereof is uncertain: and consequently no culture of the earth; no navigation, nor use of the commodities that may be imported by sea; no commodious building; no instruments of moving, and removing, such things as require much force; no knowledge of the face of the earth; no account of time; no arts; no letters; no society; and which is worst of all, continual fear, and danger of violent death; and the life of man, solitary, poor, nasty, brutish, and short.

The incommodities of such a war.

It may seem strange to some man, that has not well weighed these things; that nature should thus dissociate, and render men apt to invade, and destroy one another: and he may therefore, not trusting to this inference, made from the passions, desire perhaps to have the same confirmed by experience. Let him therefore consider with himself, when taking a journey, he arms himself, and seeks to go well accompanied; when going to sleep, he locks his doors; when even in his house he locks his chests; and this when he knows there be laws, and public officers, armed, to revenge all injuries shall be done him; what opinion he has of his fellow-subjects, when he rides armed; of his fellow citizens, when he locks his doors; and of his children, and servants, when he locks his chests. Does he not there as much accuse mankind by his actions, as I do by any words? But neither of us accuse man's nature in it. The desires, and other passions of man, are in themselves no sin. No more are the actions, that proceed from those passions, till they know a law that forbids them: which till laws be made they cannot know: nor can any law be made, till they have agreed upon the person that shall make it.

Part I.
13.

It may peradventure be thought, there was never such a time, nor condition of war as this; and I believe it was never generally so, over all the world: but there are many places, where they live so now. For the savage people in many places of America, except the government of small families, the concord whereof dependeth on natural lust, have no government at all; and live at this day in that brutish manner, as I said before. Howsoever, it may be perceived what manner of life there would be, where there were no common power to fear, by the manner of life, which men that have formerly lived under a peaceful government, use to degenerate into, a civil war.

But though there had never been any time, wherein particular men were in a condition of war one against another; yet in all times, kings, and persons of sovereign authority, because of their independency, are in continual jealousies, and in the state and posture of gladiators; having their weapons pointing, and their eyes fixed on one another; that is, their forts, garrisons, and guns upon the frontiers of their kingdoms; and continual spies upon their neighbours; which is a posture of war. But because they uphold thereby, the industry of their subjects; there does not follow from it, that misery, which accompanies the liberty of particular men.

To this war of every man, against every man, this also is consequent; that nothing can be unjust. The notions of right and wrong, justice and injustice have there no place. Where there is no common power, there is no law: where no law, no injustice. Force, and fraud, are in war the two cardinal virtues. Justice, and injustice are none of the faculties neither of the body, nor mind. If they were, they might be in a man that were alone in the world, as well as his senses, and passions. They are qualities, that relate to men in society, not in solitude. It is consequent also to the same condition, that there be no propriety, no dominion, no *mine* and *thine* distinct; but only that to be every man's, that he can get; and for so long, as he can keep it. And thus much for the ill condition, which man by mere nature is actually placed in; though with a possibility to come out of it, consisting partly in the passions, partly in his reason.

In such a war
nothing is unjust.

Part I.
13.
The passions that
incline men to
peace.

The passions that incline men to peace, are fear of death; desire of such things as are necessary to commodious living; and a hope by their industry to obtain them. And reason suggesteth convenient articles of peace, upon which men may be drawn to agreement. These articles, are they, which otherwise are called the Laws of Nature: whereof I shall speak more particularly, in the two following chapters.

Chapter XIV.
Of the First and Second Natural Laws, and of Contracts.

THE RIGHT OF NATURE, which writers commonly call *jus naturale,* is the liberty each man hath, to use his own power, as he will himself, for the preservation of his own nature; that is to say, of his own life; and consequently, of doing any thing, which in his own judgement, and reason, he shall conceive to be the aptest means thereunto.

BY LIBERTY, is understood, according to the proper signification of the word, the absence of external impediments: which impediments, may oft take away part of a man's power to do what he would; but cannot hinder him from using the power left him, according as his judgment, and reason shall dictate to him.

A LAW OF NATURE, *lex naturalis,* is a precept or general rule, found out by reason, by which a man is forbidden to do that, which is destructive of his life, or taketh away the means of preserving the same; and to omit that, by which he thinketh it may be best preserved. For though they that speak of this subject, use to confound *jus,* and *lex, right* and *law:* yet they ought to be distinguished; because RIGHT, consisteth in liberty to do, or to forbear; whereas LAW, determineth, and bindeth to one of them: so that law, and right, differ as much, as obligation, and liberty; which in one and the same matter are inconsistent.

And because the condition of man, as hath been declared in the precedent chapter, is a condition of war of every one against every one: in which case every one is governed by his own reason; and there is nothing he can make use of, that may not be a help unto him, in preserving his life against his enemies; it followeth, that in such a condition, every man has a right to every thing; even to one another's body. And therefore, as long as this natural right of every man to every thing endureth, there can be no security to any man, how strong or wise soever he be, of living out the time, which nature ordinarily alloweth men to live. And consequently it is a precept, or general rule

of reason, _that every man, ought to endeavour peace, as far as he has hope_ Part I.
of obtaining it; and when he cannot obtain it, that he may seek, and use, 14.
all helps, and advantages of war. The first branch of which rule, con-
taineth the first, and fundamental law of nature; which is, _to seek peace,_ The fundamental
and follow it. The second, the sum of the right of nature; which is, _by_ law of nature.
all means we can, to defend ourselves.

From this fundamental law of nature, by which men are com- The second law of
manded to endeavour peace, is derived this second law; _that a man be_ nature.
willing, when others are so too, as far-forth, as for peace, and defence of
himself he shall think it necessary, to lay down this right to all things; and
be contented with so much liberty against other men, as he would allow
other men against himself. For as long as every man holdeth this right,
of doing any thing he liketh; so long are all men in the condition of
war. But if other men will not lay down their right, as well as he; then
there is no reason for any one, to divest himself of his: for that were
to expose himself to prey, which no man is bound to, rather than to
dispose himself to peace. This is that law of the Gospel; _whatsoever you_
require that others should do to you, that do ye to them. And that law of
all men, _quod tibi fieri non vis, alteri ne feceris._

To _lay down_ a man's _right_ to any thing, is to _divest_ himself of the What it is to lay
liberty, of hindering another of the benefit of his own right to the same. down a right.
For he that renounceth, or passeth away his right, giveth not to any
other man a right which he had not before; because there is nothing to
which every man had not right by nature: but only standeth out of his
way, that he may enjoy his own original right, without hindrance from
him; not without hindrance from another. So that the effect which
redoundeth to one man, by another man's defect of right, is but so
much diminution of impediments to the use of his own right original.

Right is laid aside, either by simply renouncing it; or by trans- Renouncing a
ferring it to another. By _simply_ RENOUNCING; when he cares not to right, what it is.
whom the benefit thereof redoundeth. BY TRANSFERRING; when he Transferring right
intendeth the benefit thereof to some certain person, or persons. And what. Obligation.
when a man hath in either manner abandoned, or granted away his
right; then is he said to be OBLIGED, or BOUND, not to hinder those,
to whom such right is granted, or abandoned, from the benefit of it:
and that he _ought,_ and it is his DUTY, not to make void that voluntary Duty.
act of his own: and that such hindrance is INJUSTICE, and INJURY, as
being _sine jure;_ the right being before renounced, or transferred. So
that _injury,_ or _injustice,_ in the controversies of the world, is somewhat Injustice.
like to that, which in the disputations of scholars is called _absurdity._

For as it is there called an absurdity, to contradict what one maintained in the beginning: so in the world, it is called injustice, and injury, voluntarily to undo that, which from the beginning he had voluntarily done. The way by which a man either simply renounceth, or transferreth his right, is a declaration, or signification, by some voluntary and sufficient sign, or signs, that he doth so renounce, or transfer; or hath so renounced, or transferred the same, to him that accepteth it. And these signs are either words only, or actions only; or, as it happeneth most often, both words, and actions. And the same are the BONDS, by which men are bound, and obliged: bonds, that have their strength, not from their own nature, for nothing is more easily broken than a man's word, but from fear of some evil consequence upon the rupture.

Whensoever a man transferreth his right, or renounceth it; it is

Not all rights are alienable.

either in consideration of some right reciprocally transferred to himself; or for some other good be hopeth for thereby. For it is a voluntary act: and of the voluntary acts of every man, the object is some *good to himself.* And therefore there be some rights, which no man can be understood by any words, or other signs, to have abandoned, or transferred. As first a man cannot lay down the right of resisting them, that assault him by force, to take away his life; because he cannot be understood to aim thereby, at any good to himself. The same may be said of wounds, and chains, and imprisonment; both because there is no benefit consequent to such patience; as there is to the patience of suffering another to be wounded, or imprisoned: as also because a man cannot tell, when he seeth men proceed against him by violence, whether they intend his death or not. And lastly the motive, and end for which this renouncing, and transferring of right is introduced, is nothing else but the security of a man's person, in his life, and in the means of so preserving life, as not to be weary of it. And therefore if a man by words, or other signs, seem to despoil himself of the end, for which those signs were intended; he is not to be understood as if he meant it, or that it was his will; but that he was ignorant of how such words and actions were to be interpreted.

[*The section on Contracts has been deleted.*]

Part II.
Of Commonwealth.

Chapter XVII.
Of the Causes, Generation, and Definition of a Commonwealth.

The final cause, end, or design of men, who naturally love liberty, and dominion over others, in the introduction of that restraint upon themselves, in which we see them live in commonwealths, is the foresight of their own preservation, and of a more contented life thereby; that is to say, of getting themselves out from that miserable condition of war, which is necessarily consequent, as hath been shown in chapter XIII, to the natural passions of men, when there is no visible power to keep them in awe, and tie them by fear of punishment to the performance of their covenants, and observation of those laws of nature set down in the fourteenth and fifteenth chapters.

The end of commonwealth, particular security:

For the laws of nature, as *justice, equity, modesty, mercy,* and, in sum, *doing to others, as we would be done to,* of themselves, without the terror of some power, to cause them to be observed, are contrary to our natural passions, that carry us to partiality, pride, revenge, and the like. And covenants, without the sword, are but words, and of no strength to secure a man at all. Therefore notwithstanding the laws of nature, which every one hath then kept, when he has the will to keep them, when he can do it safely, if there be no power erected, or not great enough for our security; every man will, and may lawfully rely on his own strength and art, for caution against all other men. And in all places, where men have lived by small families, to rob and spoil one another, has been a trade, and so far from being reputed against the law of nature, that the greater spoils they gained, the greater was their honour; and men observed no other laws therein, but the laws of honour; that is, to abstain from cruelty, leaving to men their lives, and instruments of husbandry. And as small families did then; so now do cities and kingdoms which are but greater families, for their own security, enlarge their dominions, upon all pretences of danger, and fear of invasion, or assistance that may be given to invaders, and endeavour as much as they can, to subdue, or weaken their neighbours, by open force, and secret arts, for want of other caution, justly; and are remembered for it in after ages with honour.

Which is not to be had from the law of nature:

Part II.
17.
Nor from the
conjunction of
a few men or
families:

Nor is it the joining together of a small number of men, that gives them this security; because in small numbers, small additions on the one side or the other, make the advantage of strength so great, as is sufficient to carry the victory; and therefore gives encouragement to an invasion. The multitude sufficient to confide in for our security, is not determined by any certain number, but by comparison with the enemy we fear; and is then sufficient, when the odds of the enemy is not of so visible and conspicuous moment, to determine the event of war, as to move him to attempt.

Nor from a great
multitude, unless
directed by one
judgement:

And be there never so great a multitude; yet if their actions be directed according to their particular judgements, and particular appetites, they can expect thereby no defence, nor protection, neither against a common enemy, nor against the injuries of one another. For being distracted in opinions concerning the best use and application of their strength, they do not help but hinder one another; and reduce their strength by mutual opposition to nothing: whereby they are easily, not only subdued by a very few that agree together; but also when there is no common enemy, they make war upon each other, for their particular interests. For if we could suppose a great multitude of men to consent in the observation of justice, and other laws of nature, without a common power to keep them all in awe; we might as well suppose all mankind to do the same; and then there neither would be, nor need to be any civil government, or commonwealth at all; because there would be peace without subjection.

Nor is it enough for the security, which men desire should last all the time of their life, that they be governed, and directed by one judgement, for a limited time; as in one battle, or one war. For though they obtain a victory by their unanimous endeavour against a foreign enemy; yet afterwards, when either they have no common enemy, or he that by one part is held for an enemy, is by another part held for a friend, they must needs by the difference of their interests dissolve, and fall again into war amongst themselves.

Why certain
creatures without
reason, or speech,
do nevertheless
live in society,
without any
coercive power.

It is true, that certain living creatures, as bees, and ants, live sociably one with another, which are therefore by Aristotle numbered amongst political creatures; and yet have no other direction, than their particular judgements and appetites; nor speech, whereby one of them can signify to another, what he thinks expedient for the common benefit: and therefore some man may perhaps desire to know, why mankind cannot do the same. To which I answer,

First, that men are continually in competition for honour and dignity, which these creatures are not; and consequently amongst men there ariseth on that ground, envy and hatred, and finally war; but amongst these not so.

Secondly, that amongst these creatures, the common good differeth not from the private; and being by nature inclined to their private, they procure thereby the common benefit. But man, whose joy consisteth in comparing himself with other men, can relish nothing but what is eminent.

Thirdly, that these creatures, having not, as man, the use of reason, do not see, nor think they see any fault, in the administration of their common business; whereas amongst men, there are very many, that think themselves wiser, and abler to govern the public, better than the rest; and these strive to reform and innovate, one this way, another that way; and thereby bring it into distraction and civil war.

Fourthly, that these creatures, though they have some use of voice, in making known to one another their desires, and other affections; yet they want that art of words, by which some men can represent to others, that which is good, in the likeness of evil; and evil, in the likeness of good; and augment, or diminish the apparent greatness of good and evil; discontenting men, and troubling their peace at their pleasure.

Fifthly, irrational creatures cannot distinguish between *injury,* and *damage;* and therefore as long as they be at ease, they are not offended with their fellows: whereas man is then most troublesome, when he is most at ease: for then it is that he loves to shew his wisdom, and control the actions of them that govern the commonwealth.

Lastly, the agreement of these creatures is natural; that of men, is by covenant only, which is artificial: and therefore it is no wonder if there be somewhat else required, besides covenant, to make their agreement constant and lasting; which is a common power, to keep them in awe, and to direct their actions to the common benefit.

The only way to erect such a common power, as may be able to defend them from the invasion of foreigners, and the injuries of one another, and thereby to secure them in such sort, as that by their own industry, and by the fruits of the earth, they may nourish themselves and live contentedly; is, to confer all their power and strength upon one man, or upon one assembly of men, that may reduce all their wills, by plurality of voices, unto one will: which is as much as to say,

The generation of a commonwealth.

to appoint one man, or assembly of men, to bear their person; and every one to own, and acknowledge himself to be author of whatsoever he that so beareth their person, shall act, or cause to be acted, in those things which concern the common peace and safety; and therein to submit their wills, every one to his will, and their judgements, to his judgement. This is more than consent, or concord; it is a real unity of them all, in one and the same person, made by covenant of every man with every man, in such manner, as if every man should say to every man, *I authorise and give up my right of governing myself, to this man, or to this assembly of men, on this condition, that thou give up thy right to him, and authorise all his actions in like manner.* This done, the multitude so united in one person, is called a COMMON-WEALTH, in Latin CIVITAS. This is the generation of that great LEVIATHAN, or rather, to speak more reverently, of that *mortal god,* to which we owe under the *immortal God,* our peace and defence. For by this authority, given him by every particular man in the commonwealth, he hath the use of so much power and strength conferred on him, that by terror thereof, he is enabled to perform the wills of them all, to peace at home, and mutual aid against the enemies abroad. And

The definition of a commonwealth.

in him consisteth the essence of the commonwealth; which, to define it, is *one person, of whose acts a great multitude, by mutual covenants one with another, have made themselves every one the author, to the end he may use the strength and means of them all, as he shall think expedient, for their peace and common defence.*

Sovereign, and subject, what.

And he that carrieth this person, is called SOVEREIGN, and said to have *sovereign power;* and every one besides, his SUBJECT.

The attaining to this sovereign power, is by two ways. One, by natural force; as when a man maketh his children, to submit themselves, and their children to his government, as being able to destroy them if they refuse; or by war subdueth his enemies to his will, giving them their lives on that condition. The other, is when men agree amongst themselves, to submit to some man, or assembly of men, voluntarily, on confidence to be protected by him against all others. This latter, may be called a political commonwealth, or commonwealth by *institution;* and the former, a commonwealth by *acquisition.* And first, I shall speak of a commonwealth by institution.

Chapter XVIII.
Of the Rights of Sovereigns by Institution.

Part II.
18.

A *commonwealth* is said to be *instituted*, when a *multitude* of men do agree, and *covenant, every one, with every one*, that to whatsoever *man*, or *assembly of men*, shall be given by the major part, the *right* to *present* the person of them all, that is to say, to be their *representative*; every one, as well he that *voted for it*, as he that *voted against it*, shall *authorise* all the actions and judgements, of that man, or assembly of men, in the same manner, as if they were his own, to the end, to live peaceably amongst themselves, and be protected against other men.

The act of instituting a commonwealth, what.

From this institution of a commonwealth are derived all the *rights*, and *faculties* of him, or them, on whom sovereign power is conferred by the consent of the people assembled.

The consequences to such institution, are.

First, because they covenant, it is to be understood, they are not obliged by former covenant to anything repugnant hereunto. And consequently they that have already instituted a commonwealth, being thereby bound by covenant, to own the actions, and judgements of one, cannot lawfully make a new covenant, amongst themselves, to be obedient to any other, in any thing whatsoever, without his permission. And therefore, they that are subjects to a monarch, cannot without his leave cast off monarchy, and return to the confusion of a disunited multitude; nor transfer their person from him that beareth it, to another man, or other assembly of men: for they are bound, every man to every man, to own, and be reputed author of all, that he that already is their sovereign, shall do, and judge fit to be done: so that any one man dissenting, all the rest should break their covenant made to that man, which is injustice: and they have also every man given the sovereignty to him that beareth their person; and therefore if they depose him, they take from him that which is his own, and so again it is injustice. Besides, if he that attempteth to depose his sovereign, be killed, or punished by him for such attempt, he is author of his own punishment, as being by the institution, author of all his sovereign shall do: and because it is injustice for a man to do anything, for which he may be punished by his own authority, he is also upon that title, unjust. And whereas some men have pretended for their disobedience to their sovereign, a new covenant, made, not with men, but with God; this also is unjust: for there is no covenant with God, but by mediation of somebody that representeth God's person; which none doth but God's lieutenant, who hath the sovereignty under God. But

1. The subjects cannot change the form of government.

2. Sovereign power cannot be forfeited.

this pretence of covenant with God, is so evident a lie, even in the pretenders' own consciences, that it is not only an act of an unjust, but also of a vile, and unmanly disposition.

Secondly, because the right of bearing the person of them all, is given to him they make sovereign, by covenant only of one to another, and not of him to any of them; there can happen no breach of covenant on the part of the sovereign; and consequently none of his subjects, by any pretence of forfeiture, can be freed from his subjection. That he which is made sovereign maketh no covenant with his subjects beforehand, is manifest; because either he must make it with the whole multitude, as one party to the covenant; or he must make a several covenant with every man. With the whole, as one party, it is impossible; because as yet they are not one person: and if he make so many several covenants as there be men, those covenants after he hath the sovereignty are void; because what act soever can be pretended by any one of them for breach thereof, is the act both of himself, and of all the rest, because done in the person, and by the right of every one of them in particular. Besides, if any one, or more of them, pretend a breach of the covenant made by the sovereign at his institution; and others, or one other of his subjects, or of himself alone, pretend there was no such breach, there is in this case, no judge to decide the controversy; it returns therefore to the sword again; and every man recovereth the right of protecting himself by his own strength, contrary to the design they had in the institution. It is therefore in vain to grant sovereignty by way of precedent covenant. The opinion that any monarch receiveth his power by covenant, that is to say, on condition, proceedeth from want of understanding this easy truth, that covenants being but words and breath, have no force to oblige, contain, constrain, or protect any man, but what it has from the public sword; that is, from the untied hands of that man, or assembly of men that hath the sovereignty, and whose actions are avouched by them all, and performed by the strength of them all, in him united. But when an assembly of men is made sovereign; then no man imagineth any such covenant to have passed in the institution; for no man is so dull as to say, for example, the people of Rome made a covenant with the Romans, to hold the sovereignty on such or such conditions; which not performed, the Romans might lawfully depose the Roman people. That men see not the reason to be alike in a monarchy, and in a popular government, proceedeth from the ambition of some, that are kinder to the government of an assembly, whereof they may hope to participate, than of monarchy, which they despair to enjoy.

Thirdly, because the major part hath by consenting voices declared a sovereign; he that dissented must now consent with the rest; that is, be contented to avow all the actions he shall do, or else justly be destroyed by the rest. For if he voluntarily entered into the congregation of them that were assembled, he sufficiently declared thereby his will, and therefore tacitly covenanted, to stand to what the major part should ordain: and therefore if he refuse to stand thereto, or make protestation against any of their decrees, he does contrary to his covenant, and therefore unjustly. And whether he be of the congregation, or not; and whether his consent be asked, or not, he must either submit to their decrees, or be left in the condition of war he was in before; wherein he might without injustice be destroyed by any man whatsoever.

3. No man can without injustice protest against the institution of the sovereign declared by the major part.

Fourthly, because every subject is by this institution author of all the actions, and judgements of the sovereign instituted; it follows, that whatsoever he doth, it can be no injury to any of his subjects; nor ought he to be by any of them accused of injustice. For he that doth anything by authority from another, doth therein no injury to him by whose authority he acteth: but by this institution of a commonwealth, every particular man is author of all the sovereign doth: and consequently he that complaineth of injury from his sovereign, complaineth of that whereof he himself is author; and therefore ought not to accuse any man but himself; no, nor himself of injury; because to do injury to one's self, is impossible. It is true that they that have sovereign power may commit iniquity; but not injustice, or injury in the proper signification.

4. The sovereign's actions cannot be justly accused by the subject.

Fifthly, and consequently to that which was said last, no man that hath sovereign power can justly be put to death, or otherwise in any manner by his subjects punished. For seeing every subject is author of the actions of his sovereign; he punisheth another for the actions committed by himself.

5. Whatsoever the sovereign doth is unpunishable by the subject.

And because the end of this institution, is the peace and defence of them all; and whosoever has right to the end, has right to the means: it belongeth of right, to whatsoever man, or assembly that hath the sovereignty, to be judge both of the means of peace and defence, and also of the hindrances, and disturbances of the same; and to do whatsoever he shall think necessary to be done, both beforehand, for the

The sovereign is judge of what is necessary for the peace and defence of his subjects.

6. And judge of
what doctrines are
fit to be taught
them.

preserving of peace and security, by prevention of discord at home, and hostility from abroad; and, when peace and security are lost, for the recovery of the same. And therefore,

Sixthly, it is annexed to the sovereignty, to be judge of what opinions and doctrines are averse, and what conducing to peace; and consequently, on what occasions, how far, and what men are to be trusted withal, in speaking to multitudes of people; and who shall examine the doctrines of all books before they be published. For the actions of men proceed from their opinions; and in the well-governing of opinions, consisteth the well-governing of men's actions, in order to their peace, and concord. And though in matter of doctrine, nothing ought to be regarded but the truth; yet this is not repugnant to regulating the same by peace. For doctrine repugnant to peace, can no more be true, than peace and concord can be against the law of nature. It is true, that in a commonwealth, where by the negligence, or unskilfulness of governors, and teachers, false doctrines are by time generally received; the contrary truths may be generally offensive. Yet the most sudden, and rough bursting in of a new truth, that can be, does never break the peace, but only sometimes awake the war. For those men that are so remissly governed, that they dare take up arms to defend, or introduce an opinion, are still in war; and their condition not peace, but only a cessation of arms for fear of one another; and they live, as it were, in the precincts of battle continually. It belongeth therefore to him that hath the sovereign power, to be judge, or constitute all judges of opinions and doctrines, as a thing necessary to peace; thereby to prevent discord and civil war.

7. The right of
making rules;
whereby the sub-
jects may every
man know what is
so his own, as no
other subject can
without injustice
take it from him.

Seventhly, is annexed to the sovereignty, the whole power of prescribing the rules, whereby every man may know, what goods he may enjoy, and what actions he may do, without being molested by any of his fellow-subjects; and this is it men call *propriety*. For before constitution of sovereign power, as hath already been shown, all men had right to all things; which necessarily causeth war: and therefore this propriety, being necessary to peace, and depending on sovereign power, is the act of that power, in order to the public peace. These rules of propriety, or *meum* and *tuum*, and of *good, evil, lawful,* and *unlawful* in the actions of subjects, are the civil laws; that is to say, the laws of each commonwealth in particular; though the name of civil law be now restrained to the ancient civil laws of the city of Rome; which being the head of a great part of the world, her laws at that time were in these parts the civil law.

Eighthly, is annexed to the sovereignty, the right of judicature; that is to say, of hearing and deciding all controversies, which may arise concerning law, either civil, or natural; or concerning fact. For without the decision of controversies, there is no protection of one subject, against the injuries of another; the laws concerning *meum* and *tuum* are in vain; and to every man remaineth, from the natural and necessary appetite of his own conservation, the right of protecting himself by his private strength, which is the condition of war, and contrary to the end for which every commonwealth is instituted.

Ninthly, is annexed to the sovereignty, the right of making war and peace with other nations, and commonwealths; that is to say, of judging when it is for the public good, and how great forces are to be assembled, armed, and paid for that end; and to levy money upon the subjects, to defray the expenses thereof. For the power by which the people are to be defended, consisteth in their armies; and the strength of an army, in the union of their strength under one command; which command the sovereign instituted, therefore hath; because the command of the *militia,* without other institution, maketh him that hath it sovereign. And therefore whosoever is made general of an army, he that hath the sovereign power is always generalissimo.

Tenthly, is annexed to the sovereignty, the choosing of all counsellors, and ministers, magistrates, and officers, both in peace and war. For seeing the sovereign is charged with the end, which is the common peace and defence, he is understood to have power to use such means, as he shall think most fit for his discharge.

Eleventhly, to the sovereign is committed the power of rewarding with riches, or honour, and of punishing with corporal or pecuniary punishment, or with ignominy, every subject according to the law he hath formerly made; or if there be no law made, according as he shall judge most to conduce to the encouraging of men to serve the commonwealth, or deterring of them from doing disservice to the same.

Lastly, considering what value men are naturally apt to set upon themselves; what respect they look for from others; and how little they value other men; from whence continually arise amongst them, emulation, quarrels, factions, and at last war, to the destroying of one another, and diminution of their strength against a common enemy; it is necessary that there be laws of honour, and a public rate of the worth of such men as have deserved, or are able to deserve well of the commonwealth; and that there be force in the hands of some or other, to put those laws in execution. But it hath already been shown, that

Part II. 18.

8. To him also belongeth the right of judicature and decision of controversy.

9. And of making war, and peace, as he shall think best.

10. And of choosing all counsellors and ministers, both of peace & war.

11. And of rewarding and punishing, and that (where no former law hath determined the measure of it) arbitrarily.

12. And of honour and order.

not only the whole *militia,* or forces of the commonwealth; but also the judicature of all controversies, is annexed to the sovereignty. To the sovereign therefore it belongeth also to give titles of honour; and to appoint what order of place, and dignity, each man shall hold; and what signs of respect, in public or private meetings, they shall give to one another.

These rights are indivisible.

These are the rights, which make the essence of sovereignty; and which are the marks, whereby a man may discern in what man, or assembly of men, the sovereign power is placed, and resideth. For these are incommunicable, and inseparable. The power to coin money; to dispose of the estate and persons of infant heirs; to have preemption in markets; and all other statute prerogatives, may be transferred by the sovereign; and yet the power to protect his subjects be retained. But if he transfer the *militia,* he retains the judicature in vain, for want of execution of the laws: or if he grant away the power of raising money; the *militia* is in vain; or if he give away the government of doctrines, men will be frighted into rebellion with the fear of spirits. And so if we consider any one of the said rights, we shall presently see, that the holding of all the rest will produce no effect, in the conservation of peace and justice, the end for which all commonwealths are instituted. And this division is it, whereof it is said, *a kingdom divided in itself cannot stand:* for unless this division precede, division into opposite armies can never happen. If there had not first been an opinion received of the greatest part of England, that these powers were divided between the King, and the Lords, and the House of Commons, the people had never been divided and fallen into this civil war; first between those that disagreed in politics; and after between the dissenters about the liberty of religion; which have so instructed men in this point of sovereign right, that there be few now in England that do not see, that these rights are inseparable, and will be so generally acknowledged at the next return of peace; and so continue, till their miseries are forgotten; and no longer, except the vulgar be better taught than they have hitherto been.

And can by no grant pass away without direct renouncing of the sovereign power.

And because they are essential and inseparable rights, it follows necessarily, that in whatsoever words any of them seem to be granted away, yet if the sovereign power itself be not in direct terms renounced, and the name of sovereign no more given by the grantees to him that grants them, the grant is void: for when he has granted all he can, if we grant back the sovereignty, all is restored, as inseparably annexed thereunto.

Part II.
18.

The power and
honour of subjects
vanisheth in the
presence of the
power sovereign.

This great authority being indivisible, and inseparably annexed to the sovereignty, there is little ground for the opinion of them, that say of sovereign kings, though they be *singulis majores,* of greater power than every one of their subjects, yet they be *universis minores,* of less power than them all together. For if by *all together,* they mean not the collective body as one person, then *all together,* and *every one,* signify the same; and the speech is absurd. But if by *all together,* they understand them as one person, which person the sovereign bears, then the power of all together, is the same with the sovereign's power; and so again the speech is absurd: which absurdity they see well enough, when the sovereignty is in an assembly of the people; but in a monarch they see it not; and yet the power of sovereignty is the same in whomsoever it be placed.

And as the power, so also the honour of the sovereign, ought to be greater, than that of any, or all the subjects. For in the sovereignty is the fountain of honour. The dignities of lord, earl, duke, and prince are his creatures. As in the presence of the master, the servants are equal, and without any honour at all; so are the subjects, in the presence of the sovereign. And though they shine some more, some less, when they are out of his sight; yet in his presence, they shine no more than the stars in the presence of the sun.

Sovereign power
not so hurtful as
the want of it,
and the hurt
proceeds for the
greatest part from
the submitting
readily to a less.

But a man may here object, that the condition of subjects is very miserable; as being obnoxious to the lusts, and other irregular passions of him, or them that have so unlimited a power in their hands. And commonly they that live under a monarch, think it the fault of monarchy; and they that live under the government of democracy, or other sovereign assembly, attribute all the inconvenience to that form of commonwealth; whereas the power in all forms, if they be perfect enough to protect them, is the same: not considering that the state of man can never be without some incommodity or other; and that the greatest, that in any form of government can possibly happen to the people in general, is scarce sensible, in respect to the miseries, and horrible calamities, that accompany a civil war, or that dissolute condition of masterless men, without subjection to laws, and a coercive power to tie their hands from rapine and revenge: nor considering that the greatest pressure of sovereign governors, proceedeth not from any delight, or profit they can expect in the damage or weakening of their subjects, in whose vigour, consisteth their own strength and glory; but in the restiveness of themselves, that unwillingly contributing to their own defence, make it necessary for their governors to draw from them what they can in time of peace, that they may have means on any emergent occasion, or sudden need, to resist, or take advantage on their enemies. For all men are by nature provided of notable multiplying glasses, that is their passions and self-love, through which, every little payment appeareth a great grievance; but are destitute of those prospective glasses, namely moral and civil science, to see afar off the miseries that hang over them, and cannot without such payments be avoided.

Chapter XXI.
Of the Liberty of Subjects.

LIBERTY, or FREEDOM, signifieth, properly, the absence of opposition; by opposition, I mean external impediments of motion; and may be applied no less to irrational, and inanimate creatures, than to rational. For whatsoever is so tied, or environed, as it cannot move but within a certain space, which space is determined by the opposition of some external body, we say it hath not liberty to go further. And so of all living creatures, whilst they are imprisoned, or restrained, with walls, or chains; and of the water whilst it is kept in by banks, or vessels, that otherwise would spread itself into a larger space, we use to say, they are not at liberty to move in such manner, as without those external impediments they would. But when the impediment of motion, is in the constitution of the thing itself, we use not to say; it wants the liberty; but the power to move; as when a stone lieth still, or a man is fastened to his bed by sickness.

And according to this proper, and generally received meaning of the word, a FREEMAN, *is he, that in those things, which by his strength and wit he is able to do, is not hindered to do what he has a will to.* But when the words *free,* and *liberty,* are applied to any thing but *bodies,* they are abused; for that which is not subject to motion, is not subject to impediment: and therefore, when it is said, for example, the way is free, no liberty of the way is signified, but of those that walk in it without stop. And when we say a gift is free, there is not meant any liberty of the gift, but of the giver, that was not bound by any law or covenant to give it. So when we *speak freely,* it is not the liberty of voice, or pronunciation, but of the man, whom no law hath obliged to speak otherwise than he did. Lastly, from the use of the word *free-will,* no liberty can be inferred of the will, desire, or inclination, but the liberty of the man; which consisteth in this, that he finds no stop, in doing what he has the will, desire, or inclination to do.

Fear and liberty are consistent; as when a man throweth his goods into the sea for *fear* the ship should sink, he doth it nevertheless very willingly, and may refuse to do it if he will: it is therefore the action of one that was *free:* so a man sometimes pays his debt, only for *fear* of imprisonment, which because nobody hindered him from detaining, was the action of a man at *liberty.* And generally all actions which men do in commonwealths, for *fear* of the law, are actions, which the doers had *liberty* to omit.

Liberty, and *necessity* are consistent: as in the water, that hath not only *liberty,* but *a necessity* of descending by the channel; so likewise in the actions which men voluntarily do: which, because they proceed from their will, proceed from *liberty;* and yet, because every act of man's will, and every desire, and inclination proceedeth from some cause, and that from another cause, in a continual chain, whose first link is in the hand of God the first of all causes, proceed from *necessity.* So that to him that could see the connexion of those causes, the *necessity* of all men's voluntary actions, would appear manifest. And therefore God, that seeth, and disposeth all things, seeth also that the *liberty* of man in doing what he will, is accompanied with the *necessity* of doing that which God will, and no more, nor less. For though men may do many things, which God does not command, nor is therefore author of them; yet they can have no passion, nor appetite to anything, of which appetite God's will is not the cause. And did not his will assure the *necessity* of man's will, and consequently of all that on man's will dependeth, the *liberty* of men would be a contradiction, and impediment to the omnipotence and *liberty* of God. And this shall suffice, as to the matter in hand, of that natural *liberty,* which only is properly called *liberty.*

But as men, for the attaining of peace, and conservation of themselves thereby, have made an artificial man, which we call a commonwealth; so also have they made artificial chains, called *civil laws,* which they themselves, by mutual covenants, have fastened at one end, to the lips of that man, or assembly, to whom they have given the sovereign power; and at the other end to their own ears. These bonds, in their own nature but weak, may nevertheless be made to hold, by the danger, though not by the difficulty of breaking them.

Part II.
21.
Liberty of sub-
jects consisteth
in liberty from
covenants.

In relation to these bonds only it is, that I am to speak now, of the *liberty* of *subjects*. For seeing there is no commonwealth in the world, wherein there be rules enough set down, for the regulating of all the actions, and words of men; as being a thing impossible: it followeth necessarily, that in all kinds of actions by the laws praetermitted, men have the liberty, of doing what their own reasons shall suggest, for the most profitable to themselves. For if we take liberty in the proper sense, for corporal liberty; that is to say, freedom from chains and prison; it were very absurd for men to clamour as they do, for the liberty they so manifestly enjoy. Again, if we take liberty, for an exemption from laws, it is no less absurd, for men to demand as they do, that liberty, by which all other men may be masters of their lives. And yet, as absurd as it is, this is it they demand; not knowing that the laws are of no power to protect them, without a sword in the hands of a man, or men, to cause those laws to be put in execution. The liberty of a subject, lieth therefore only in those things, which in regulating their actions, the sovereign hath praetermitted: such as is the liberty to buy, and sell, and otherwise contract with one another; to choose their own abode, their own diet, their own trade of life, and institute their children as they themselves think fit; and the like.

Liberty of the
subject consis-
tent with the
unlimited
power of the
sovereign.

Nevertheless we are not to understand, that by such liberty, the sovereign power of life and death, is either abolished, or limited. For it has been already shown, that nothing the sovereign representative can do to a subject, on what pretence soever, can properly be called injustice, or injury; because every subject is author of every act the sovereign doth; so that he never wanteth right to anything, otherwise, than as he himself is the subject of God, and bound thereby to observe the laws of nature. And therefore it may, and doth often happen in commonwealths, that a subject may be put to death, by the command of the sovereign power; and yet neither do the other wrong: as when Jephtha caused his daughter to be sacrificed: in which, and the like cases, he that so dieth, had liberty to do the action, for which he is nevertheless, without injury put to death. And the same holdeth also in a sovereign prince, that putteth to death an innocent subject. For though the action be against the law of nature, as being contrary to equity, as was the killing of Uriah, by David; yet it was not an injury to Uriah, but to God. Not to Uriah, because the right to do what he pleased was given him by Uriah himself: and yet to God, because David was God's subject, and prohibited all iniquity by the law of nature: which distinction, David himself, when he repented the fact, evidently confirmed, saying, *To thee only have I sinned.* In the same manner, the people of Athens, when they banished the most potent of their commonwealth for ten years, thought they committed no injustice; and yet they never questioned what crime he had done; but what hurt he would do: nay they commanded the banishment of they knew not whom; and every citizen bringing his oystershell into the market place, written with the name of him he desired should be banished, without actually accusing him, sometimes banished an Aristides, for his reputation of justice; and sometimes a scurrilous jester, as Hyperbolus, to make a jest of it. And yet a man cannot say, the sovereign people of Athens wanted right to banish them; or an Athenian the liberty to jest, or to be just.

The liberty, whereof there is so frequent and honourable mention, in the histories, and philosophy of the ancient Greeks, and Romans, and in the writings, and discourse of those that from them have received all their learning in the politics, is not the liberty of particular men; but the liberty of the commonwealth: which is the same with that which every man then should have, if there were no civil laws, nor commonwealth at all. And the effects of it also be the same. For as amongst masterless men, there is perpetual war, of every man against his neighbour; no inheritance, to transmit to the son, nor to expect from the father; no propriety of goods, or lands; no security; but a full and absolute liberty in every particular man: so in states, and commonwealths not dependent on one another, every commonwealth, not every man, has an absolute liberty, to do what it shall judge, that is to say, what that man, or assembly that representeth it, shall judge most conducing to their benefit. But withal, they live in the condition of a perpetual war, and upon the confines of battle, with their frontiers armed, and cannons planted against their neighbours round about. The Athenians, and Romans were free; that is, free commonwealths: not that any particular men had the liberty to resist their own representative; but that their representative had the liberty to resist, or invade other people. There is written on the turrets of the city of Lucca in great characters at this day, the word LIBERTAS; yet no man can thence infer, that a particular man has more liberty, or immunity from the service of the commonwealth there, than in Constantinople. Whether a commonwealth be monarchical, or popular, the freedom is still the same.

But it is an easy thing, for men to be deceived, by the specious name of liberty; and for want of judgement to distinguish, mistake

Part II.
21.

The liberty which writers praise, is the liberty of sovereigns; not of private men.

The liberty which writers praise, is the liberty of sovereigns; not of private men.

that for their private inheritance, and birth-right, which is the right of the public only. And when the same error is confirmed by the authority of men in reputation for their writings on this subject, it is no wonder if it produce sedition, and change of government. In these western parts of the world, we are made to receive our opinions concerning the institution, and rights of commonwealths, from Aristotle, Cicero, and other men, Greeks and Romans, that living under popular states, derived those rights, not from the principles of nature, but transcribed them into their books, out of the practice of their own commonwealths, which were popular; as the grammarians describe the rules of language, out of the practice of the time; or the rules of poetry, out of the poems of Homer and Virgil. And because the Athenians were taught, to keep them from desire of changing their government, that they were freemen, and all that lived under monarchy were slaves; therefore Aristotle puts it down in his *Politics, (lib.* 6. *cap.* ii*) In democracy,* LIBERTY *is to be supposed: for it is commonly held, that no man is* FREE *in any other government.* And as Aristotle; so Cicero, and other writers have grounded their civil doctrine, on the opinions of the Romans, who were taught to hate monarchy, at first, by them that having deposed their sovereign, shared amongst them the sovereignty of Rome; and afterwards by their successors. And by reading of these Greek, and Latin authors, men from their childhood have gotten a habit, under a false show of liberty, of favouring tumults, and of licentious controlling the actions of their sovereigns, and again of controlling those controllers; with the effusion of so much blood, as I think I may truly say, there was never any thing so dearly bought, as these western parts have bought the learning of the Greek and Latin tongues.

Liberty of subjects
how to be
measured.

　　To come now to the particulars of the true liberty of a subject; that is to say, what are the things, which though commanded by the sovereign, he may nevertheless, without injustice, refuse to do; we are to consider, what rights we pass away, when we make a commonwealth; or, which is all one, what liberty we deny ourselves, by owning all the actions, without exception, of the man, or assembly we make our sovereign. For in the act of our *submission,* consisteth both our *obligation,* and our *liberty;* which must therefore be inferred by arguments taken from thence; there being no obligation on any man, which ariseth not from some act of his own; for all men equally, are by nature free. And because such arguments, must either be drawn from the express words, *I authorize all his actions,* or from the intention of him that submitteth himself to his power, which intention is to be understood by the end for which he so submitteth: the obligation, and liberty of the subject, is to be derived, either from those words, or others equivalent: or else from the end of the institution of sovereignty, namely, the peace of the subjects within themselves, and their defence against a common enemy.

Part II. 21.

First therefore, seeing sovereignty by institution, is by covenant of every one to every one; and sovereignty by acquisition, by covenants of the vanquished to the victor, or child to the parent; it is manifest, that every subject has liberty in all those things, the right whereof cannot by covenant be transferred. I have shewn before in the 14th chapter, that covenants, not to defend a man's own body, are void. Therefore,

Subjects have liberty to defend their own bodies, even against them that lawfully invade them.

If the sovereign command a man, though justly condemned, to kill, wound, or maim himself; or not to resist those that assault him; or to abstain from the use of food, air, medicine, or any other thing, without which we cannot live; yet hath that man the liberty to disobey.

Are not bound to hurt themselves.

If a man be interrogated by the sovereign, or his authority, concerning a crime done by himself, he is not bound, without assurance of pardon, to confess it; because no man, as I have shown in the same chapter, can be obliged by covenant to accuse himself.

Again, the consent of a subject to sovereign power, is contained in these words, *I authorize, or take upon me, all his actions;* in which there is no restriction at all, of his own former natural liberty: for by allowing him to *kill me,* I am not bound to kill myself when he commands me. It is one thing to say, *kill me, or my fellow, if you please;* another thing to say, *I will kill myself, or my fellow.* It followeth therefore, that

No man is bound by the words themselves, either to kill himself, or any other man; and consequently, that the obligation a man may sometimes have, upon the command of the sovereign to execute any dangerous, or dishonourable office, dependeth not on the words of our submission; but on the intention, which is to be understood by the end thereof. When therefore our refusal to obey, frustrates the end for which the sovereignty was ordained; then there is no liberty to refuse: otherwise there is.

Upon this ground, a man that is commanded as a soldier to fight against the enemy, though his sovereign have right enough to punish his refusal with death, may nevertheless in many cases refuse, without

Nor to warfare, unless they voluntarily undertake it.

injustice; as when he substituteth a sufficient soldier in his place: for in this case he deserteth not the service of the commonwealth. And there is allowance to be made for natural timorousness; not only to women, of whom no such dangerous duty is expected, but also to men of feminine courage. When armies fight, there is on one side, or both, a running away; yet when they do it not out of treachery, but fear, they are not esteemed to do it unjustly, but dishonourably. For the same reason, to avoid battle, is not injustice, but cowardice. But he that inrolleth himself a soldier, or taketh imprest money, taketh away the excuse of a timorous nature: and is obliged, not only to go to the battle, but also not to run from it, without his captain's leave. And when the defence of the commonwealth, requireth at once the help of all that are able to bear arms, every one is obliged; because otherwise the institution of the commonwealth, which they have not the purpose, or courage to preserve, was in vain.

To resist the sword of the commonwealth, in defence of another man, guilty, or innocent, no man hath liberty; because such liberty, takes away from the sovereign, the means of protecting us: and is therefore destructive of the very essence of government. But in case a great many men together, have already resisted the sovereign power unjustly, or committed some capital crime, for which every one of them expecteth death, whether have they not the liberty then to join together, and assist, and defend one another? Certainly they have: for they but defend their lives, which the guilty man may as well do, as the innocent. There was indeed injustice in the first breach of their duty; their bearing of arms subsequent to it, though it be to maintain what they have done, is no new unjust act. And if it be only to defend their persons, it is not unjust at all. But the offer of pardon taketh from them, to whom it is offered, the plea of self-defence, and maketh their perseverance in assisting, or defending the rest, unlawful.

The greatest liberty of subjects, dependeth on the silence of the law.

As for other liberties, they depend on the silence of the law. In cases where the sovereign has prescribed no rule, there the subject hath the liberty to do, or forbear, according to his own discretion. And therefore such liberty is in some places more, and in some less; and in some times more, in other times less, according as they that have the sovereignty shall think most convenient. As for example, there was a time, when in England a man might enter into his own land, and dispossess such as wrongfully possessed it, by force. But in aftertimes, that liberty of forcible entry, was taken away by a statute made, by the king, in parliament. And in some places of the world, men have the liberty of many wives: in other places, such liberty is not allowed.

If a subject have a controversy with his sovereign, of debt, or of right of possession of lands or goods, or concerning any service required at his hands, or concerning any penalty, corporal, or pecuniary, grounded on a precedent law; he hath the same liberty to sue for his right, as if it were against a subject; and before such judges, as are appointed by the sovereign. For seeing the sovereign demandeth by force of a former law, and not by virtue of his power; he declareth thereby, that he requireth no more, than shall appear to be due by that law. The suit therefore is not contrary to the will of the sovereign; and consequently the subject hath the liberty to demand the hearing of his cause; and sentence, according to that law. But if he demand, or take anything by pretence of his power; there lieth, in that case, no action of law; for all that is done by him in virtue of his power, is done by the authority of every subject, and consequently he that brings an action against the sovereign, brings it against himself.

If a monarch, or sovereign assembly, grant a liberty to all, or any of his subjects, which grant standing, he is disabled to provide for their safety, the grant is void; unless he directly renounce, or transfer the sovereignty to another. For in that he might openly, if it had been his will, and in plain terms, have renounced, or transferred it, and did not; it is to be understood it was not his will, but that the grant proceeded from ignorance of the repugnancy between such a liberty and the sovereign power; and therefore the sovereignty is still retained; and consequently all those powers, which are necessary to the exercising thereof; such as are the power of war, and peace, of judicature, of appointing officers, and councillors, of levying money, and the rest named in the 18th chapter.

The obligation of subjects to the sovereign, is understood to last as long, and no longer, than the power lasteth, by which he is able to protect them. For the right men have by nature to protect themselves, when none else can protect them, can by no covenant be relinquished. The sovereignty is the soul of the commonwealth; which once departed from the body, the members do no more receive their motion from it. The end of obedience is protection; which, wheresoever a man seeth it, either in his own, or in another's sword, nature applieth his obedience to it, and his endeavour to maintain it. And though sovereignty, in the intention of them that make it, be immortal; yet it is in its own

In what cases subjects are absolved of their obedience to their sovereign.

nature, not only subject to violent death, by foreign war; but also through the ignorance, and passions of men, it hath in it, from the very institution, many seeds of a natural mortality, by intestine discord.

In case of captivity.

If a subject be taken prisoner in war; or his person, or his means of life be within the guards of the enemy, and hath his life and corporal liberty given him, on condition to be subject to the victor, he hath liberty to accept the condition; and having accepted it, is the subject of him that took him; because he had no other way to preserve himself. The case is the same, if he be detained on the same terms, in a foreign country. But if a man be held in prison, or bonds, or is not trusted with the liberty of his body; he cannot be understood to be bound by covenant to subjection; and therefore may, if he can, make his escape by any means whatsoever.

In case the sovereign cast off the government from himself and his heirs.

If a monarch shall relinquish the sovereignty, both for himself, and his heirs; his subjects return to the absolute liberty of nature; because, though nature may declare who are his sons, and who are the nearest of his kin; yet it dependeth on his own will, as hath been said in the precedent chapter, who shall be his heir. If therefore he will have no heir, there is no sovereignty, nor subjection. The case is the same, if he die without known kindred, and without declaration of his heir. For then there can no heir be known, and consequently no subjection be due.

In case of banishment.

If the sovereign banish his subject; during the banishment, he is not subject. But he that is sent on a message, or hath leave to travel, is still subject; but it is, by contract between sovereigns, not by virtue of the covenant of subjection. For whosoever entereth into another's dominion, is subject to all the laws thereof; unless he have a privilege by the amity of the sovereigns, or by special licence.

In case the sovereign render himself subject to another.

If a monarch subdued by war, render himself subject to the victor; his subjects are delivered from their former obligation, and become obliged to the victor. But if he be held prisoner, or have not the liberty of his own body; he is not understood to have given away the right of sovereignty; and therefore his subjects are obliged to yield obedience to the magistrates formerly placed, governing not in their own name, but in his. For, his right remaining, the question is only of the administration; that is to say, of the magistrates and officers; which, if he have not means to name, he is supposed to approve those, which he himself had formerly appointed.

from *The Turkish Embassy Letters*

Lady Mary Wortley Montagu

Letter 26

To Her Royal Highness the P____¹

*Adrianople,*² **April 1, O. S. 1717**

I have now, Madam, past a journey that has not been undertaken by any Christian since the time of the Greek emperors, and I shall not regret all the fatigues I have suffered in it, if it gives me an opportunity of amusing Your Royal Highness by an account of places utterly unknown amongst us; the Emperor's ambassadors, and those few English that have come hither, always going on the Danube to Nicopolis.³ But that river was now frozen, and Mr. [W]—— so zealous for the service of His Majesty, he would not defer his journey to wait for the conveniency of that passage.⁴ We crossed the deserts of Servia, almost quite overgrown with wood, though a country naturally fertile, and the inhabitants industrious, but the oppression of the peasants is so great, they are forced to abandon their houses and neglect their tillage, all they have being a prey to the janissaries whenever they please to seize upon it. We had a guard of five hundred of them, and I was almost in tears every day to see their insolences in the poor villages through which we passed.

After seven days travelling through thick woods, we came to Nissa,⁵ once the capital of Servia, situate in a fine plain on the river Nissava, in a very good air, and so fruitful a soil that the great plenty is hardly credible. I was certainly assured that the quantity of wine last vintage was so prodigious, they were forced to dig holes in the earth to put it in, not having vessels enough in the town to hold it. The happiness of this plenty is scarce perceived by the oppressed people. I saw here a new occasion for my compassion. The wretches that had provided twenty wagons for our baggage from Belgrade hither for a certain hire, being all sent back without payment, some of their horses lamed and others killed, without any satisfaction made for them. The poor fellows came round the house weeping and tearing their hair and beards in a most pitiful manner without getting anything but drubs from the insolent soldiers. I cannot express to Your Royal Highness how much I was moved at this scene. I would have paid them the money out of my own pocket with all my heart, but it had been only giving so much to the Aga, who would have taken it from them without any remorse.

After four days journey from this place over the mountains we came to Sophia situate in a large beautiful plain, on the river Isca,[6] surrounded with distant mountains. 'Tis hardly possible to see a more agreeable landscape. The city itself is very large and extremely populous. Here are hot baths, very famous for their medicinal virtues.[7] Four days journey from hence we arrived at Philippopoli after having passed the ridges between the mountains of Haemus and Rhodophe,[8] which are always covered with snow. This town is situate on a rising ground near the river Hebrus, and is almost wholly inhabited by Greeks. Here are still some ancient Christian churches. They have a bishop; and several of the richest Greeks live here, but they are forced to conceal their wealth with great care, the appearance of poverty (which includes part of its inconveniencies) being all their security against feeling it in earnest. The country from hence to Adrianople is the finest in the world. Vines grow wild on all the hills, and the perpetual spring they enjoy makes everything gay and flourishing, but this climate, as happy as it seems, can never be preferred to England with all its snows and frosts, while we are blessed with an easy government under a king who makes his own happiness consist in the liberty of his people, and chooses rather to be looked upon as their father, than their master.—This theme would carry me very far, and I am sensible I have already tired out Your Royal Highness's patience, but my letter is in your hands, and you may make it as short as you please, by throwing it into the fire when you are weary of reading it. I am, Madam, with the greatest respect etc.

Letter 27

To the Lady_____ [9]

Adrianople, April 1, O. S. 1717

I am now got into a new world where everything I see appears to me a change of scene, and I write to Your Ladyship with some content of mind, hoping at least that you will find the charm of novelty in my letters, and no longer reproach me that I tell you nothing extraordinary. I won't trouble you with a relation of our tedious journey, but I must not omit what I saw remarkable at

Sophia, one of the most beautiful towns in the Turkish Empire and famous for its hot baths that are resorted to both for diversion and health. I stopped here one day on purpose to see them. Designing to go *incognito*, I hired a Turkish coach; these *voitures* are not at all like ours, but much more convenient for the country, the heat being so great that glasses would be very troublesome. They are made a good deal in the manner of the Dutch coaches, having wooden lattices painted and gilded, the inside being painted with baskets and nosegays of flowers, intermixed commonly with little poetical mottos. They are covered all over with scarlet cloth, lined with silk, and very often richly embroidered and fringed. This covering entirely hides the persons in them, but may be thrown back at pleasure, and the ladies peep through the lattices. They hold four people very conveniently, seated on cushions, but not raised.

In one of these covered wagons I went to the *bagnio* about ten o'clock. It was already full of women. It is built of stone, in the shape of a dome, with no windows but in the roof, which gives light enough. There was five of these domes joined together, the outmost being less than the rest, and serving only as a hall, where the portress stood at the door. Ladies of quality generally give this woman the value of a crown or ten shillings, and I did not forget that ceremony. The next room is a very large one, paved with marble, and all round it raised two sofas of marble, one above another. There were four fountains of cold water in this room, falling first into marble basins, and then running on the floor in little channels made for that purpose, which carried the streams into the next room, something less than this, with the same sort of marble sofas, but so hot with steams of sulphur proceeding from the baths joining to it, 'twas impossible to stay there with one's clothes on. The two other domes were the hot baths, one of which had cocks of cold water turning into it, to temper it to what degree of warmth the bathers have a mind to.

I was in my travelling habit, which is a riding dress, and certainly appeared very extraordinary to them, yet there was not one of them that showed the least surprise or impertinent curiosity, but received me with all the obliging civility possible. I know no European court where the ladies would have behaved themselves in so polite a manner to such a stranger. I believe in the whole there were two hundred women, and yet none of those disdainful smiles, or satiric whispers that never fail in our assemblies, when anybody appears that is not dressed exactly in the fashion. They repeated over and over to me, *Uzelle, pek uzelle*, which is nothing but *Charming, very charming*. The first sofas were covered with cushions and rich carpets, on which sat the ladies, and on the second their slaves behind 'em, but without any distinction of rank by their dress, all being in the state of nature, that is, in plain English, stark naked, without any beauty or defect concealed, yet there was not the least wanton smile or immodest gesture amongst them. They walked, and moved with the same majestic grace which Milton describes of our General Mother.[10] There were many amongst them as exactly proportioned as ever any goddess was drawn by the pencil of Guido or Titian, and most of their skins shiningly white, only adorned by their beautiful hair divided into many tresses hanging on their shoulders, braided either with pearl or ribbon, perfectly representing the figures of the Graces.

I was here convinced of the truth of a reflection that I had often made, that if it was the fashion to go naked, the face would be hardly observed. I perceived that the ladies with the finest skins and most delicate shapes had the greatest share of my admiration, though their faces were sometimes less beautiful than those of their companions. To tell you the truth, I had wickedness enough to wish secretly that Mr. Gervase[11] could have been there invisible. I fancy it would have very much improved his art to see so many fine women naked, in different postures, some in conversation, some working, others drinking coffee or sherbet, and many negligently lying on their cushions, while their slaves (generally pretty girls of seventeen or eighteen) were employed in braiding their hair in several pretty manners. In short, 'tis the woman's coffee-house, where all the news of the Town is told, scandal invented, etc.[12]

They generally take this diversion once a week, and stay there at least four or five hours without getting cold by immediate coming out of the hot-bath into the cool room, which was very surprising to me. The lady that seemed the most considerable amongst them entreated me to sit by her, and would fain have undressed me for the bath. I excused myself with some difficulty, they being all so earnest in persuading me. I was at last forced to open my skirt and show them my stays, which satisfied them very well, for I saw they believed I was so locked up in that machine that it was not in my own power to open it, which contrivance they attributed to my husband.[13] I was charmed with their civility and beauty, and should have been very glad to pass more time with them, but Mr. W—— resolving to pursue his journey next morning early, I was in haste to see the ruins of Justinian's church, which did not afford me so agreeable a prospect as I had left, being little more than a heap of stones.[14] Adieu, Madam. I am sure I have now entertained you with an account of such a sight as you never saw in your life, and what no book of travels could inform you of. 'Tis no less than death for a man to be found in one of these places.[15]

Letter 28

To the Abbot _____.[16]

Adrianople, **April 1, O. S. 1717**

You see that I am very exact in keeping the promise you engaged me to make, but I know not whether your curiosity will be satisfied with the accounts I shall give you, though I can assure you that the desire I have to oblige you to the utmost of my power has made me very diligent in my inquiries and observations. 'Tis certain we have but very imperfect relations of the manners and religion of these people, this part of the world being seldom visited but by merchants who mind little but their own affairs, or travellers who make too short a stay to be able to report anything exactly of their own knowledge. The Turks are too proud to converse familiarly with merchants or etc., who can only pick up some confused informations which are generally false, and they can give no better an account of the ways here than a French *refugée*, lodging in a garret in Greek Street,[17] could write of the Court of England. The journey we have made from Belgrade hither by land cannot possibly be passed by any out of a public character. The desert woods of Servia are the common refuge of thieves who rob fifty in a company, that we had need of all our guards to secure us, and the villages so poor that only force could exhort from them necessary provisions. Indeed, the janissaries had no mercy on their poverty, killing all the poultry and sheep they could find, without asking who they belonged to, while the wretched owners durst not put in their claim for fear of being beaten. Lambs just fallen, geese and turkeys big with egg, all massacred without distinction! I fancied I heard the complaints of Meliboeus for the hope of his flock.[18] When the bassas travel 'tis yet worse. Those oppressors are not content with eating all that is to be eaten belonging to the peasants; after they have crammed themselves and their numerous retinue, they have the impudence to exact what they call *teeth money*, a contribution for the use of their teeth, worn with doing them the honour of devouring their meat. This is literal known truth, however extravagant it seems, and such is the natural corruption of a military government, their religion not allowing of this barbarity any more than ours does.

I had the advantage of lodging three weeks at Belgrade with a principal effendi, that is to say, a scholar. This set of men are equally capable of preferments in the law or the Church, those two sciences being cast into one, a lawyer and a priest being the same word.[19] They are the only men really considerable in the Empire; all the profitable employments and church revenues are in their hands. The Grand Signor, though general heir to his people, never presumes to touch their lands or money, which goes in an uninterrupted succession to their children. 'Tis true they lose this privilege by accepting a place at Court or the title of bassa, but there are few examples of such fools amongst them. You may easily judge of the power of these men who have engrossed all the learning and almost all the wealth of the Empire. 'Tis they that are the real authors, though the soldiers are the actors of revolutions. They deposed the late Sultan Mustapha, and their power is so well known, 'tis the Emperor's interest to flatter them.[20]

This is a long digression. I was going to tell you that an intimate daily conversation with the effendi Achmet-Beg gave me an opportunity of knowing their religion and morals in a more particular manner than perhaps any Christian ever did. I explained to him the difference between the religion of England and Rome, and he was pleased to hear there were Christians that did not worship images, or adore the Virgin Mary. The ridicule of transubstantiation appeared very strong to him. Upon comparing our creeds together, I am convinced that if our friend Dr. _____ [21] had free liberty of preaching here, it would be very easy to persuade the generality to Christianity, whose notions are very little different from his. Mr. Wh_____ [22] would make a very good apostle here; I don't doubt but his zeal will be much fired if you communicate this account to him, but tell him he must first have the gift of tongues before he could possibly be of any use.

Mahometism is divided into as many sects as Christianity, and the first institution as much neglected and obscured by interpretations. I cannot here forbear reflecting on the natural inclination of mankind, to make mysteries and novelties. The *Zeidi, Kadari, Jabari*, etc. put me in mind of the Catholic, Lutheran, and Calvinist, etc., and are equally zealous against one another.[23] But the most prevailing opinion, if you search into the secret of the effendis is plain deism,[24] but this is kept from the people, who are amused with a thousand different notions, according to the different interests of their preachers. There are very few amongst them (Achmet-Beg denied there were any) so absurd as to set up for wit by declaring they believe no God at all. Sir Paul Rycaut is mistaken[25] (as he commonly is) in calling the sect *Muserin* (i.e., the secret with us) atheists, they being deists, and their impiety consists in making a jest of their prophet.[26] Achmet-Beg did not own to me that he was of this opinion, but made no scruple of deviating from some part of Mahomet's Law by drinking wine with the same freedom we did. When I asked how he came to allow himself that liberty, he made answer, all the creatures of God were good and designed for the use of man; however, that the prohibition of wine was a very wise maxim and meant for the common people, being the source of all disorders amongst them, but that the prophet never designed to confine those that knew how to use it with moderation; however, scandal ought to be avoided, and that he never drank it in public. This is the general way of thinking amongst them, and very few forbear drinking wine, that are able to afford it. He assured me that if I understood Arabic I should be very well pleased with reading the Alcoran, which is so far from the nonsense we charge it with, 'tis the purest morality delivered in the very best language. I have since heard impartial Christians speak of it in the same manner, and I don't doubt but all our translations are from copies got from the Greek priests, who would not fail to falsify it with the extremity of malice. No body of men ever were more ignorant and more corrupt, yet they differ so little from the Romish Church, I confess there is nothing gives me a greater abhorrence of the cruelty of your clergy than the barbarous persecutions of them, whenever they have been their masters, for no other reason than not acknowledging the Pope. The dissenting in that one article has got them the titles of heretics, schismatics, and what is worse, the same treatment. I found at Philippopoli a sect of Christians that call themselves Paulines.[27] They show an old church where, they say, St. Paul preached, and he is their favourite saint after the same manner as St. Peter is at Rome; neither do they forget to give him the same preference over the rest of the Apostles.

But of all the religions I have seen the Arnounts seem to me the most particular. They are natives of Arnountlick, the ancient Macedonia, and still retain the courage and hardiness, though they have lost the name of Macedonians, being the best militia in the Turkish Empire and the only check upon the janissaries.[28] They are foot soldiers. We had a guard of them, relieved in every considerable town we passed. They are all clothed and armed at their own expense, generally lusty young fellows, dressed in clean white coarse cloth, carrying guns of a prodigious length, which they run with upon their shoulders as if they did not feel the weight of them, the leader singing a sort of a rude tune not unpleasant, and the rest making up the chorus. These people living between Christians and Mahometans, and not being skilled in controversy, declare that they are utterly unable to judge which religion is best; but to be certain of not entirely rejecting the truth, they very prudently follow both, and go to the mosque on Fridays, and the church on Sundays, saying for their excuse, that at the Day of Judgement they are sure of protection from the True Prophet, but which that is they are not able to determine in this world. I believe there is no other race of mankind, who have so modest an opinion of their own capacity. These are the remarks I have made on the diversity of religions I have seen. I don't ask your pardon for the liberty I have taken in speaking of the Roman. I know you equally condemn the quackery of all churches, as much as you revere the sacred truths in which we both agree.

You will expect I should say something to you of the antiquities of this country, but there are few remains of ancient Greece. We passed near the piece of an arch, which is commonly called Trajan's Gate,[29] as supposing he made it to shut up the passage over the mountains between Sophia and Philippopoli, but I rather believe it the remains of some triumphal arch (though I could not see any inscription), for if that passage had been shut up there are many others, that would serve for the march of an army; and notwithstanding the story of Baldwin, Earl of Flanders,[30] being overthrown in these straits after he won Constantinople, I don't fancy the Germans would find themselves stopped by them. 'Tis true, the road is now made (with great industry) as commodious as possible for the march of the Turkish army. There is not one ditch or puddle between this place and Belgrade that has not a large strong bridge of planks built over it. But the precipices were not so terrible as I had heard them represented. At the foot of these mountains we lay at the little village of Kiskoi, wholly inhabited by Christians, as all the peasants of Bulgaria are. Their houses are nothing but little huts raised of dirt, baked in the sun, and they leave them and fly into the mountains some months before the march of the Turkish army, who would else entirely ruin them by driving away their whole flocks. This precaution secures them in a sort of plenty, for such vast tracts of land lying in common, they have liberty of sowing what they please, and are generally very industrious husbandmen. I drank here several sorts of delicious wine. The women dress themselves in a great variety of coloured glass-beads, and are not ugly, but of tawny complexions. I have now told you all that is worth telling you, (and perhaps more) relating to my journey. When I am at Constantinople, I'll try to pick up some curiosities and then you shall hear again from etc.[31]

Letter 30

To the Countess of ____ [32]

Adrianople, **April 1, O. S. 1717**

I wish to God (dear Sister) that you was as regular in letting me have the pleasure of knowing what passes on your side of the globe, as I am careful in endeavouring to amuse you by the account of all I see that I think you care to hear of. You content yourself in telling me over and over that the town is very dull; it may possibly be dull to you, when every day does not present you with something new, but for me, that am in arrear at least two months news, all that seems very stale with you would be fresh and sweet here. Pray let me into more particulars, I will try to awaken your gratitude by giving you a full and true relation of the novelties of this place, none of which would surprise you more than a sight of my person as I am now in my Turkish habit, though I believe you would be of my opinion that his admirably becoming. I intend to send you my picture; in the mean time accept of it here.[33]

The first piece of my dress is a pair of drawers, very full, that reach to my shoes, and conceal the legs more modestly than your petticoats. They are of a thin rose coloured damask, brocaded with silver flowers. My shoes are of white kid leather, embroidered with gold. Over this hangs my smock of a fine while silk gauze, edged with embroidery. This smock has wide sleeves hanging half-way down my arm and is closed at the neck with a diamond button, but the shape and colour of the bosom very well to be distinguished through it.—The *antery* is a waistcoat made close to the shape, of white and gold damask, with very long sleeves falling back and fringed with deep gold fringe, and should have diamond or pearl buttons. My *caftan*, of the same stuff with my drawers, is a robe exactly fitted to my shape and reaching to my feet, with very long strait falling sleeves. Over this is the girdle, of about four fingers broad, which all that can afford have entirely of diamonds or other precious stones. Those that will not be at that expense, have it of exquisite embroidery on satin, but it must be fastened before with a clasp of diamonds. The *curdée* is a loose robe they throw off or put on according to the weather, being of a rich brocade (mine is green and gold) either lined with ermine or sables; the sleeves reach very little below the shoulders. The headdress is composed of a cap, called *talpock*, which is in winter of fine velvet embroidered with pearls or diamonds, and in summer of a light shining silver stuff. This is fixed on one side of the head, hanging a little way down with a gold tassel, and bound on either with a circle of diamonds (as I have seen several) or a rich embroidered handker-chief. On the other side of the head, the hair is laid flat, and here the ladies are at liberty to show their fancies, some putting flowers, others a plume of heron's feathers, and, in short, what they please; but the most general fashion is, a large bouquet of jewels, made like natural flowers, that is, the buds of pearls, the roses of different coloured rubies, the jessamines of diamonds, the jonquils of topazes, etc. so well set and enamelled, 'tis hard to imagine anything of that kind so beautiful. The hair hangs at its full length behind, divided into tresses braided with pearl or ribbon, which is always in great quantity.

I never saw in my life, so many fine heads of hair. I have counted 110 of these tresses of one lady's, all natural, but it must be owned that every beauty is more common here than with us. 'Tis surprising to see a young woman that is not very handsome. They have naturally the most beautiful complexions in the world and generally large black eyes. I can assure you with great truth, that the Court of England (though I believe it the fairest in Christendom) cannot show so many beauties as are under our protection here. They generally shape their eye-brows, and the Greeks and Turks have the custom of putting round their eyes on the inside a black tincture that, at a distance, or by candlelight, adds very much to the blackness of them. I fancy many of our ladies would be overjoyed to know this secret, but 'tis too visible by day. They dye their nails a rose-colour; I own I cannot enough accustom myself to this fashion to find any beauty in it.

As to their morality or good conduct, I can say, like Harlequin, that 'tis just as 'tis with you,[34] and the Turkish ladies don't commit one sin the less for not being Christians. Now I am a little acquainted with their ways, I cannot for-bear admiring either the exemplary discretion or extreme stupidity of all the writers that have given accounts of them.[35] 'Tis very easy to see, they have more liberty than we have, no woman of what rank soever being permitted to go in the streets without two muslins, one that covers her face all but her eyes, and another that hides the whole dress of her head, and hangs half way down her back; and their shapes are also wholly concealed by a thing they call a *ferigée*, which no woman of any sort appears without. This has strait sleeves that reach-es to their fingers' ends, and it laps all round them, not unlike a riding-hood. In winter 'tis of cloth, and in summer plain stuff or silk. You may guess how effectually this disguises them, that there is no distinguishing the great lady from her slave, and his impossible for the most jealous husband to know his wife when he meets her, and no man dare either touch or follow a woman in the street.

This perpetual masquerade gives them entire liberty of following their inclinations without danger of discovery.[36] The most usual method of intrigue is to send an appointment to the lover to meet the lady at a Jew's shop, which are as notoriously convenient as our Indian houses,[37] and yet even those that don't make that use of them do not scruple to go to buy pennorths[38] and tumble over rich goods, which are chiefly to be found amongst that sort of people. The great ladies seldom let their gallants know who they are, and 'tis so difficult to find it out that they can very seldom guess at her name, they have corresponded with above half a year together. You may easily imagine the number of faithful wives very small in a country where they have nothing to fear from their lovers' indiscretion, since we see so many that have the courage to expose themselves to that in this world, and all the threatened punishment of the next, which is never preached to the Turkish damsels. Neither have they much to apprehend from the resentment of their husbands, those ladies that are rich having all their money in their own hands, which they take with them upon a divorce, with an addition which he is obliged to give them."[39] Upon the whole, I look upon the Turkish women as the only free people in the Empire. The very Divan pays a respect to them, and the Grand Signor himself, when a *bassa* is executed, never violates the privileges of the *haram*,[40] (or women's apartment) which remains unsearched entire to the widow. They are queens of their slaves, whom the husband has no permission so much as to look upon, except it be an old woman or two that his lady chooses. 'Tis true their law permits them four wives, but there is no instance of a man of quality that makes use of this liberty, or of a woman of rank that would suffer it. When a husband happens to be inconstant (as those things will happen) he keeps his mistress in a house apart, and visits her as privately as he can, just as 'tis with you. Amongst all the great men here, I only know the *Tefterdar*[41] (i.e., treasurer) that keeps a number of she-slaves for his own use (that is, on his own side of the house, for a slave, once given to serve a lady, is entirely at her disposal) and he is spoke of as a libertine, or what we should call a rake, and his wife won't see him, though she continues to live in his house.[42] Thus you see, dear Sister, the manners of mankind do not differ so widely as our voyage writers would make us believe. Perhaps it would be more entertaining to add a few surprising customs of my own invention, but nothing seems to me so agreeable as truth, and I believe nothing so acceptable to you. I conclude with repeating the great truth of my being, dear Sister, etc.

Letter 32

To Mrs. S. C_____ [43]

Adrianople, **April 1, O. S. 1717**

In my opinion, dear S., I ought rather to quarrel with you for not answering my Nimeguen[44] letter of August till December than to excuse my not writing again until now. I am sure there is on my side a very good excuse for silence, having gone such tiresome land journeys, though I don't find the conclusion of them so bad as you seem to imagine. I am very easy here, and not in the solitude you fancy me; the great quantity of Greek, French, English and Italians that are under our protection make their court to me from morning till night, and I'll assure you are many of them very fine ladies, for there is no possibility for a Christian to live easily under this government but by the protection of an ambassador, and the richer they are the greater their danger.

Those dreadful stories you have heard of the plague have very little foundation in truth.[45] I own I have much ado to reconcile myself to the sound of a word, which has always given me such terrible ideas. Though I am convinced there is little more in it than a fever, as a proof of which we passed through two or three towns most violently infected. In the very next house where we lay in one of them, two persons died of it. Luckily for me, I was so well deceived that I knew nothing of the matter, and I was made believe, that our second cook who fell ill there had only a great cold. However, we left our doctor to take care of him and yesterday they both arrived here in good health, and I am now let into the secret that he has had the plague. There are many that escape of it, neither is the air ever infected. I am persuaded it would be as easy to root it out here as out of Italy and France, but it does so little mischief, they are not very solicitous about it and are content to suffer this distemper instead of our variety, which they are utterly unacquainted with.

Apropos of distempers, I am going to tell you a thing that I am sure will make you wish yourself here. The smallpox so fatal and so general amongst us is here entirely harmless by the invention of engrafting (which is the term they give it).[46] There is a set of old women who make it their business to perform the operation. Every autumn in the month of September when the great heat is abated, people send to one another to know if any of their family has a mind to have the smallpox. They make parties for this purpose, and when they are met (commonly fifteen or sixteen together) the old woman comes with a nutshell full of the matter of the best sort of smallpox and asks what vein you please to have opened. She immediately rips open that you offer to her with a large needle (which gives you no more pain than a common scratch) and puts into the vein as much venom as can lie upon the head of her needle and after binds up the little wound with a hollow bit of shell and in this manner opens four or live veins. The Grecians have commonly the superstition of opening one in the middle of the forehead, in each arm and on the breast to mark the sign of the cross, but this has a very ill effect all these wounds leaving little scars, and is not done by those that are not superstitious, who choose to have them in the legs or that part of the arm that is concealed. The children or young patients play together all the rest of the day and are in perfect health till the eighth. Then the fever begins to seize them, and they keep their beds two days, very seldom three. They have very rarely above twenty or thirty in their faces, which never mark, and in eight days time they are as well as before their illness. Where they are wounded there remains running sores during the distemper, which I don't doubt is a great relief to it. Every year thousands undergo this operation, and the French Ambassador says pleasantly that they take the smallpox here by way of diversion as they take the waters in other countries. There is no example of any one that has died in it, and you may believe I am very well satisfied of the safety of the experiment since I intend to try it on my dear little son. I am patriot enough to take pains to bring this useful invention into fashion in England, and I should not fail to write to some of our doctors very particularly about it if I knew any one of them that I thought had virtue enough to destroy such a considerable branch of their revenue for the good of mankind, but that distemper is too beneficial to them, not to expose to all their resentment the hardy wight that should undertake to put an end to it.[47] Perhaps if I live to return I may, however, have courage to war with them. Upon this occasion, admire the heroism in the heart of your friend etc.

Letter 33

To Mrs. T____ [48]

Adrianople, **April 1, O. S., 1717**

I can now tell dear Mrs. T that I am safely arrived at the end of my very long journey. I will not tire you with my account of the many fatigues I have suffered. You would rather hear something of what I see here; and a letter out of Turkey that has nothing extraordinary in it would be as great a disappointment as my visitors will receive at London if I return thither without any rarities to show them. What shall I tell you of? You never saw camels in your life and perhaps the description of them will appear new to you. I can assure you the first sight of them was very much so to me, and though I have seen hundreds of pictures of those animals, I never saw any that was resembling enough to give me a true idea of them. I am going to make a bold observation, and possibly a false one, because nobody has ever made it before me, but I do take them to be of the stag-kind; their legs, bodies, and necks are exactly shaped like them, and their colour very near the same. 'Tis true, they are much larger, being a great deal higher than a horse, and so swift, that, after the defeat of Peterwaradin, they far out-run the swiftest horses and brought the first news of the loss of the battle to Belgrade.[49] They are never thoroughly tamed. The drivers take care to tie them one to another with strong ropes, fifty in a string, led by an ass on which the driver rides. I have seen three hundred in one caravan. They carry the third part more than any horse, but 'tis a particular art to load them because of the bunch on their backs. They seem to me very ugly creatures, their heads being ill formed and dis-proportioned to their bodies. They carry all the burdens, and the beasts destined to the plough are buffaloes, an animal you are also unacquainted with. They are larger and more clumsy than an ox. They have short black horns close to their heads, which grow turning backwards. They say this horn looks very beautiful when 'tis well polished. They are all black with very short hair on their hides and extreme little white eyes that make them look like devils. The country people dye their tails and the hair of their foreheads red by way of ornament. Horses are not put here to any laborious work, nor are they at all fit for it. They are beautiful and full of spirit, but generally little and not so strong as the breed of colder countries, very gentle with all their vivacity, swift and sure-footed. I have a little white favourite that I would not part with on any terms. He prances under me with so much fire you would think that I had a great deal of courage to dare mount him, yet I'll assure you I never rid a horse in my life so much at my command.[50] My sidesaddle is the first was ever seen in this part of the world and gazed at with as much wonder as the ship of Columbus was in America. Here are some birds held in a sort of religious reverence, and for that reason multiply prodigiously: turtles on the account of their innocence, and storks because they are supposed to make every winter the pilgrimage to Mecca.[51] To say truth, they are the happiest subjects under the Turkish government, and are so sensible of their privileges they walk the streets without fear and generally build in the low parts of houses. Happy are those that are so distinguished, the vulgar Turks are perfectly persuaded that they will not be that year either attacked by fire or pestilence. I have the happiness of one of their sacred nests just under my chamber window.

Now I am talking of my chamber, I remember the description of the houses here would be as new to you as any of the birds or beasts. I suppose you have read in most of our accounts of Turkey that their houses are the most miserable pieces of building in the world. I can speak very learnedly on that subject, having been in so many of them, and I assure you 'tis no such thing. We are now lodged in a palace belonging to the Grand Signor. I really think the manner of building here very agreeable and proper for the country. 'Tis true they are not at all solicitous to beautify the outsides of their houses, and they are generally built of wood, which I own is the cause of many inconveniences, but this is not to be charged on the ill taste of the people but the oppression of the government. Every house upon the death of its master is at the Grand Signor's disposal, and therefore no man cares to make a great expense which he is not sure his family will be the better for. All their design is to build a house commodious and that will last their lives and are very indifferent if it falls down the year after. Every house, great and small, is divided into two distinct parts, which only join together by a narrow passage. The first house has a large court before it and open galleries all round it, which is to me a thing very agreeable. This gallery leads to all the chambers, which are commonly large and with two rows of windows, the first being of painted glass. They seldom build above two stories, each of which has such galleries. The stairs are broad and not often above thirty steps. This is the house belonging to the lord and the adjoining one is called the haram that is the ladies' apartment, for the name of Seraglio is peculiar to the Grand Signor's. It has also a gallery running round it towards the garden to which all the windows are turned, and the same number of chambers as the other, but more gay and splendid both in painting and furniture. The second row of windows are very low, with grates like those of convents.

The rooms are all spread with Persian carpets and raised at one end of them (my chamber is raised at both ends) about two foot. This is the sofa and is laid with a richer sort of carpet, and all round it a sort of couch raised half a foot, covered with rich silk according to the fancy or magnificence of the owner. Mine is of scarlet cloth with a gold fringe. Round this are placed, standing against the wall, two rows of cushions, the first very large and the next little ones, and here the Turks display their greatest magnificence. They are generally brocade or embroidery of gold wire upon satin. Nothing can look more gay and splendid. These seats are also so convenient and easy I shall never endure chairs as long as I live. The rooms are low, which I think no fault, and the ceiling is always of wood, generally inlaid or painted and gilded. They use no hangings, the rooms being all wainscoted with cedar set off with nails or painted with flowers, which open in many places, with folding doors and serve for cabinets, I think more conveniently than ours. Between the windows are little arches to set pots of perfume or baskets of flowers, but what pleases me best is the fashion of having marble fountains in the lower part of the room which throws up several spouts of water, giving at the same time an agreeable coolness and a pleasant dashing sound falling from one basin to another. Some of these fountains are very magnificent. Each house has a bagnio, which is generally of two or three little rooms leaded on the top, paved with marble, with basins, cocks of water, and all conveniences for either hot or cold baths.

You will perhaps be surprised at an account so different from what you have been entertained with by the common voyage-writers, who are very fond of speaking of what they don't know. It must be under a very particular character, or on some extraordinary occasion, when a Christian is admitted into the house of a man of quality, and their harams are always forbidden ground.[52] Thus they can only speak of the outside, which makes no great appearance, and the women's apartments are all built backward, removed from sight, and have no other prospect than the gardens, which are enclosed with very high walls. There is none of our parterres[53] in them, but they are planted with high trees, which give an agreeable shade and, to my fancy, a pleasing view. In the midst of the garden is the *chiosk*, that is, a large room, commonly beautified with a fine fountain in the midst of it. It is raised nine or ten steps and enclosed with gilded lattices, round which vines, jessamines and honey-suckles twining make a sort of green wall. Large trees are planted round this place, which is the scene of their greatest pleasures, and where the ladies spend most of their hours, employed by their music or embroidery. In the public gardens, there are public chiosks where people go that are not so well accommodated at home and drink their coffee, sherbet, etc. Neither are they ignorant of a more durable manner of building. Their mosques are all of free stone, and the public *hans* or inns extremely magnificent, many of them taking up a large square, built round with shops under stone arches, where poor artificers are lodged grails. They have always a mosque joining to them, and the body of the han is a most noble hall, capable of holding three or four hundred persons, the court extreme spacious, and cloisters round it, that give it the air of our colleges. I own, I think these foundations a more reasonable piece of charily than the founding of convents. I think I have now told you a great deal for once. If you don't like my choice of subjects, tell me what you would have me write upon. There is nobody more desirous to entertain you than, dear Mrs. T, etc.

Letter 38

To the Lady_____ [54]

Belgrade Village, June 17, O. S. 1717

I heartily beg Your ladyship's pardon, but I really could not forbear laughing heartily at your letter and the commissions you are pleased to honour me with. You desire me to buy you a Greek slave who is to be mistress of a thousand good qualities. The Greeks are subjects and not slaves. Those who are to be bought in that manner are either such as are taken in war or stolen by the Tartars from Russia, Circassia, or Georgia, and are such miserable awkward, poor wretches, you would not think any of them worthy to be your housemaid. 'Tis true that many thousands were taken in the Morea,[55] but they have been most of them redeemed by the charitable contributions of the Christians or ransomed by their own relations at Venice. The fine slaves that wait upon the great ladies, or serve the pleasures of the great men, are all bought at the age of eight or nine year old and educated with great care to accomplish them in singing, dancing, embroidery, etc. They are commonly Circassians, and their patron never sells them, except it is as a punishment for some very great fault. If ever they grow weary of them, they either present them to a friend or give them their freedoms. Those that are exposed to sale at the markets are always either guilty of some crime or so entirely worthless that they are of no use at all. I am afraid you'll doubt the truth of this account, which I own is very different from our common notions in England, but it is not less truth for all that.

Your whole letter is full of mistakes from one end to the other. I see you have taken your ideas of Turkey from that worthy author Dumont,[56] who has writ with equal ignorance and confidence. 'Tis a particular pleasure to me here to read the voyages to the Levant, which are generally so far removed from truth and so full of absurdities, I am very well diverted with them. They never fail giving you an account of the women, which 'tis certain they never saw, and talking very wisely of the genius of the men, into whose company they are never admitted, and very often describe mosques, which they dare not peep into. The Turks are very proud and will not converse with a stranger they are not assured is considerable in his own country. I speak of the men of distinction, for as to the ordinary fellows, you may imagine what ideas their conversation can give of the general genius of the people.

As to the balm of Mecha,[57] I will certainly send you some; but it is not so easily got as you suppose it, and I cannot in conscience advise you to make use of it. I know not how it comes to have such universal applause. All the ladies of my acquaintance at London and Vienna have begged me to send pots of it to them. I have had a present of a small quantity (which I'll assure you is very valuable) of the best sort, and with great joy applied it to my face, expecting some wonderful effect to my advantage. The next morning the change indeed was wonderful; my face was swelled to a very extraordinary size, and all over as red as my Lady [ ]'s.[58] It remained in this lamentable state three days, during which you may be sure I passed my time very ill. I believed it would never be otherwise, and to add to my mortification Mr. W_____ reproached my indiscretion without ceasing. However, my face is since in statu quo; nay, I'm told by the ladies here, that 'tis much mended by the operation, which I confess I cannot perceive in my looking glass. Indeed, if one was to form an opinion of this balm from their faces, once should think very well of it. They all make use of it, and have the loveliest bloom in the world. From my part, I never intend to endure the pain of it again; let my complexion take its natural course, and decay in its own due time. I have very little esteem for medicines of this nature; but do as you please, Madam, only remember before you use it that your face will not be such as you'll care to show in the drawing room for some days after.

If one was to believe the women in this country, there is a surer way of making one's self beloved than by becoming handsome, though you know that's our method. But they pretend to the knowledge of secrets that by way of enchantment give them the entire empire over whom they please. For me, that am not very apt to believe in wonders, I cannot find faith for this. I disputed the point last night with a lady who really talks very sensibly on any other subject, but she was downright angry with me that she did not perceive she had persuaded me of the truth of forty stories she told me of this kind, and at last mentioned several ridiculous marriages that there could be no other reason assigned for. I assured her that in England, where we were entirely ignorant of all magic, where the climate is not half so warm, nor the women half so handsome, we were not without our ridiculous marriages, and that we did not look upon it as anything supernatural when a man played the fool for the sake of a woman. But my arguments could not convince her against (as she said) her certain knowledge, though she added that she scrupled making use of charms herself, but that she could do it whenever she pleased; and staring in my face said (with a very learned air) that no enchantments would have their effect upon me, and that there were some people exempt from their power, but very few. You may imagine how I laughed at this discourse, but all the women are of the same opinion. They don't pretend to any commerce with the devil, but that there are certain compositions to inspire love. If one could send over a shipload of them, I fancy it would be a very quick way of raising an estate. What would not some ladies of our acquaintance give for such merchandise?

Adieu my dear Lady _____, I cannot conclude my letter with a subject that affords more delightful scenes to imagination. I leave you to figure to yourself the extreme court that will be made to me at my return if my travels should furnish me with such a useful piece of learning. I am, dear Madam, etc.

Letter 39

To Mrs. T_____ [59]

Pera of Constantinople, Jan 4, O. S. 1718[60]

I am infinitely obliged to you, dear Mrs. T_____, for your entertaining letter. You are the only one of my correspondents that have judged right enough to think I would gladly be informed of the news amongst you. All the rest of them tell me (almost in the same words) that they suppose I know everything. Why they are pleased to suppose in this manner I can guess no reason except they are persuaded that the breed of Mahomet's pigeon[61] still subsists in this country, and that I receive supernatural intelligence. I wish I could return your goodness with some diverting accounts from hence, but I know not what part of the scenes here would gratify your curiosity or whether you have any curiosity at all for things so far distant. To say the truth, I am at this present writing not very much turned for the recollection of what is diverting, my head being wholly filled with the preparations necessary for the increase of my family, which I expect every day.[62] You may easily guess at my uneasy situation, but I am, however, in some degree comforted by the glory that accrues to me from it, and a reflection on the contempt I should otherwise fall under. You won't know what to make of this speech, but in this country 'tis more despicable to be married and not fruitful than 'tis with us to be fruitful before marriage. They have a notion that whenever a woman leaves off bringing children 'tis because she is too old for that business, whatever her face says to the contrary, and this opinion makes the ladies here so ready to make proofs of their youth (which is as necessary in order to be a received beauty as it is to show the proofs of nobility to be admitted Knight of Malta[63]) that they do not content themselves with using the natural means, but fly to all sort of quackeries to avoid the scandal of being past child-bearing and often kill themselves by them. Without any exaggeration, all the women of my acquaintance that have been married ten year have twelve or thirteen children, and the old ones boast of having had five and twenty or thirty apiece, and are respected according to the number they have produced. When they are with child, 'tis their common expression to say they hope God will be so merciful to them to send two this time, and when I have asked them sometimes how they expected to provide for such a flock as they desire, they answer that the plague will certainly kill half of them, which, indeed, generally happens without much concern to the parents, who are satisfied with the vanity of having brought forth so plentifully. The French Ambassadress is forced to comply with this fashion as well as myself. She has not been here much above a year, and has lain in once and is big again.[64] What is most wonderful is the exemption they seem to enjoy from the curse entailed on the sex. They see all company the day of their delivery, and at the fortnight's end return visits, set out in their jewels and new clothes.

I wish I may find the influence of the climate in this particular, but I fear I shall continue an English woman in that affair as well as I do in my dread of fire and plague, which are two things very little feared here, most families having had their houses burnt down once or twice, occasioned by their extraordinary way of warming themselves, which is neither by chimneys nor stoves but a certain machine called a tendour, the height of two foot in the form of a table, covered with a fine carpet or embroidery. This is made only of wood, and they put into it a small quantity of hot ashes and sit with their legs under the carpet. At this table they work, read, and, very often sleep; and if they chance to dream, kick down the tendour and the hot ashes commonly sets the house on-fire. There was five hundred houses burnt in this manner about a fortnight ago, and I have seen several of the owners since who seem not at all moved at so common a misfortune. They put their goods into a bark, and see their houses burn with great philosophy, their persons being very seldom endangered, having no stairs to descend.

But having entertained you with things I don't like, 'tis but just I should tell you something that pleases me. The climate is delightful in the extremist degree. I am now sitting, this present 4th of January, with the windows open, enjoying the warm shine of the sun, while you are freezing over a sad sea-coal fire; and my chamber set out with carnations, roses, and jonquils, fresh from my garden.[65] I am also charmed with many points of the Turkish law, to our shame be it spoken, better designed and better executed than ours, particularly the punishment of convicted liars (triumphant criminals in our country, God knows). They are burnt in the forehead with a hot iron, being proved authors of any notorious falsehood. How many white foreheads should we see disfigured? How many fine gentlemen would be forced to wear their wigs low as their eyebrows were this law in practice with us? I should go on to tell you many other parts of justice, but I must send for my midwife.

Letter 43

To the Countess of____[66]

I am now preparing to leave Constantinople, and perhaps you will accuse me of hypocrisy when I tell you 'tis with regret, but I am used to the air and have learnt the language. I am easy here, and as much as I love travelling, I tremble at the inconveniencies attending so great a journey with a numerous family and a little infant hanging at the breast. However, I endeavour upon this occasion to do as I have hitherto done in all the odd turns of my life; turn them, if I can, to my diversion. In order to this, I ramble every day wrapped up in my *ferace* and *yashmak*[67] about Constantinople and amuse myself with seeing all that is curious in it. I know you'll expect that this declaration should be followed with some account of what I have seen, but I am in no humour to copy what has been writ so often over. To what purpose should I tell you that Constantinople is the ancient Byzantium, that 'tis at present the conquest of a race of people supposed Scythians,[68] that there is five or six thousand mosques in it, that Sancta Sophia was founded by Justinian, etc.? I'll assure you 'tis not want of learning that I forbear writing all these bright things. I could also, with little trouble, run over Knolles and Sir Paul Rycaut to give you a list of Turkish Emperors, but I will not tell you what you may find in every author that has writ of this country.[69] I am more inclined, out of a true female spirit of contradiction, to tell you the falsehood of a great part of what you find in authors. As for example the admirable Mr. Hill, who so gravely asserts that he saw in Sancta Sophia, a sweating pillar very balsamic for disordered heads.[70] There is not the least tradition of any such matter, and I suppose it was revealed to him in vision during his wonderful stay in the Egyptian Catacombs, for I am sure he never heard of any such miracle here. 'Tis also very pleasant to observe how tenderly he and all his brethren voyage-writers lament on the miserable confinement of the Turkish ladies,[71] who are (perhaps) freer than any ladies in the universe,[72] and are the only women in the world that lead a life of uninterrupted pleasure, exempt from cares, their whole time being spent in visiting, bathing, or the agreeable amusement of spending money and inventing new fashions. A husband would be thought mad that exacted any degree of economy from his wife, whose expenses are no way limited but by her own fancy. 'Tis his business to get money and hers to spend it, and this noble prerogative extends itself to the very meanest of the sex. Here is a fellow that carries embroidered handkerchiefs upon his back to sell, as miserable a figure as you may suppose such a mean dealer, yet I'll assure you his wife scorns to wear anything less than cloth of gold, has her ermine furs, and a very handsome set of jewels for her head. They go abroad when and where they please. 'Tis true they have no places but the bagnios, and there can only be seen by their own sex; however that is a diversion they take great pleasure in.

I was three days ago at one of the finest in the town and had the opportunity of seeing a Turkish bride received there and all the ceremonies used on that occasion, which made me recollect the epilthalamium of Helen by Theocritus,[73] and it seems to me that the same customs have continued ever since. All the she-friends, relations and acquaintance of the two families newly allied meet at the bagnio; several others go out of curiosity, and I believe there was that day at least two hundred women. Those that were or had been married placed themselves round the rooms on the marble sofas, but the virgins very hastily threw off their clothes, and appeared without other ornament or covering than their own long hair braided with pearl or ribbon. Two of them met the bride at the door, conducted by her mother and another grave relation. She was a beautiful maid of about seventeen, very richly dressed and shining with jewels, but was presently reduced by them to the state of nature. Two others filled silver gilt pots with perfume and begun the procession, the rest following in pairs, to the number of thirty. The leaders sung an epithalamium, answered by the others in chorus, and the two last led the fair bride, her eyes fixed on the ground with a charming affectation of modesty. In this order they marched round the three large rooms of the bagnio. 'Tis not easy to represent to you the beauty of this sight, most of them being well proportioned and white skinned, all of them perfectly smooth and polished by the frequent use of bathing. After having made their tour, the bride was again led to every matron round the rooms, who saluted her with a compliment and a present, some of jewels, others pieces of stuff, handkerchiefs, or little gallantries of that nature, which she thanked them for by kissing their hands.[74]

I was very well pleased with having seen this ceremony, and you may believe me that the Turkish ladies have at least as much wit and civility, nay liberty, as ladies among us.[75] 'Tis true the same customs that give them so many opportunities of gratifying their evil inclinations (if they have any) also puts it very fully in the power of their husbands to revenge them if they are discovered, and I do not doubt but they suffer sometimes for their indiscretions in a very severe manner. About two months ago there was found at day break not very far from my house, the bleeding body of a young woman, naked, only wrapped in a coarse sheet, with two wounds with a knife, one in her side, and another in her breast. She was not yet quite cold, and was so surprisingly beautiful that there were very few men in Pera that did not go to look upon her; but it was not possible for anybody to know her, no woman's face being known. She was supposed to be brought in dead of night from the Constantinople side and laid there. Very little inquiry was made about the murderer, and the corpse privately buried without noise. Murder is never pursued by the King's officers as with us. 'Tis the business of the next relations to revenge the dead person, and if they like better to compound the matter for money (as they generally do) there is no more said of it. One would imagine this defect in their government should make such tragedies very frequent, yet they are extremely rare, which is enough to prove the people not naturally cruel. Neither do I think in many other particulars they deserve the barbarous character we give them.

I am well acquainted with a Christian woman of quality who made it her choice to live with a Turkish husband, and is a very agreeable sensible lady. Her story is so extraordinary I cannot forbear relating it, but I promise you it shall be in as few words as I can possibly express it. She is a Spaniard and was at Naples with her family when that kingdom was part of the Spanish dominion.[76] Coming from thence in a felucca,[77] accompanied by her brother, they were attacked by the Turkish admiral, boarded and taken; and now how shall I modestly tell you the rest of her adventure? The same accident happened to her that happened to the fair Lucretia[78] so many years before her, but she was too good a Christian to kill herself as that heathenish Roman did. The admiral was so much more charmed with the beauty and long-suffering of the fair captive that as his first compliment he gave immediate liberty to her brother and attendants, who made haste to Spain and in a few months sent the sum of £4,000 sterling as a ransom for his sister. The Turk took the money, which he presented to her, and told her she was at liberty, but the lady very discreetly weighed the different treatment she was likely to find in her native country. Her Catholic relations, as the kindest thing they could do for her in her present circumstances, would certainly confine her to a nunnery for the rest of her days. Her infidel lover was very handsome, very tender, fond of her, and lavished at her feet all the Turkish magnificence. She answered him very resolutely that her liberty was not so precious to her as her honour, that he could no way restore that but by marrying her. She desired him to accept the ransom as her portion and give her the satisfaction of knowing that no man could boast of her favours without being her husband. The admiral was transported at this kind offer and sent back the money to her relations, saying he was too happy in her possession. He married her and never took any other wife, and (as she says herself) she never had any reason to repent the choice she made. He left her some years after one of the richest widows in Constantinople, but there is no remaining honourably a single woman, and that consideration has obliged her to marry the present Captain Bassa (i.e., admiral), his successor.[79] I am afraid you will think that my friend fell in love with her ravisher, but I am willing to take her word for it that she acted wholly on principles of honour, though I think she might be reasonably touched at his generosity, which is often found amongst the Turks of rank.[80]

'Tis a degree of generosity to tell the truth, and 'tis very rare that any Turk will assert a solemn falsehood. I don't speak of the lowest sort, for as there is a great deal of ignorance, there is very little virtue amongst them, and false witnesses are much cheaper than in Christendom, those wretches not being punished (even when they are publicly detected) with the rigour they ought to be. Now I am speaking of their law, I don't know whether I have ever mentioned to you one custom peculiar to this country. I mean adoption, very common amongst the Turks, and yet more amongst the Greeks and Armenians. Not having it in their power to give their estates to a friend or distant relation,[81] to avoid its falling into the Grand Signor's treasury, when they are not likely to have children of their own, they choose some pretty child of either sex amongst the meanest people, and carry the child and its parents before the cadi, and there declare they receive it for their heir. The parents at the same time renounce all future claim to it, a writing is drawn and witnessed, and a child thus adopted cannot be disinherited. Yet I have seen some common beggars that have refused to part with their children in this manner to some of the richest amongst the Greeks. So powerful is the instinctive fondness natural to parents! Though the adopting fathers are generally very tender to these children of their souls as they call them. I own this custom pleases me much better than our absurd following our name. Methinks 'tis much more reasonable to make happy and rich an infant whom I educate after my own manner, brought up (in the Turkish phrase) upon my knees, and who has learnt to look upon me with a filial respect, than to give an estate to a creature without other merit or relation to me than by a few letters. Yet this is an absurdity we see frequently practiced.

Now I have mentioned the Armenians, perhaps it will be agreeable to tell you something of that nation, with which I am sure you are utterly unacquainted. I will not trouble you with the geographical account of the situation of their country, which you may see in the map, or a relation of their ancient greatness, which you may read in the Roman history. They are now subject to the Turks, and, being very industrious in trade, and increasing and multiplying, are dispersed in great numbers through all the Turkish dominions. They were (as they say) converted to the Christian religion by St. Gregory,[82] and are (perhaps) the devoutest Christians in the whole world. The chief precepts of their priests enjoin the strict keeping of their Lents, which are at least seven months in every year, and are not to be dispensed with on the most emergent necessity. No occasion whatever can excuse them if they touch anything more than mere herbs or roots (without oil) and plain dry bread. That is their Lenten diet. Mr. W____ has one of his interpreters of this nation, and the poor fellow was brought so low with the severity of his fasts that his life was despaired of, yet neither his master's commands or the doctor's entreaties (who declared nothing else could save his life) were powerful enough to prevail with him to take two or three spoonfuls of broth. Excepting this, which may rather be called custom than an article of faith, I see very little in their religion different from ours. 'Tis true they seem to incline very much to Mr. Wh____'s doctrine;[83] neither do I think the Greek church very distant from it, since 'tis certain the insisting on the Holy Spirit only proceeding from the Father is making a plain subordination in the Son. But the Armenians have no notion of transubstantiation, whatever account Sir Paul Rycaut gives of them (which account I am apt to believe was designed to compliment our court in 1679)[84] and they have a great horror for those amongst them that change to the Roman religion.

What is most extraordinary in their customs is their matrimony, a ceremony I believe unparalleled all over the world. They are always promised very young, but the espoused never see one another till three days after their marriage. The bride is carried to church with a cap on her head in the fashion of a large trencher, and over it a red silken veil which covers her all over to her feet. The priest asks the bridegroom whether he is contented to marry that woman, be she deaf, be she blind? These are the literal words, to which having answered yes, she is led home to his house accompanied with all the friends and relations on both sides, singing and dancing, and is placed on a cushion in the corner of the sofa, but her veil never lifted up, not even by her husband, till she has been three days married.[85] There is something so odd and monstrous in these ways that I could not believe them till I had enquired of several Armenians myself, who all assured me of the truth of them, particularly one young fellow who wept when he spoke of it, being promised by his mother to a girl that he must marry in this manner, though he protested to me he had rather die than submit to this slavery, having already figured his bride to himself with all the deformities in nature—.

I fancy I see you bless yourself at this terrible relation. I cannot conclude my letter with a more surprising story yet 'tis as seriously true as that I am, dear Sister,[86] your etc.[87]

Notes

[1] To the Princess of Wales. Caroline of Anspach (1683–1737) married George Augustus in 1705 and succeeded as Queen consort in 1727. Like Lady Mary, she was known for her intelligence and beauty, and was also an avid reader, owned an extensive library, and survived smallpox. She was instrumental in the spread of Lady Mary's smallpox inoculation. Convincing the court of its efficacy, the Princess had three of her own children inoculated.

[2] Adrianople is the English name for present day Turkish city of Edirne, which lies close to the Greek and Bulgarian border. It was the capital of the Ottoman Empire (1365–1453) prior to the conquest of Constantinople; Mustapha II (1695–1703) resided in Edirne most of the time, a decision that outraged Istanbul. On taking power, Ahmet III promised never to reside there (see Mansel 180), but it remained an important city. Wortley first met with the Grand Vizier in Adrianople.

[3] Preveza, Greece. Nikopolis is the ancient name for the city. As Halsband notes (1.310n3), Lady Mary is exaggerating; "Christians had made the journey by land as early as the sixteenth century." However, she is likely the first Christian woman to write about the route.

[4] Halsband (1.310n4) gives Wortley's account, which suggests the river was not frozen.

[5] Niš is one of the oldest cities in the Balkans, the medieval capital, and the birthplace of Constantine the Great.

[6] Sofia and the Iskar River, Bulgaria.

[7] Both the Romans and Ottomans built public baths around the thermal mineral springs that are still enjoyed today. See Letter 27, where Lady Mary describes her visit to them.

[8] Plovdiv, Bulgaria. The Greek name was Philippoupolis and the Turkish name Filibe.

[9] To Lady____. The addressee of this crucial letter is not specified. Although the letter is addressed from Adrianople, Lady Mary is relating events that happened in Sofia. This letter inspired the famous orientalist painting, *Le Bain turc* (1862) by Jean-Auguste-Dominique Ingres (1780–1867), who copied several passages from it in his notebook. See p. 118, note 74.

[10] John Milton, *Paradise Lost* (1667) 4.304–18:

She, as a veil down to the slender waist,
Her unadorned golden tresses wore
Dishevell'd, but in wanton ringlets wav'd
As the vine curls her tendrils—which implied

Subjection, but requir'd with gentle sway,
And by her yielded, by him best receiv'd,
Yielded with coy submission, modest pride,
And sweet, reluctant, amorous delay.
Nor those mysterious parts were then conceal'd:
Then was not guilty shame. Dishonest Shame
Of Nature's works, Honour dishonourable,
Sin-bred, how have ye troubl'd mankind
With shows instead, mere shows of seeming pure,
And banish'd from man's life his happiest life,
Simplicity and spotless innocence!

[11] Charles Jervas (c. 1675–1739), an Irish portrait painter who painted many of London's intellectuals including Pope and Swift, became the Principal Portrait Painter to King George I in 1723. He painted Lady Mary in 1716.

[12] The coffee houses in England (the first opened in 1637, almost a hundred years after the first coffee house in Istanbul) were mostly closed to women clients during this period, although women could own them and did serve in them.

[13] Halsband (1.314n3) notes: "In 1741, when LM met Joseph Spence in Rome, she related this episode, and quoted the lady's remark that 'the Husbands in England were much worse than in the East; for that they ty'd up their Wives in little Boxes, of the shape of their bodies.'" Working against the tradition of male travel literature that emphasized the enslavement of Turkish women, Lady Mary instead offers herself up as a figure in need of saving.

[14] Lady Mary is referring to the few remains of antiquity left in the ancient city of Sardica, the church founded by the Emperor Justinian I (ruled from 527 to 565).

[15] Male travelers had no access to women's quarters, yet fantastical accounts of the abuse of Turkish women in the harem are standard tropes of seventeenth- and eighteenth-century travel narratives to the Levant.

[16] To the Abbé Conti. Antonio Schinella Conti (1677–1749) was a Venetian cleric and literary figure from Padua who visited England in 1715 and in 1717–18. While in England he became a member of the Royal Society and adjudicated in the controversy between Leibniz and Newton over the invention of differential calculus. Princess Caroline received him, and throughout 1715 he attended Lady Mary's weekly suppers of authors and intellectuals. They were reacquainted when Lady Mary moved to Venice in 1739, and he translated nine of her poems and one essay into Italian. See Grundy 89 and 405 . . . for a letter she wrote to him in French.

[17] A street in Soho, London. An area that was populated by French Protestant refugees (Huguenots) that escaped to England after the revocation of the Edict of Nantes in 1685.

[18] See Virgil, *Eclogue I*. In Virgil, Meliboeus, who had his farm expropriated by a veteran in Octavian's army, bemoans the effects of officially sanctioned extortion. For

many of Lady Mary's readers this passage and the reference to Virgil would have resonated with on-going debates regarding the corruptibility and the danger of a standing army. England was one of the last European powers to institute a standing military.

[19] Kadi or Islamic judge.

[20] The "abdication" of Mustapha II in 1703 in favour of his brother, the reigning Sultan Ahmed III, was known as the Edirne Incident. Istanbul citizens, unpaid Janissaries, and most religious leaders (the *ulema*), all participated in the revolt against the deposed Sultan.

[21] Dr. Samuel Clarke (1675–1729), Rector of St. James's Church, Piccadilly, was criticized by more orthodox churchmen for promulgating deism to his congregation. He was a close acquaintance of Lady Mary, whom he had met in 1715. See p. 102, note 22.

[22] The English mathematician, historian, and theologian William Whiston (1667–1752) held that the early church believed in Arianism, a doctrine that held that Christ was created and therefore separate and inferior to God. He was expelled from Cambridge for his views. He was a close friend of Clarke and also part of Lady Mary's circle.

[23] The two main sects of Islam are Sunni and Shi'a, but within these two there are many other smaller divisions. Zaidiyah and Kadariyah are the ones to which Lady Mary is referring. Jabari may be Jafariyah, a subset of Kadariyah (although Halsband [I.317n4] has it listed as Djabariya). For more on Muslim sects see Ibn Tāhir al-Baghdadi.

[24] Deists believe in a supreme being on purely rational grounds without any reliance on revealed religion.

[25] Sir Paul Rycaut (1629–1700) was a prominent member of the embassy to the Ottoman Porte from 1660–65. While carrying out his duties for the Levant Company, he compiled the information that would eventually be published as *The Present State of the Ottoman Empire* (1686). Printed as a continuation of Richard Knolles's *The Generalie Historie of the Turkes* (1603), Rycaut's text was one of the most influential works about the Ottomans.

[26] Rycaut (129) had claimed that the Muserin (Mu'tazila) were atheists, but Lady Mary is more accurate when she describes them as deists as this sect holds that knowledge is derived from reason and that the Qur'an as created could not be co-terminous with the eternal.

[27] See p. 98, note 8 on her visit. The Paulicians formed a new centre in Philippopoli; they were a dualistic and heretical sect who venerated the apostle St. Paul.

[28] Arnauts were Albanians who were highly regarded as mercenary soldiers in the Ottoman military, but who never fully embraced either Islam or Christianity and were fiercely independent.

[29] A historic mountain pass at Ihtiman, Bulgaria.

[30] Baldwin I (1172–1205), Count of Flanders, was Emperor of the Latin Empire of Constantinople. He was captured by the Bulgarians at the Battle of Adrianople (1205) and died later that year.

[31] This is the end of the first volume of the 1763 edition.

[32] To Lady Mar.

[33] During her stay, Lady Mary had her portrait painted twice by Jean-Baptiste Vanmour, who had been based in Istanbul since 1699. In the one she had done for her sister, she is alone, and in the other she is with her son.

[34] In Aphra Brim's *The Emperor of the Moon* (1687), Harlequin declares the same moral codes exist on the moon as those on earth (III. i).

[35] A common theme in the travel and histories of the Ottoman Empire and Turkey was the oppression of Muslim women and the comparative freedom of European women. Jean de Thevenot (1637) writes: "the Turks do not believe that Women go to Heaven, and hardly account them Rational Creatures; the truth is, they take them only for their service as they would a Horse" (56–57). Aaron Hill in his 1709 account wrongly reports that Turkish women are denied entry into Paradise and promises to give "British ladies, an enlivening taste of Turkish arrogance" in order that they will see "how little cause [they] have to grieve" as in contrast British men "posses a just and mild pre-eminence by nature's laws and those of matrimony" (42). He further informs the reader that Turks "boast a sort of unconfined authority, which makes their wives submissively obedient" (97). Around the question of women's confinement, Hill (97) and Dumont (268) erroneously declare that women are strictly sequestered. Dumont remarks that "There is no Slavery equal to that of the Turkish Women. . . . The Door of the Womens Apartment is a *Ne plus ultra* for every thing that looks like a Man, and the utmost limit of the Womens Liberty" (268). In contrast, Joseph de Tournefort in his *Relation d'un voyage du Levant* (1717) states that most women could pursue their affairs without detection.

[36] Masquerades were a very popular aristocratic entertainment throughout Europe and England at this time. In the literature and art of the period, they were often depicted as places of sexual intrigue.

[37] Lady Mary had suggested she and Edward secretly meet at an Indian house—rooms that were let out to distressed lovers—when they were engaged in their clandestine courtship that led to their elopement.

[38] In this context, pennyworths means bargains.

[39] Refers to married Muslim women's rights to own property; the Qur'an established women's right to the *mahr*, which is granted to the bride on her marriage. In contrast, the English dowry was given to the husband and British women were subject to the doctrine of "coverture," where wives and all their assets were the property of and under the control of their husbands.

[40] Harem means sanctuary or sacred place.

[41] A defterdar or book-keeper was a high ranking official in charge of the finances of the Ottoman Empire.

[42] Wortley makes similar observations in a private letter to Joseph Addison: "The men of Consideration among the Turks appear in their conversation as much civilized as any I have met with in Italy and are not unlike the Italians in their Carriage. Those that are in good credit have but one wife. She has commonly several slaves, which the Husband does not see; if he does it makes an intire breach with the wife. But they frequently keep women at private places. The wives who go abroad with their faces hid are thought to take as much liberty as they do in Italy. The Privilege of having more wives than one is very rarely made use of unless by those that travel into distant Countries" (22 August 1717, Tickell MS; quoted in Halsband 1.329 n3).

[43] To Sarah Chiswell. In Malcolm Jack's edition, Letters 32–35 have the wrong date: they are listed as 1718 and should be 1717.

[44] Lady Mary is referring to Letter 3, dated 13 August 1716.

[45] See in contrast Alexander William Kinglake, in chapter 18 of his *Eothen* (1844), for a very exaggerated and orientalist account of the plague in Cairo. Reports on the plague were commonplace both in travel literature and in diplomatic dispatches. Lady Mary underestimates the virulence of the plague, which killed large numbers in both Europe (last major outbreak in 1720 in Marseilles) and in the Ottoman Empire; port towns were particularly vulnerable.

[46] Lady Mary was disfigured by smallpox in 1715 and her brother had died of it two years earlier. She had her son Edward (1713–76) inoculated in Turkey and later her daughter Mary (1718–94) in 1721, when an outbreak was sweeping England.

[47] Her attempts to introduce inoculation into England were met with resistance and Lady Mary correctly predicted that she would have to "wage war" with the English doctors. Reports of the success of smallpox inoculation in the East were already circulating in England from about 1700 but were largely ignored despite the presentation of the practice to the Royal Society.

[48] To Mrs. Thistlethwayte.

[49] By referring to it as a "loss," Lady Mary betrays her sympathies for the Turkish powers. Shortly after the date of this letter Prince Eugene would initiate a successful campaign against Belgrade that would have a significant impact on Wortley's diplomatic mission. See Letter 39.

[50] Originating in the Arabian Peninsula and one of the oldest breeds in the world, the Arabian horse was much sought after to improve other breeds. Lady Mary returned with four horses. See Donna Landry on Arabian horses and Lady Mary.

[51] Revered in Islam, storks are believed to incarnate the souls of Muslims who failed to make the pilgrimage to Mecca and thus now make it as a bird.

[52] Jean-Baptiste Tavernier, Jean Dumont, and Ottaviano Bon are among the many male travel writers who reported on the lascivious goings on in harems, despite the fact they had no access to them.

[53] A formal garden, usually with a symmetrical pattern.

[54] This is how the address line reads in the letter-book. Wharncliffe identifies the addressee as Lady Rich (2.35), but the addressee is unidentified in Halsband.

[55] The Peloponnesian peninsula in southern Greece. The peninsula was captured by the Venetians in the Morean War or the sixth Ottoman-Venetian War (1684–99), but the Ottomans recaptured it in 1715.

[56] Jean Dumont (1667–1727) was the author of *Nouveau Voyage du Levant* (1694, trans. 1696).

[57] Also known as the Balm of Gilead, a cosmetic made from resin of a tree that grows especially around the Red Sea. The anonymous work *The Duties of a Lady's Maid* (1825) has an entry under cosmetics that explains how to use it (267–71). Lady Mary is describing an allergic reaction, a possible side effect.

[58] The letter-book is illegible here. It may be "TS."

[59] To Mrs. Thistlethwayte. This is one of three letters in the letter-book that is not in Lady Mary's hand. Lady Mary inscribed the heading and the date and retroactively crossed out the name Thistlethwayte. The rest of the letter is in a copyist's hand.

[60] There is a gap of over six months between Letters 38 and 39. During this interlude Wortley's ambassadorial actions were undermined by English rivals at the Viennese court. Wortley was endeavoring to achieve a peace treaty by the autumn of 1717, but Prince Eugene besieged Belgrade and utterly razed the city in late August. As Grundy notes, the fate of Lady Mary's friend Achmet-Beg is unknown; thus this gap in the letters carries a certain affective weight, especially in light of her remarks on the aftermath of Petrovaradin. After the fall of Belgrade, news of Wortley's recall arrived and threw his household finances into chaos. Although criticized for being too pro-Turk, the terms on which Wortley negotiated peace were eventually adopted and he had the humiliating experience of being excluded from the congress at which the treaty was signed. The gap in the letters means that Lady Mary doesn't have to address these reverses in her husband's career. Grundy also notes that Lady Mary was pregnant and gave birth to her daughter Mary Wortley Montagu during this period. (See Grundy, 155–58.)

[61] Halsband (1.371n3) glosses this passage by referring to Joseph Pitts, *A Faithful Account of the Religion and Manners of the Mahometans* (1704): "The Story of the *Pidgeon*, which is said to have been taught by Mahomet to pick Corn out of his Ear, and which the vulgar took to be the whispers of the Holy Ghost, hath no better Foundation, that ever I could learn than a Castle . . . in the Air."

[62] Lady Mary was pregnant with her daughter Mary, the future Lady Bute.

[63] The Knights of Malta, a chivalric military and religious order dating back to the Crusades, were drawn only from nobility, and their lineage was strictly scrutinized. They were based in Rhodes from 1310 to 1530, when they were defeated by Suleyman the Magnificent. From Rhodes they retreated to Malta and remained a prominent force in the Mediterranean from 1530 to 1798. The Knights fought against the Turks on numerous occasions, most notably at the Battle of Lepanto in 1571.

[64] She gave birth to François-Armand de Bonnac (1716–82) in Istanbul on 7 December.

[65] See "Verses written in the Chiosk of the British Palace at Pera."

[66] Wharncliffe identifies the addressee as the Countess of Bristol (2.68). Halsband leaves the addressee blank, but guesses at the date (which is also not given) as May 1718. There is no place designation. Crossed out in the letter-book are the first lines: "Your Ladyship may be assured I received yours with very great pleasure. I am very glad to hear that our friends are in good health, particularly Mr. Congreve, who I heard was ill of the gout."

[67] Outer coat and veil.

[68] The history of the Scythians continues to be debated. Various theories suggest they originated in either Turkestan and Western Siberia or the Pontic-Caspian steppe.

[69] See p. 102, note 25.

[70] There is a sweating pillar in the Aya Sophia, and the moisture is rumoured to have healing properties. Aaron Hill states in *A Full and Just Account* (1709) that "you may see great numbers of promiscuous People wiping off the Moisture with their Cloaths or Foreheads, some expecting by its sovereign Power, to be protected from the least Misfortune" (138).

[71] The depiction of the Muslim woman as oppressed is a standard trope that continues to the present day.

[72] Many female travel writers after Lady Mary, including Lady Craven in *A Journey Through the Crimea to Constantinople* (1789), commented on the "freedom" of Turkish women largely because Muslim women had the right to own property. The Qur'an established women's right to the *mahr*, which is granted to the bride on her marriage, unlike the English dowry that was given to the husband. British women were subject to the doctrine of "coverture," where wives and all their assets were under the control of their husbands. To her future husband's inquiries about her dowry, Lady Mary responded: "People in my way are sold like slaves, and I cannot tell what price my Master will put on me" (Halsband 64).

[73] The 18th Idyll of Theocritus (3rd century BCE) celebrates the mythological wedding of Menelaus and Helen.

[74] This passage was also copied by Ingres in his notebook and influenced his orientalist painting *Le Bain turc* (1862). See p. 98, note 9.

[75] Hill's comment, accusing Turkish women of lewd and lascivious behaviour, is again typical among the male travelers: "'tis no wonder they have no more regard to their *Vertue* or their *Honour*." A persistent myth that circulated in these narratives is that cucumbers were cut up before they were allowed into the harem to prevent the women from using them wantonly.

[76] Naples was ruled by Spain from 1506 to 1714.

[77] A narrow sailing vessel used in the Mediterranean Sea.

[78] The revenge taken for the rape and ensuing suicide of the legendary Roman matron Lucretia is said to have led to the overthrow of the Roman monarchy and the establishment of the Roman republic.

[79] Halsband (1.409n1) suggests that the admiral in this tale is Ibrahim Pasha, Lord Admiral 1706–09 and 1717–18.

[80] Judith Tucker, in a presentation at Yale (May 2012) entitled "Women, Men, and Violence: Middle East Piracy From a Gendered Perspective," considered the agency of women in ransom negotiations (forthcoming in *JMEWS*, 2013). Also, see her *Women, Family, and Gender in Islamic Law* for a broader discussion of women and marriage.

[81] Laws of entailment that aristocratic estates in England would not be broken up or fall into a female line; thus these lands would be inherited by the male progenitor (the nearest male descendent). Edward Wortley Montagu refused to agree to this condition to entail his estate to a male heir, which is one of the reasons Lady Mary had to elope with Edward. See Halsband 1.51–52 for Lady Mary's letter to Wortley that discusses this matter. Worley eventually disinherited his son Edward.

[82] Saint Gregory is credited with converting Armenians from paganism to Christianity; Armenia was the first nation to adopt Christianity officially in 301 CE.

[83] William Whiston. See p. 102, note 22

[84] Rycaut wrote that Armenians, like Catholics, believed in transubstantiation in his *The Present State of the Greek and Armenian Churches*, which was written "at the command of Charles II" and published in 1679 in the midst of the Exclusion Crisis (1678–81). The Exclusion Bill sought to prevent Charles's brother James from succeeding to the throne for fear of his Catholicism. The Whigs (like Lady Mary) supported the Bill, while the court party, the Tories, opposed it.

[85] Armenian marriage practices were often commented on in travel narratives and histories, including in the works of Sandys and Rycaut.

[86] The letter begins addressed to the Countess and concludes with salutations to her sister. The crossed-out lines at the opening of the letter suggest a discrepancy between the initial address and the closing salutation.

[87] This is the end of the second volume of the 1763 edition.

Lines Written in Early Spring

William Wordsworth

I heard a thousand blended notes,
While in a grove I sate reclined,
In that sweet mood when pleasant thoughts
Bring sad thoughts to the mind.

To her fair works did Nature link
The human soul that through me ran;
And much it grieved my heart to think
What man has made of man.

Through primrose tufts, in that green bower,
The periwinkle trailed its wreaths;
And 'tis my faith that every flower
Enjoys the air it breathes.

The birds around me hopped and played,
Their thoughts I cannot measure:—
But the least motion which they made
It seemed a thrill of pleasure.

The budding twigs spread out their fan,
To catch the breezy air;
And I must think, do all I can,
That there was pleasure there.

If this belief from heaven be sent,
If such be Nature's holy plan,
Have I not reason to lament
What man has made of man?

The Boy of Winander

William Wordsworth

There was a Boy; ye knew him well, ye cliffs
And islands of Winander!—many a time,
At evening, when the earliest stars began
To move along the edges of the hills,
Rising or setting, would he stand alone,
Beneath the trees, or by the glimmering lake;
And there, with fingers interwoven, both hands
Pressed closely palm to palm and to his mouth
Uplifted, he, as through an instrument,
Blew mimic hootings to the silent owls,   10
That they might answer him.—And they would shout
Across the watery vale, and shout again,
Responsive to his call,—with quivering peals,
And long halloos, and screams, and echoes loud
Redoubled and redoubled; concourse wild
Of jocund din! And, when there came a pause
Of silence such as baffled his best skill:
Then, sometimes, in that silence, while he hung
Listening, a gentle shock of mild surprise
Has carried far into his heart the voice   20
Of mountain-torrents; or the visible scene
Would enter unawares into his mind
With all its solemn imagery, its rocks,
Its woods, and that uncertain heaven received
Into the bosom of the steady lake.
This boy was taken from his mates, and died
In childhood, ere he was full twelve years old.

Pre-eminent in beauty is the vale
Where he was born and bred: the churchyard hangs
Upon a slope above the village-school;   30
And, through that church-yard when my way has led
On summer-evenings, I believe, that there
A long half-hour together I have stood
Mute—looking at the grave in which he lies!

London

William Blake

I wander thro' each charter'd street,
Near where the charter'd Thames does flow,
And mark in every face I meet
Marks of weakness, marks of woe.

In every cry of every Man,
In every Infants cry of fear,
In every voice: in every ban,
The mind-forg'd manacles I hear.

How the Chimney-sweeper's cry
Every blackning Church appalls;
And the hapless Soldier's sigh
Runs in blood down Palace walls.

But most thro' midnight streets I hear
How the youthful Harlot's curse
Blasts the new-born Infants tear,
And blights with plagues the Marriage hearse.

Jerusalem
["And did those feet in ancient time"]

William Blake

And did those feet in ancient time
Walk upon England's mountains green:
And was the holy Lamb of God,
On England's pleasant pastures seen!

And did the Countenance Divine,
Shine forth upon our clouded hills?
And was Jerusalem builded here,
Among these dark Satanic Mills?

Bring me my Bow of burning gold:
Bring me my arrows of desire:
Bring me my Spear: O clouds unfold!
Bring me my Chariot of fire!

I will not cease from Mental Fight,
Nor shall my sword sleep in my hand:
Till we have built Jerusalem,
In England's green & pleasant Land.

She Walks in Beauty

Lord Byron (George Gordon)

She walks in beauty, like the night
  Of cloudless climes and starry skies;
And all that's best of dark and bright
  Meet in her aspect and her eyes;
Thus mellowed to that tender light
  Which heaven to gaudy day denies.

One shade the more, one ray the less,
  Had half impaired the nameless grace
Which waves in every raven tress,
  Or softly lightens o'er her face;
Where thoughts serenely sweet express,
  How pure, how dear their dwelling-place.

And on that cheek, and o'er that brow,
  So soft, so calm, yet eloquent,
The smiles that win, the tints that glow,
  But tell of days in goodness spent,
A mind at peace with all below,
  A heart whose love is innocent!

On First Looking into Chapman's Homer

John Keats

Much have I travell'd in the realms of gold,
   And many goodly states and kingdoms seen;
   Round many western islands have I been
Which bards in fealty to Apollo hold.
Oft of one wide expanse had I been told
   That deep-brow'd Homer ruled as his demesne;
   Yet did I never breathe its pure serene
Till I heard Chapman speak out loud and bold:
Then felt I like some watcher of the skies
   When a new planet swims into his ken;
Or like stout Cortez when with eagle eyes
   He star'd at the Pacific—and all his men
Look'd at each other with a wild surmise—
   Silent, upon a peak in Darien.

On Seeing the Elgin Marbles

John Keats

My spirit is too weak—mortality
  Weighs heavily on me like unwilling sleep,
  And each imagined pinnacle and steep
Of godlike hardship tells me I must die
Like a sick eagle looking at the sky.
  Yet 'tis a gentle luxury to weep
  That I have not the cloudy winds to keep
Fresh for the opening of the morning's eye.
Such dim-conceived glories of the brain
  Bring round the heart an undescribable feud;
So do these wonders a most dizzy pain,
  That mingles Grecian grandeur with the rude
Wasting of old time—with a billowy main—
  A sun—a shadow of a magnitude.

Ozymandias

Percy Bysshe Shelley

I met a traveller from an antique land,
Who said—"Two vast and trunkless legs of stone
Stand in the desert. . . . Near them, on the sand,
Half sunk a shattered visage lies, whose frown,
And wrinkled lip, and sneer of cold command,
Tell that its sculptor well those passions read
Which yet survive, stamped on these lifeless things,
The hand that mocked them, and the heart that fed;
And on the pedestal, these words appear:
My name is Ozymandias, King of Kings;
Look on my Works, ye Mighty, and despair!
Nothing beside remains. Round the decay
Of that colossal Wreck, boundless and bare
The lone and level sands stretch far away."

The Lace-Makers

Louise Otto-Peters
Translated by Melanie Archangeli and Patricia A. Herminghouse

See the lace-makers sitting at their pillows
    Their cheeks pale and their eyes red—
All toiling for a bite,
    A bite of black bread.

Grandmother has lost her sight,
    And waits for death to set her free,
In silent prayer she wrings her hands:
    God protect us in these difficult times!

The children move their little hands,
    The bobbins flying up and down
To the toil and sorrow there is no end, no end!
    Here is their future course of life.

All the maidens, God grant them mercy,
    They know not the pleasure of life's youth,
Misery holds them in its arms,
    Privation nestles in their breast!

See them sitting at their pillows,
    See the lace that they have made:
Rich men, great men—has your conscience
    Never trembled in your soul?

You live in luxury and debauchery while they perish,
    You enjoy life carousing and feasting,
Meantime they will die of hunger,
    Thanking God the torture is over.

You see them sitting at their pillows
    And still speak of faith in God?
You have torn it from our souls:
    We only see your godlessness.

You see them sitting at their pillows
    And feel no mercy in such a time:
Then shall your own death-pillow be
    The curse of poverty and all its pain!

from *The Social Contract*

or
Principles of Political Right

Jean-Jacques Rousseau
Translated by Maurice Cranston

—foederis aequas
Dicamus leges
AENEID, XI

Foreword

This little treatise is part of a larger work which I undertook many years ago without thinking of the limitations of my powers, and have long since abandoned. Of the various fragments that might have been taken from what I wrote, this is the most considerable, and the one I think the least unworthy of being offered to the public. The rest no longer exists.

Book I

My purpose is to consider if, in political society, there can be any legitimate and sure principle of government, taking men as they are and laws as they might be. In this inquiry I shall try always to bring together what right permits with what interest prescribes so that justice and utility are in no way divided.

I start without seeking to prove the importance of my subject. I may be asked whether I am a prince or a legislator that I should be writing about politics. I answer no: and indeed that that is my reason for doing so. If I were a prince or a legislator I should not waste my time saying what ought to be done; I should do it or keep silent.

Born as I was the citizen of a free state and a member of its sovereign body, the very right to vote imposes on me the duty to instruct myself in public affairs, however little influence my voice may have in them. And whenever I reflect upon governments, I am happy to find that my studies always give me fresh reasons for admiring that of my own country.

Chapter I

The subject of Book I

Man was born free, and he is everywhere in chains. Those who think themselves the masters of others are indeed greater slaves than they. How did this transformation come about? I do not know. How can it be made legitimate? That question I believe I can answer. If I were to consider only force and the effects of force, I should say: 'So long as a people is constrained to obey, and obeys, it does well; but as soon as it can shake off the yoke, and shakes it off, it does better; for since it regains its freedom by the same right as that which removed it, a people is either justified in taking back its freedom, or there is no justifying those who took it away.' But the social order is a sacred right which serves as a basis for all other rights. And as it is not a natural right, it must be one founded on covenants. The problem is to determine what those covenants are. But before we pass on to that question, I must substantiate what I have so far said.

Chapter 2

The First Societies

The oldest of all societies, and the only natural one, is that of the family; yet children remain tied to their father by nature only so long as they need him for their preservation. As soon as this need ends, the natural bond is dissolved. Once the children are freed from the obedience they owe their father, and the father is freed from his responsibilities towards them, both parties equally regain their independence. If they continue to remain united, it is no longer nature, but their own choice, which unites them; and the family as such is kept in being only by agreement.

This common liberty is a consequence of man's nature. Man's first law is to watch over his own preservation; his first care he owes to himself; and as soon as he reaches the age of reason, he becomes the only judge of the best means to preserve himself; he becomes his own master.

The family may therefore perhaps be seen as the first model of political societies: the head of the state bears the image of the father, the people the image of his children, and all, being born free and equal, surrender their freedom only when they see advantage in doing so. The only difference is that in the family, a father's love for his children repays him for the care he bestows on them, while in the state, where the ruler can have no such feeling for his people, the pleasure of commanding must take the place of love.

Grotius denies that all human government is established for the benefit of the governed, and he cites the example of slavery. His characteristic method of reasoning is always to offer fact as a proof of right.[1] It is possible to imagine a more logical method, but not one more favourable to tyrants.

According to Grotius, therefore, it is doubtful whether humanity belongs to a hundred men, or whether these hundred men belong to humanity, though he seems throughout his book to lean to the first of these views, which is also that of Hobbes. These authors show us the human race divided into herds of cattle, each with a master who preserves it only in order to devour its members.

Just as a shepherd possesses a nature superior to that of his flock, so do those shepherds of men, their rulers, have a nature superior to that of their people. Or so, we are told by Philo, the Emperor Caligula argued, concluding, reasonably enough on this same analogy, that kings were gods or alternatively that the people were animals.

The reasoning of Caligula coincides with that of Hobbes and Grotius. Indeed Aristotle, before any of them, said that men were not at all equal by nature, since some were born for slavery and others born to be masters.

Aristotle was right; but he mistook the effect for the cause. Anyone born in slavery is born for slavery—nothing is more certain. Slaves, in their bondage, lose everything, even the desire to be free. They love their servitude even as the companions of Ulysses loved their life as brutes.[2] But if there are slaves by nature, it is only because there has been slavery against nature. Force made the first slaves; and their cowardice perpetuates their slavery.

I have said nothing of the King Adam or of the Emperor Noah, father of the three great monarchs who shared out the universe between them, like the children of Saturn, with whom some authors have identified them. I hope my readers will be grateful for this moderation, for since I am directly descended from one of those princes, and perhaps in the eldest line, how do I know that if the deeds were checked, I might not find myself the legitimate king of the human race? However that may be, there is no gainsaying that Adam was the king of the world, as was Robinson Crusoe of his island, precisely because he was the sole inhabitant; and the great advantage of such an empire was that the monarch, secure upon his throne, had no occasion to fear rebellions, wars or conspirators.

Chapter 3

The Right of the Strongest

The strongest man is never strong enough to be master all the time, unless he transforms force into right and obedience into duty. Hence 'the right of the strongest'—a 'right' that sounds like something intended ironically, but is actually laid down as a principle. But shall we never have this phrase explained? Force is a physical power; I do not see how its effects could produce morality. To yield to force is an act of necessity, not of will; it is at best an act of prudence. In what sense can it be a moral duty?

Let us grant, for a moment, that this so-called right exists. I suggest it can only produce a tissue of bewildering nonsense; for once might is made to be right, cause and effect are reversed, and every, force which overcomes another force inherits the right which belonged to the vanquished. As soon as man can disobey with impunity, his disobedience becomes legitimate; and as the strongest is always right, the only problem is how to become the strongest. But what can be the validity of a right which perishes with the force on which it rests? If force compels obedience, there is no need to invoke a duty to obey, and if force ceases to compel obedience, there is no longer any obligation. Thus the word 'right' adds nothing to what is said by 'force'; it is meaningless.

'Obey those in power.' If this means 'yield to force' the precept is sound, but superfluous; it will never, I suggest, be violated. All power comes from God, I agree; but so does every disease, and no one forbids us to summon a physician. If I am held up by a robber at the edge of a wood, force compels me to hand over my purse. But if I could somehow contrive to keep the purse from him, would I still be obliged in conscience to surrender it? After all, the pistol in the robber's hand is undoubtedly a *power*.

Surely it must be admitted, then, that might does not make right, and that the duty of obedience is owed only to legitimate powers. Thus we are constantly led back to my original question.

Chapter 4

Slavery

Since no man has any natural authority over his fellows, and since force alone bestows no right, all legitimate authority among men must be based on covenants.

Grotius says: 'If an individual can alienate his freedom and become the slave of a master, why may not a whole people alienate its freedom and become the subject of a king?' In this remark there are several ambiguous words which call for explanation; but let us confine ourselves to one—to 'alienate'. To alienate is to give or sell. A man who becomes the slave of another does not give himself, he sells himself in return for at least a subsistence. But in return for what could a whole people be said to sell itself? A king, far from nourishing his subjects, draws his nourishment from them; and kings, according to Rabelais, need more than a little nourishment. Do subjects, then, give their persons to the king on condition that he will accept their property as well? If so, I fail to see what they have left to preserve.

It will be said that a despot gives his subjects the assurance of civil tranquillity. Very well, but what does it profit them, if those wars against other powers which result from a despot's ambition, if his insatiable greed, and the oppressive demands of his administration, cause more desolation than civil strife would cause? What do the people gain if their very condition of civil tranquillity is one of their hardships? There is peace in dungeons, but is that enough to make dungeons desirable? The Greeks lived in peace in the cave of Cyclops awaiting their turn to be devoured.

To speak of a man giving himself in return for nothing is to speak of what is absurd, unthinkable; such an action would be illegitimate, void, if only because no one who did it could be in his right mind. To say the same of a whole people is to conjure up a nation of lunatics; and right cannot rest on madness.

Even if each individual could alienate himself, he cannot alienate his children. For they are born men; they are born free; their liberty belongs to them; no one but they themselves has the right to dispose of it. Before they reach the years of discretion, their father may, in their name, make certain rules for their protection and their welfare, but he cannot give away their liberty irrevocably and unconditionally, for such a gift would be contrary to the ends of nature and an abuse of paternal right. Hence, an arbitrary government would be legitimate only if every new generation were able to accept or reject it, and in that case the government would cease to be arbitrary.

To renounce freedom is to renounce one's humanity, one's rights as a man and equally one's duties. There is no possible *quid pro quo* for one who renounces everything; indeed such renunciation is contrary to man's very nature; for if you take away all freedom of the will, you strip a man's actions of all moral significance. Finally, any covenant which stipulated absolute dominion for one party and absolute obedience for the other would be illogical and nugatory. Is it not evident that he who is entitled to demand everything owes nothing? And does not the single fact of there being no reciprocity, no mutual obligation, nullify the act? For what right can my slave have against me? If everything he has belongs to me, his right is *my* right, and it would be nonsense to speak of my having a right *against* myself.

Grotius and the rest claim to find in war another justification for the so-called right of slavery. They argue that the victor's having the right to kill the vanquished implies that the vanquished has the right to purchase his life at the expense of his liberty—a bargain thought to be the more legitimate because it is advantageous to both parties.

But it is clear that this so-called right to kill the vanquished cannot be derived from the state of war. For this reason alone, that men living in their primitive condition of independence have no intercourse regular enough to constitute either a state of peace or a state of war; and men are not naturally enemies. It is conflicts over things, not quarrels between men which constitute war, and the state of war cannot arise from mere personal relations, but only from property relations. Private wars between one man and another can exist neither in a state of nature, where there is no fixed property, nor in society, where everything is under the authority of law.

Private fights, duels, skirmishes, do not constitute any kind of state; and as for the private wars that were permitted by the ordinances of Louis IX, King of France, and suspended by the Peace of God, these were no more than an abuse of feudal government, an irrational system if there ever was one, and contrary both to natural justice and to all sound polity.

War, then, is not a relation between men, but between states; in war individuals are enemies wholly by chance, not as men, not even as citizens,[3] but only as soldiers; not as members of their country, but only as its defenders. In a word, a state can have as an enemy only another state, not men, because there can be no real relation between things possessing different intrinsic natures.

This principle conforms to the established rules of all tunes and to the constant practice of every political society. Declarations of war are warnings not so much to governments as to their subjects. The foreigner—whether he is a king, a private person or a whole people—who robs, kills or detains the subjects of another prince without first declaring war against that prince, is not an enemy but a brigand. Even in the midst of war, a just prince, seizing what he can of public property in the enemy's territory, nevertheless respects the persons and possessions of private individuals; he respects the principles on which his own rights are based. Since the aim of war is to subdue a hostile state, a combatant has the right to kill the defenders of that state while they are armed; but as soon as they lay down their arms and surrender, they cease to be either enemies or instruments of the enemy; they become simply men once more, and no one has any longer the right to take their lives. It is sometimes possible to destroy a state without killing a single one of its members, and war gives no right to inflict any more destruction than is necessary for victory. These principles were not invented by Grotius, nor are they founded on the authority of the poets; they are derived from the nature of things; they are based on reason.

The right of conquest has no other foundation than the law of the strongest. And if war gives the conqueror no right to massacre a conquered people, no such right can be invoked to justify their enslavement. Men have the right to kill their enemies only when they cannot enslave them, so the right of enslaving cannot be derived from the right to kill. It would therefore be an iniquitous barter to make the vanquished purchase with their liberty the lives over which the victor has no legitimate claim. An argument basing the right over life and death on the right to enslave, and the right to enslave on the right over life and death, is an argument trapped in a vicious circle.

Even if we assumed that this terrible right of massacre did exist, then slaves of war, or a conquered people, would be under no obligation to obey their master any further than they were forced to do so. By taking an equivalent of his victim's life, the victor shows him no favour; instead of destroying him unprofitable he destroys him by exploiting him. Hence, far from the victor having acquired some further authority besides that of force over the vanquished, the state of war between them continues; their mutual relation is the effect of war, and the continuation of the rights of war implies that there has been no treaty of peace. An agreement has assuredly been made, but that agreement, far from ending the state of war, presupposes its continuation.

Thus, however we look at the question, the 'right' of slavery is seen to be void; void, not only because it cannot be justified, but also because it is nonsensical, because it has no meaning. The words 'slavery' and 'right' are contradictory, they cancel each other out. Whether as between one man and another, or between one man and a whole people, it would always be absurd to say: 'I hereby make a covenant with you which is wholly at your expense and wholly to my advantage; I will respect it so long as I please and you shall respect it so long as I wish.'

Chapter 5

That We Must Always Go Back To an Original Covenant

Even if I were to concede all that I have so far refuted, the champions of despotism would be no better off. There will always be a great difference between subduing a multitude and ruling a society. If one man successively enslaved many separate individuals, no matter how numerous, he and they would never bear the aspect of anything but a master and his slaves, not at all that of a people and their ruler; an aggregation, perhaps, but certainly not an association, for they would neither have a common good nor be a body politic. Even if such a man were to enslave half the world, he would remain a private individual, and his interest, always distinct from that of the others, would never be more than a personal interest. When he died, the empire he left would be scattered for lack of any bond of union, even as an oak crumbles and falls into a heap of ashes when fire has consumed it.

'A people,' says Grotius, 'may give itself to a king.' Therefore, according to Grotius a people is *a people* even before the gift to the king is made. The gift itself is a civil act; it presupposes public deliberation. Hence, before considering the act by which a people submits to a king, we ought to scrutinize the act by which people become *a* people, for that act, being necessarily antecedent to the other, is the real foundation of society.

In fact, if there were no earlier agreement, how, unless the election were unanimous, could there be any obligation on the minority to accept the decision of the majority? What right have the hundred who want to have a master to vote on behalf of the ten who do not? The law of majority-voting itself rests on an agreement, and implies that there has been on at least one occasion unanimity.

Chapter 6

The Social Pact

I assume that men reach a point where the obstacles to their preservation in a state of nature prove greater than the strength that each man has to preserve himself in that state. Beyond this point, the primitive condition cannot endure, for then the human race will perish if it does not change its mode of existence.

Since men cannot create new forces, but merely combine and control those which already exist, the only way in which they can preserve themselves is by uniting their separate powers in a combination strong enough to overcome any resistance, uniting them so that their powers are directed by a single motive and act in concert.

Such a sum of forces can be produced only by the union of separate men, but as each man's own strength and liberty are the chief instruments of his preservation, how can he merge his with others' without putting himself in peril and neglecting the care he owes to himself? This difficulty, in terms of my present subject, may be expressed in these words:

'How to find a form of association which will defend the person and goods of each member with the collective force of all, and under which each individual, while uniting himself with the others, obeys no one but himself, and remains as free as before.' This is the fundamental problem to which the social contract holds the solution.

The articles of this contract are so precisely determined by the nature of the act, that the slightest modification must render them null and void; they are such that, though perhaps never formally stated, they are everywhere the same, everywhere tacitly admitted and recognized; and if ever the social pact is violated, every man regains his original rights and, recovering his natural freedom, loses that civil freedom for which he exchanged it.

These articles of association, rightly understood, are reducible to a single one, namely the total alienation by each associate of himself and all his rights to the whole community. Thus, in the first place, as every individual gives himself absolutely, the conditions are the same for all, and precisely because they are the same for all, it is in no one's interest to make the conditions onerous for others.

Secondly, since the alienation is unconditional, the union is as perfect as it can be, and no individual associate has any longer any rights to claim; for if rights were left to individuals, in the absence of any higher authority to judge between them and the public, each individual, being his own judge in some causes, would soon demand to be his own judge in all; and in this way the state of nature would be kept in being, and the association inevitably become either tyrannical or void.

Finally, since each man gives himself to all, he gives himself to no one; and since there is no associate over whom he does not gain the same rights as others gain over him, each man recovers the equivalent of everything he loses, and in the bargain he acquires more power to preserve what he has.

If, then, we eliminate from the social pact everything that is not essential to it, we find it comes down to this: 'Each one of us puts into the community his person and all his powers under the supreme direction of the general will; and as a body, we incorporate every member as an indivisible part of the whole.'

Immediately, in place of the individual person of each contracting party, this act of association creates an artificial and corporate body composed of as many members as there are voters in the assembly, and by this same act that body acquires its unity, its common *ego*, its life and its will. The public person thus formed by the union of all other persons was once called the *city*,[4] and is now known as the *republic* or the *body politic*. In its passive role it is called the *state*, when it plays an active role it is the *sovereign*; and when it is compared to others of its own kind, it is a *power*. Those who are associated in it take collectively the name of *a people*, and call themselves individually *citizens*, in that they share in the sovereign power, and *subjects*, in that they put themselves under the laws of the state. However, these words are often confused, each being mistaken for another; but the essential thing is to know how to recognize them when they are used in their precise sense.

Chapter 7

The Sovereign

This formula shows that the act of association consists of a reciprocal commitment between society and the individual, so that each person, in making a contract, as it were, with himself, finds himself doubly committed, first, as a member of the sovereign body in relation to individuals, and secondly as a member of the state in relation to the sovereign. Here there can be no invoking the principle of civil law which says that no man is bound by a contract with himself, for there is a great difference between having an obligation to oneself and having an obligation to something of which one is a member. We must add that a public decision can impose an obligation on all the subjects towards the sovereign, by reason of the two aspects under which each can be seen, while, contrariwise, such decisions cannot impose an obligation on the sovereign towards itself; and hence it would be against the very nature of a political body for the sovereign to set over itself a law which it could not infringe. The sovereign, bearing only one single and identical aspect, is in the position of a private person making a contract with himself, which shows that there neither is, nor can be, any kind of fundamental law binding on the people as a body, not even the social contract itself. This does not mean that the whole body cannot incur obligations to other nations, so long as those obligations do not infringe the contract; for in relation to foreign powers, the body politic is a simple entity, an individual.

However, since the body politic, or sovereign, owes its being to the sanctity of the contract alone, it cannot commit itself, even in treaties with foreign powers, to anything that would derogate from the original act of association; it could not, for example, alienate a part of itself or submit to another sovereign. To violate the act which has given it. existence would be to annihilate itself; and what is nothing can produce nothing.

As soon as the multitude is united thus in a single body, no one can injure any one of the members without attacking the whole, still less injure the whole without each member feeling it. Duty and self-interest thus equally oblige the two contracting parties to give each other mutual aid; and the same men should seek to bring together in this dual relationship, all the advantages that flow from it.

Now, as the sovereign is formed entirely of the individuals who compose it, it has not, nor could it have, any interest contrary to theirs; and so the sovereign has no need to give guarantees to the subjects, because it is impossible for a body to wish to hurt all of its members, and, as we shall see, it cannot hurt any particular member. The sovereign by the mere fact that it is, is always all that it ought to be.

But this is not true of the relation of subject to sovereign. Despite their common interest, subjects will not be bound by their commitment unless means are found to guarantee their fidelity.

For every individual as a man may have a private will contrary to, or different from, the general will that he has as a citizen. His private interest may speak with a very different voice from that of the public interest; his absolute and naturally independent existence may make him regard what he owes to the common cause as a gratuitous contribution, the loss of which would be less painful for others than the payment is onerous for him; and fancying that the artificial person which constitutes the state is a mere fictitious entity (since it is not a man), he might seek to enjoy the rights of a citizen without doing the duties of a subject The growth of this kind of injustice would bring about the ruin of the body politic.

Hence, in order that the social pact shall not be an empty formula, it is tacitly implied in that commitment—which alone can give force to all others—that whoever refuses to obey the general will shall be constrained to do so by the whole body, which means nothing other than that he shall be forced to be free; for this is the necessary condition which, by giving each citizen to the nation, secures him against all personal dependence, it is the condition which shapes both the design and the working of the political machine, and which alone bestows justice on civil contracts—without it, such contracts would be absurd, tyrannical and liable to the grossest abuse.

Chapter 8

Personal interest

Civil Society

The passing from the state of nature to the civil society produces a remarkable change in man; it puts justice as a rule of conduct in the place of instinct, and gives his actions the moral quality they previously lacked. It is only then, when the voice of duty has taken the place of physical impulse, and right that of desire, that man, who has hitherto thought only of himself, finds himself compelled to act on other principles, and to consult his reason rather than study his inclinations. And although in civil society man surrenders some of the advantages that belong to the state of nature, he gains in return far greater ones; his faculties are so exercised and developed, his mind is so enlarged, his sentiments so ennobled, and his whole spirit so elevated that, if the abuse of his new condition did not in many cases lower him to something worse than what he had left, he should constantly bless the happy hour that lifted him for ever from the state of nature and from a stupid, limited animal made a creature of intelligence and a man.

Suppose we draw up a balance sheet, so that the losses and gains may be readily compared. What man loses by the social contract is his natural liberty and the absolute right to anything that tempts him and that he can take; what he gains by the social contract is civil liberty and the legal right of property in what he possesses. If we are to avoid mistakes in weighing the one side against the other, we must clearly distinguish between *natural* liberty, which has no limit but the physical power of the individual concerned, and *civil* liberty, which is limited by the general will; and we must distinguish also between *possession*, which is based only on force or 'the right of the first occupant', and *property*, which must rest on a legal title. *the group, common good*

We might also add that man acquires with civil society, moral freedom, which alone makes man the master of himself; for to be governed by appetite alone is slavery, while obedience to a law one prescribes to oneself is freedom. However, I have already said more than enough on this subject, and the philosophical meaning of the word 'freedom' is no part of my subject here.

Chapter 9

Of Property

Every member of the community gives himself to it at the moment it is brought into being just as he is—he himself, with all his resources, including all his goods. This is not to say that possession by this act changes its nature in changing, hands and becomes property in the grasp of the sovereign; but rather, that as the resources of the nation are incomparably greater than those of an individual, public possession is in simple fact more secure and more irrevocable than private possession, without being any more legitimate—at any rate, in the eyes of foreigners; for the state, *vis-à-vis* its own members, becomes master of all their goods by virtue of the social contract, which serves, within the state, as the basis of all other rights; while *vis-à-vis* other nations, the state has only the 'right of the first occupant', which it derives from individuals.

The 'right of the first occupant', although more real than the 'right of the strongest', does not become a true right until the institution of property. Every man has a natural right to what he needs; but the positive act which makes a man the proprietor of any estate excludes him from everything else. His share having once been settled, he must confine himself to it, and he has no further right against the community. Thus we see how 'the right of the first occupant', weak as it is in the state of nature, compels in political society the respect of all men. What this right makes one aware of is less what belongs to others than what does *not* belong to oneself.

As a general rule, to justify the right of the first occupant to any piece of land whatever, the following conditions must obtain: first, that the land shall not already be inhabited by anyone else; secondly, that the claimant occupies no more than he needs for subsistence; thirdly, that he takes possession, not by an idle ceremony, but by actually working and cultivating the soil—the only sign of ownership which need be respected by other people in the absence of a legal title.

It can, indeed, be said that tying 'the right of the first occupant' to need and work is stretching it as far as it will go. Can one really avoid setting limits on the right? Is it enough to put one's feet on a piece of common land in order to claim it at once as one's own? Is it enough to have the power to keep other men off for one moment in order to deprive them of the right ever to return? How could a man or a people seize a vast territory and keep out the rest of the human race except by a criminal usurpation—since the action would rob the rest of mankind of the shelter and the food that nature has given them all in common? When Nunez Balbao stood on the shore and took possession of the southern seas and of South America in the name of the crown of Castille, was that enough to dispossess all the inhabitants and to exclude all the other princes of the world? If so, such idle ceremonies would have had no end; and the Catholic King might without leaving his royal chamber have taken possession of the whole universe, only excepting afterwards those parts of his empire already belonging to other princes.

We can see how the lands of private persons, when they are united and contiguous, become public territory; and how the right of sovereignty, extending from the subjects to the soil they occupy, covers both property and persons; it makes the owners all the more dependent, and turns their own strength into the guarantee of their fidelity. This advantage seems to have eluded the ancient monarchs, who, in calling themselves simply the King of the Persians or the Scythians or the Macedonians, appear to have regarded themselves rather as rulers of men than as masters of their countries. Monarchs of the present day call themselves more shrewdly the King of France, or of Spain, or of England and so on; in holding thus the land, they are very sure of holding the inhabitants.

What is unique about the alienation entailed by the social contract is that the community in accepting the goods of an individual is far from depriving him of them; on the contrary it simply assures him of their lawful possession; it changes usurpation into valid right and mere enjoyment into legal ownership. Since every owner is regarded as a trustee of the public property, his rights are respected by every other member of the state, and protected with its collective force against foreigners; men have, by a surrender which is advantageous to the public and still more to themselves, acquired, so to speak, all that they have given up—a paradox which is easily explained by the distinction between the rights which the sovereign has and which the owner has over the same property, as will be seen later.

It may also happen that men begin to unite before they possess anything, and spreading over a territory large enough for them all, proceed to enjoy it in common, or, alternatively, divide it among themselves either equally or in shares determined by the sovereign. In whatever manner this acquisition is made, the right of any individual over his own estate is always subordinate to the right of the community over everything; for without this there would be neither strength in the social bond nor effective force in the exercise of sovereignty.

I shall end this chapter—and Book I—with an observation which might serve as a basis for the whole social system: namely, that the social pact, far from destroying natural equality, substitutes, on the contrary, a moral and lawful equality for whatever physical inequality that nature may have imposed on mankind; so that however unequal in strength and intelligence, men become equal by covenant and by right.[5]

Notes

[1.] 'Learned researches on public law are often only the history of ancient abuses, and one is misled when one gives oneself the trouble of studying them too closely.' *Traité manuscrit des intérêts de la France avec ses voisins* par M. L. M. d'A. This is exactly what Grotius does. [Rousseau's quotation is from the Marquis d'Argenson. *Trans.*]

[2.] See a short treatise of Plutarch entitled: *That Animals use Reason.*

[3.] The Romans, who understood and respected the rights of war better than any other nation, carried their scruples on this subject so far that a citizen was forbidden to volunteer without engaging himself expressly against the enemy and against an enemy specifically named. When the legion in which the younger Cato fought his first campaign under Popilius was re-formed, the elder Cato wrote to Popilius saying that if he wished his son to continue to serve under him, he should administer a fresh military oath, on the grounds that his son's first oath was annulled, and that he could no longer bear arms against the enemy. Cato also wrote to his son warning him not to go into battle without first taking the oath.

I realize that the siege of Clusium and other incidents from Roman history may be quoted against me, but I am citing laws and customs. No nation has broken its own laws less frequently than the Romans, and no nation has ever had such excellent laws. [Footnote added in the Edition of 1782.]

[4.] The real meaning of this word has been almost entirely lost in the modern world, when a town and a city are thought to be identical, and a citizen the same as a burgess. People forget that houses may make a town, while only citizens can make a city. The Carthaginians once paid dearly for this mistake. I have never read of the title *cives* being given to the subject of any prince, not even to the Macedonians in ancient times or the English today, in spite of their being closer to liberty than any other people. The French alone treat the same 'Citizen' with familiarity, and that is because they do not know what it means, as their Dictionaries prove; if they did know, they would be guilty, in usurping it, of *lèse-majesté*; as it is, they use the word to designate social status and not legal right. When Bodin wanted to speak of citizens and burgesses, he made the gross error of mistaking the one for the other. Monsieur d' Alembert avoids this mistake; and in his article on 'Geneva' he correctly distinguishes between the four orders of men (five, if aliens are included) which are found in our town, and of which only two compose the republic. No other French author to my knowledge has understood the real meaning of the word 'citizen'.

5. Under a bad government, this equality is only an appearance and an illusion; it serves only to keep the poor in their wretchedness and sustain the rich in their usurpation. In truth, laws are always useful to those with possessions and harmful to those who have nothing; from which it follows that the social state is advantageous to men only when all possess something and none has too much.

from *A Vindication of the Rights of Woman,* Vol. I

Mary Wollstonecraft

Introduction

After considering the historic page, and viewing the living world with anxious solicitude, the most melancholy emotions of sorrowful indignation have depressed my spirits, and I have sighed when obliged to confess, that either nature has made a great difference between man and man, or that the civilization which has hitherto taken place in the world has been very partial. I have turned over various books written on the subject of education, and patiently observed the conduct of parents and the management of schools; but what has been the result?—a profound conviction that the neglected education of my fellow-creatures is the grand source of the misery I deplore; and that women, in particular, are rendered weak and wretched by a variety of concurring causes, originating from one hasty conclusion. The conduct and manners of women, in fact, evidently prove that their minds are not in a healthy state; for, like the flowers which are planted in too rich a soil, strength and usefulness are sacrificed to beauty; and the flaunting leaves, after having pleased a fastidious eye, fade, disregarded on the stalk, long before the season when they ought to have arrived at maturity. One cause of this barren blooming I attribute to a false system of education, gathered from the books written on this subject by men who, considering females rather as women than human creatures, have been more anxious to make them alluring mistresses than affectionate wives and rational mothers; and the understanding of the sex has been so bubbled by this specious homage, that the civilized women of the present century, with a few exceptions, are only anxious to inspire love, when they ought to cherish a nobler ambition, and by their abilities and virtues exact respect.

In a treatise, therefore, on female rights and manners, the works which have been particularly written for their improvement must not be overlooked; especially when it is asserted, in direct terms, that the minds of women are enfeebled by false refinement; that the books of instruction, written by men of genius, have had the same tendency as more frivolous productions; and that, in the true style of Mahometanism, they are treated as a kind of subordinate beings, and not as a part of the human species, when improveable reason is allowed to be the dignified distinction which raises men above the brute creation, and puts a natural sceptre in a feeble hand.

Yet, because I am a woman, I would not lead my readers to suppose that I mean violently to agitate the contested question respecting the equality or inferiority of the sex; but as the subject lies in my way, and I cannot pass it over without subjecting the main tendency of my reasoning to misconstruction, I shall stop a moment to deliver, in a few words, my opinion. In the government of the physical world it is observable that the female in point of strength is, in general, inferior to the male. This is the law of nature; and it does not appear to be suspended or abrogated in favour of woman. A degree of physical superiority cannot, therefore, be denied—and it is a noble prerogative! But not content with this natural preeminence, men endeavour to sink us still lower, merely to render us alluring objects for a moment; and women, intoxicated by the adoration which men, under the influence of their senses, pay them, do not seek to obtain a durable interest in their hearts, or to become the friends of the fellow creatures who find amusement in their society.

I am aware of an obvious inference: from every quarter have I heard exclamations against masculine women; but where are they to be found? If by this appellation men mean to inveigh against their ardour in hunting, shooting, and gaming, I shall most cordially join in the cry; but if it be against the imitation of manly virtues, or, more properly speaking, the attainment of those talents and virtues, the exercise of which ennobles the human character, and which raise females in the scale of animal being, when they are comprehensively termed mankind; all those who view them with a philosophic eye must, I should think, wish with me, that they may every day grow more and more masculine.

This discussion naturally divides the subject. I shall first consider women in the grand light of human creatures, who, in common with men, are placed on this earth to unfold their faculties; and afterwards I shall more particularly point out their peculiar designation.

I wish also to steer clear of an error which many respectable writers have fallen into; for the instruction which has hitherto been addressed to women, has rather been applicable to *ladies*, if the little indirect advice, that is scattered through Sandford and Merton, be excepted; but, addressing my sex in a firmer tone, I pay particular attention to those in the middle class, because they appear to be in the most natural state. Perhaps the seeds of false-refinement, immorality, and vanity, have ever been shed by the great. Weak, artificial beings, raised above the common wants and affections of their race, in a premature unnatural manner, undermine the very foundation of virtue, and spread corruption through the whole mass of society! As a class of mankind they have the strongest claim to pity; the education of the rich tends to render them vain and helpless, and the unfolding mind is not strengthened by the practice of those duties which dignify the human character. They only live to amuse themselves, and by the same law which in nature invariably produces certain effects, they soon only afford barren amusement.

But as I purpose taking a separate view of the different ranks of society, and of the moral character of women, in each, this hint is, for the present, sufficient; and I have only alluded to the subject, because it appears to me to be the very essence of an introduction to give a cursory account of the contents of the work it introduces.

My own sex, I hope, will excuse me, if I treat them like rational creatures, instead of flattering their *fascinating* graces, and viewing them as if they were in a state of perpetual childhood, unable to stand alone. I earnestly wish to point out in what true dignity and human happiness consists—I wish to persuade women to endeavour to acquire strength, both of mind and body, and to convince them that the soft phrases, susceptibility of heart, delicacy of sentiment, and refinement of taste, are almost synonymous with epithets of weakness, and that those beings who are only the objects of pity and that kind of love, which has been termed its sister, will soon become objects of contempt.

Dismissing then those pretty feminine phrases, which the men condescendingly use to soften our slavish dependence, and despising that weak elegancy of mind, exquisite sensibility, and sweet docility of manners, supposed to be the sexual characteristics of the weaker vessel, I wish to shew that elegance is inferior to virtue, that the first object of laudable ambition is to obtain a character as a human being, regardless of the distinction of sex; and that secondary views should be brought to this simple touchstone.

This is a rough sketch of my plan; and should I express my conviction with the energetic emotions that I feel whenever I think of the subject, the dictates of experience and reflection will be felt by some of my readers. Animated by this important object, I shall disdain to cull my phrases or polish my style; I aim at being useful, and sincerity will render me unaffected; for, wishing rather to persuade by the force of my arguments, than dazzle by the elegance of my language, I shall not waste my time in rounding periods, or in fabricating the turgid bombast of artificial feelings, which, coming from the head, never reach the heart. I shall be employed about things, not words!—and, anxious to render my sex more respectable members of society, I shall try to avoid that flowery diction which has slided from essays into novels, and from novels into familiar letters and conversation.

These pretty superlatives, dropping glibly from the tongue, vitiate the taste, and create a kind of sickly delicacy that turns away from simple unadorned truth; and a deluge of false sentiments and overstretched feelings, stifling the natural emotions of the heart, render the domestic pleasures insipid, that ought to sweeten the exercise of those severe duties, which educate a rational and immortal being for a nobler field of action.

The education of women has, of late, been more attended to than formerly; yet they are still reckoned a frivolous sex, and ridiculed or pitied by the writers who endeavour by satire or instruction to improve them. It is acknowledged that they spend many of the first years of their lives in acquiring a smattering of accomplishments; meanwhile strength of body and mind are sacrificed to libertine notions of beauty, to the desire of establishing themselves—the only way women can rise in the world—by marriage. And this desire making mere animals of them, when they marry they act as such children may be expected to act: they dress; they paint, and nickname God's creatures. Surely these weak beings are only fit for a seraglio!—Can they be expected to govern a family with judgment, or take care of the poor babes whom they bring into the world?

If then it can be fairly deducted from the present conduct of the sex, from the prevalent fondness for pleasure which takes place of ambition and those nobler passions that open and enlarge the soul; that the instruction which women have hitherto received has only tended, with the constitution of civil society, to render them insignificant objects of desire—mere propagators of fools!—if it can be proved that in aiming to accomplish them, without cultivating their understandings, they are taken out of their sphere of duties, and made ridiculous and useless when the short-lived bloom of beauty is over.[1] I presume that *rational* men will excuse me for endeavouring to persuade them to become more masculine and respectable.

Indeed the word masculine is only a bugbear: there is little reason to fear that women will acquire too much courage or fortitude; for their apparent inferiority with respect to bodily strength, must render them, in some degree, dependent on men in the various relations of life; but why should it be increased by prejudices that give a sex to virtue, and confound simple truths with sensual reveries?

Women are, in fact, so much degraded by mistaken notions of female excellence, that I do not mean to add a paradox when I assert, that this artificial weakness produces a propensity to tyrannize, and gives birth to cunning, the natural opponent of strength, which leads them to play off those contemptible infantine airs that undermine esteem even whilst they excite desire. Let men become more chaste and modest, and if women do not grow wiser in the same ratio, it will be clear that they have weaker understandings. It seems scarcely necessary to say, that I now speak of the sex in general. Many individuals have more sense than their male relatives; and, as nothing preponderates where there is a constant struggle for an equilibrium, without it has naturally more gravity, some women govern their husbands without degrading themselves, because intellect will always govern.

Chap. II
The Prevailing Opinion of a Sexual Character Discussed

To account for, and excuse the tyranny of man, many ingenious arguments have been brought forward to prove, that the two sexes, in the acquirement of virtue, ought to aim at attaining a very different character: or, to speak explicitly, women are not allowed to have sufficient strength of mind to acquire what really deserves the name of virtue. Yet it should seem, allowing them to have souls, that there is but one way appointed by Providence to lead *mankind* to either virtue or happiness.

If then women are not a swarm of ephemeron triflers, why should they be kept in ignorance under the specious name of innocence? Men complain, and with reason, of the follies and caprices of our sex, when they do not keenly satirize our headstrong passions and groveling vices. Behold, I should answer, the natural effect of ignorance! The mind will ever be unstable that has only prejudices to rest on, and the current will run with destructive fury when there are no barriers to break its force. Women are told from their infancy, and taught by the example of their mothers, that a little knowledge of human weakness, justly termed cunning, softness of temper, *outward* obedience, and a scrupulous attention to a puerile kind of propriety, will obtain for them the protection of man; and should they be beautiful, every thing else is needless, for, at least, twenty years of their lives.

Thus Milton describes our first frail mother; though when he tells us that women are formed for softness and sweet attractive grace, I cannot comprehend his meaning, unless, in the true Mahometan strain, he meant to deprive us of souls, and insinuate that we were beings only designed by sweet attractive grace, and docile blind obedience, to gratify the senses of man when he can no longer soar on the wing of contemplation.

How grossly do they insult us who thus advise us only to render ourselves gentle, domestic brutes! For instance, the winning softness so warmly, and frequently, recommended, that governs by obeying. What childish expressions, and how insignificant is the being—can it be an immortal one? who will condescend to govern by such sinister methods! 'Certainly,' says Lord Bacon, 'man is of kin to the beasts by his body; and if he be not of kin to God by his spirit, he is a base and ignoble creature!' Men, indeed, appear to me to act in a very unphilosophical manner when they try to secure the good conduct of women by attempting to keep them always in a state of childhood. Rousseau was more consistent when he wished to stop the progress of reason in both sexes, for if men eat of the tree of knowledge, women will come in for a taste; but, from the imperfect cultivation which their understandings now receive, they only attain a knowledge of evil.

Children, I grant, should be innocent; but when the epithet is applied to men, or women, it is but a civil term for weakness. For if it be allowed that women were destined by Providence to acquire human virtues, and by the exercise of their understandings, that stability of character which is the firmest ground to rest our future hopes upon, they must be permitted to turn to the fountain of light, and not forced to shape their course by the twinkling of a mere satellite. Milton, I grant, was of a very different opinion; for he only bends to the indefeasible right of beauty, though it would be difficult to render two passages which I now mean to contrast, consistent. But into similar inconsistencies are great men often led by their senses.

'To whom thus Eve with *perfect beauty* adorn'd.
'My Author and Disposer, what thou bidst
'*Unargued* I obey; So God ordains;
'God is *thy law*, thou mine: to know no more
'Is Woman's *happiest* knowledge and her *praise*.'

These are exactly the arguments that I have used to children; but I have added, your reason is now gaining strength, and, till it arrives at some degree of maturity, you must look up to me for advice—then you ought to *think*, and only rely on God.

Yet in the following lines Milton seems to coincide with me; when he makes Adam thus expostulate with his Maker.

'Hast thou not made me here thy substitute,
'And these inferior far beneath me set?
'Among *unequals* what society
'Can sort, what harmony or true delight?

'Which must be mutual, in proposition due
'Giv'n and receiv'd; but in *disparity*
'The one intense, the other still remiss
'Cannot well suit with either, but soon prove
'Tedious alike: of *fellowship* I speak
'Such as I seek, fit to participate
'All rational delight—'

In treating, therefore, of the manners of women, let us, disregarding sensual arguments, trace what we should endeavour to make them in order to co-operate, if the expression be not too bold, with the supreme Being.

By individual education, I mean, for the sense of the word is not precisely defined, such an attention to a child as will slowly sharpen the senses, form the temper, regulate the passions as they begin to ferment, and set the understanding to work before the body arrives at maturity; so that the man may only have to proceed, not to begin, the important task of learning to think and reason.

To prevent any misconstruction, I must add, that I do not believe that a private education can work the wonders which some sanguine writers have attributed to it. Men and women must be educated, in a great degree, by the opinions and manners of the society they live in. In every age there has been a stream of popular opinion that has carried all before it, and given a family character, as it were, to the century. It may then fairly be inferred, that, till society be differently constituted, much cannot be expected from education. It is, however, sufficient for my present purpose to assert, that, whatever effect circumstances have on the abilities, every being may become virtuous by the exercise of its own reason; for if but one being was created with vicious inclinations, that is positively bad, what can save us from atheism? or if we worship a God, is not that God a devil?

Consequently, the most perfect education, in my opinion, is such an exercise of the understanding as is best calculated to strengthen the body and form the heart. Or, in other words, to enable the individual to attain such habits of virtue as will render it independent. In fact, it is a farce to call any being virtuous whose virtues do not result from the exercise of its own reason. This was Rousseau's opinion respecting men: I extend it to women, and confidently assert that they have been drawn out of their sphere by false refinement, and not by an endeavour to acquire masculine qualities. Still the regal homage which they receive is so intoxicating, that till the manners of the times are changed, and formed on more reasonable principles, it may be impossible to convince them that the illegitimate power, which they obtain, by degrading themselves, is a curse, and that they must return to nature and equality, if they wish to secure the placid satisfaction that unsophisticated affections impart. But for this epoch we must wait—wait, perhaps, till kings and nobles, enlightened by reason, and, preferring the real dignity of man to childish state, throw off their gaudy hereditary trappings: and if then women do not resign the arbitrary power of beauty—they will prove that they have *less* mind than man.

I may be accused of arrogance; still I must declare what I firmly believe, that all the writers who have written on the subject of female education and manners from Rousseau to Dr. Gregory, have contributed to render women more artificial, weak characters, than they would otherwise have been; and, consequently, more useless members of society. I might have expressed this conviction in a lower key; but I am afraid it would have been the whine of affectation, and not the faithful expression of my feelings, of the clear result, which experience and reflection have led me to draw. When I come to that division of the subject, I shall advert to the passages that I more particularly disapprove of, in the works of the authors I have just alluded to; but it is first necessary to observe, that my objection extends to the whole purport of those books, which tend, in my opinion, to degrade one half of the human species, and render women pleasing at the expense of every solid virtue.

Though, to reason on Rousseau's ground, if man did attain a degree of perfection of mind when his body arrived at maturity, it might be proper, in order to make a man and his wife *one,* that she should rely entirely on his understanding; and the graceful ivy, clasping the oak that supported it, would form a whole in which strength and beauty would be equally conspicuous. But, alas! husbands, as well as their helpmates, are often only overgrown children; nay, thanks to early debauchery, scarcely men in their outward form—and if the blind lead the blind, one need not come from heaven to tell us the consequence.

Many are the causes that, in the present corrupt state of society, contribute to enslave women by cramping their understandings and sharpening their senses. One, perhaps, that silently does more mischief than all the rest, is their disregard of order.

To do every thing in an orderly manner, is a most important precept, which women, who, generally speaking, receive only a disorderly kind of education, seldom attend to with that degree of exactness that men, who from their infancy are broken into method, observe. This negligent kind of guess-work, for what other epithet can be used to point out the random exertions of a sort of instinctive common sense, never brought to the test of reason? prevents their generalizing matters of fact—so they do to-day, what they did yesterday, merely because they did it yesterday.

This contempt of the understanding in early life has more baneful consequences than is commonly supposed; for the little knowledge which women of strong minds attain, is, from various circumstances, of a more desultory kind than the knowledge of men, and it is acquired more by sheer observations on real life, than from comparing what has been individually observed with the results of experience generalized by speculation. Led by their dependent situation and domestic employments more into society, what they learn is rather by snatches; and as learning is with them, in general, only a secondary thing, they do not pursue any one branch with that persevering ardour necessary to give vigour to the faculties, and clearness to the judgment. In the present state of society, a little learning is required to support the character of a gentleman; and boys are obliged to submit to a few years of discipline. But in the education of women, the cultivation of the understanding is always subordinate to the acquirement of some corporeal accomplishment; even while enervated by confinement and false notions of modesty, the body is prevented from attaining that grace and beauty which relaxed half-formed limbs never exhibit. Besides, in youth their faculties are not brought forward by emulation; and having no serious scientific study, if they have natural sagacity it is turned too soon on life and manners. They dwell on effects, and modifications, without tracing them back to causes; and complicated rules to adjust behaviour are a weak substitute for simple principles.

As a proof that education gives this appearance of weakness to females, we may instance the example of military men, who are, like them, sent into the world before their minds have been stored with knowledge or fortified by principles. The consequences are similar; soldiers acquire a little superficial knowledge, snatched from the muddy current of conversation, and, from continually mixing with society, they gain, what is termed a knowledge of the world; and this acquaintance with manners and customs has frequently been confounded with a knowledge of the human heart. But can the crude fruit of casual observation, never brought to the test of judgment, formed by comparing speculation and experience, deserve such a distinction? Soldiers, as well as women, practice the minor virtues with punctilious politeness. Where is then the sexual difference, when the education has been the same? All the difference that I can discern, arises from the superior advantage of liberty, which enables the former to see more of life.

It is wandering from my present subject, perhaps, to make a political remark; but, as it was produced naturally by the train of my reflections, I shall not pass it silently over.

Standing armies can never consist of resolute, robust men; they may be well disciplined machines, but they will seldom contain men under the influence of strong passions, or with very vigorous faculties. And as for any depth of understanding, I will venture to affirm, that it is as rarely to be found in the army as amongst women; and the cause, I maintain, is the same. It may be further observed, that officers are also particularly attentive to their persons, fond of dancing, crowded rooms, adventures, and ridicule.[2] Like the *fair* sex, the business of their lives is gallantry. They were taught to please, and they only live to please. Yet they do not lose their rank in the distinction of sexes, for they are still reckoned superior to women, though in what their superiority consists, beyond what I have just mentioned, it is difficult to discover.

The great misfortune is this, that they both acquire manners before morals, and a knowledge of life before they have, from reflection, any acquaintance with the grand ideal outline of human nature. The consequence is natural; satisfied with common nature, they become a prey to prejudices, and taking all their opinions on credit, they blindly submit to authority. So that, if they have any sense, it is a kind of instinctive glance, that catches proportions, and decides with respect to manners; but fails when arguments are to be pursued below the surface, or opinions analyzed.

May not the same remark be applied to women? Nay, the argument may be carried still further, for they are both thrown out of a useful station by the unnatural distinctions established in civilized life. Riches and hereditary honours have made cyphers of women to give consequence to the numerical figure; and idleness has produced a mixture of gallantry and despotism into society, which leads the very men who are the slaves of their mistresses to tyrannize over their sisters, wives, and daughters. This is only keeping them in rank and file, it is true. Strengthen the female mind by enlarging it, and there will be an end to blind obedience; but, as blind obedience is ever sought for by power, tyrants and sensualists are in the right when they endeavour to keep women in the dark, because the former only want slaves, and the latter a plaything. The sensualist, indeed, has been the most dangerous of tyrants, and women have been duped by their lovers, as princes by their ministers, whilst dreaming that they reigned over them.

I now principally allude to Rousseau, for his character of Sophia is, undoubtedly, a captivating one, though it appears to me grossly unnatural; however it is not the superstructure, but the foundation of her character, the principles on which her education was built, that I mean to attack; nay, warmly as I admire the genius of that able writer, whose opinions I shall often have occasion to cite, indignation always takes place of admiration, and the rigid frown of insulted virtue effaces the smile of complacency, which his eloquent periods are wont to raise, when I read his voluptuous reveries. Is this the man, who, in his ardour for virtue, would banish all the soft arts of peace, and almost carry us back to Spartan discipline? Is this the man who delights to paint the useful struggles of passion, the triumphs of good dispositions, and the heroic flights which carry the flowing soul out of itself? How are these mighty sentiments lowered when he describes the pretty foot and enticing airs of his little favourite! But, for the present, I wave the subject, and, instead of severely reprehending the transient effusions of overweening sensibility, I shall only observe, that whoever has cast a benevolent eye on society, must often have been gratified by the sight of a humble mutual love, not dignified by sentiment, or strengthened by a union in intellectual pursuits. The domestic trifles of the day have afforded matters for cheerful converse, and innocent caresses have softened toils which did not require great exercise of mind or stretch of thought: yet, has not the sight of this moderate felicity excited more tenderness than respect? An emotion similar to what we feel when children are playing, or animals sporting, whilst the contemplation of the noble struggles of suffering merit has raised admiration, and carried our thoughts to that world where sensation will give place to reason.

Women are, therefore, to be considered either as moral beings, or so weak that they must be entirely subjected to the superior faculties of men.

Let us examine this question. Rousseau declares that a woman should never, for a moment, feel herself independent, that she should be governed by fear to exercise her natural cunning, and made a coquetish slave in order to render her a more alluring object of desire, a *sweeter* companion to man, whenever he chooses to relax himself. He carries the arguments, which he pretends to draw from the indications of nature, still further, and insinuates that truth and fortitude, the corner stones of all human virtue, should be cultivated with certain restrictions, because, with respect to the female character, obedience is the grand lesson which ought to be impressed with unrelenting rigour.

What nonsense! When will a great man arise with sufficient strength of mind to puff away the fumes which pride and sensuality have thus spread over the subject! If women are by nature inferior to men, their virtues must be the same in quality, if not in degree, or virtue is a relative idea; consequently, their conduct should be founded on the same principles, and have the same aim.

Connected with man as daughters, wives, and mothers, their moral character may be estimated by their manner of fulfilling those simple duties; but the end, the grand end of their exertions should be to unfold their own faculties and acquire the dignity of conscious virtue. They may try to render their road pleasant; but ought never to forget, in common with man, that life yields not the felicity which can satisfy an immortal soul. I do not mean to insinuate, that either sex should be so lost in abstract reflections or distant views, as to forget the affections and duties that lie before them, and are, in truth, the means appointed to produce the fruit of life; on the contrary, I would warmly recommend them, even while I assert, that they afford most satisfaction when they are considered in their true, sober light.

Probably the prevailing opinion, that woman was created for man, may have taken its rise from Moses's poetical story, yet, as very few, it is presumed, who have bestowed any serious thought on the subject, ever supposed that Eve was, literally speaking, one of Adam's ribs, the deduction must be allowed to fall to the ground; or, only be so far admitted as it proves that man, from the remotest antiquity, found it convenient to exert his strength to subjugate his companion, and his invention to shew that she ought to have her neck bent under the yoke, because the whole creation was only created for his convenience or pleasure.

Let it not be concluded that I wish to invert the order of things; I have already granted, that, from the constitution of their bodies, men seem to be designed by Providence to attain a greater degree of virtue. I speak collectively of the whole sex; but I see not the shadow of a reason to conclude that their virtues should differ in respect to their nature. In fact, how can they, if virtue has only one eternal standard? I must therefore, if I reason consequentially, as strenuously maintain that they have the same simple direction, as that there is a God.

It follows then that cunning should not be opposed to wisdom, little cares to great exertions, or insipid softness, varnished over with the name of gentleness, to that fortitude which grand views alone can inspire.

I shall be told that woman would then lose many of her peculiar graces, and the opinion of a well known poet might be quoted to refute my unqualified assertion. For Pope has said, in the name of the whole male sex,

'Yet ne'er so sure our passion to create,
'As when she touch'd the brink of all we hate.'

In what light this sally places men and women, I shall leave to the judicious to determine; meanwhile I shall content myself with observing, that I cannot discover why, unless they are mortal, females should always be degraded by being made subservient to love or lust.

To speak disrespectfully of love is, I know, high treason against sentiment and fine feelings; but I wish to speak the simple language of truth, and rather to address the head than the heart. To endeavour to reason love out of the world, would be to out Quixote Cervantes, and equally offend against common sense; but an endeavour to restrain this tumultuous passion, and to prove that it should not be allowed to dethrone superior powers, or to usurp the sceptre which the understanding should ever coolly wield, appears less wild.

Youth is the season for love in both sexes; but in those days of thoughtless enjoyment provision should be made for the more important years of life, when reflection takes place of sensation. But Rousseau, and most of the male writers who have followed his steps, have warmly inculcated that the whole tendency of female education ought to be directed to one point: to render them pleasing.

Let me reason with the supporters of this opinion who have any knowledge of human nature, do they imagine that marriage can eradicate the habitude of life? The woman who has only been taught to please will soon find that her charms are oblique sunbeams, and that they cannot have much effect on her husband's heart when they are seen every day, when the summer is passed and gone. Will she then have sufficient native energy to look into herself for comfort, and cultivate her dormant faculties? or, is it not more rational to expect that she will try to please other men; and, in the emotions raised by the expectation of new conquests, endeavour to forget the mortification her love or pride has received? When the husband ceases to be a lover—and the time will inevitably come, her desire of pleasing will then grow languid, or become a spring of bitterness; and love, perhaps, the most evanescent of all passions, gives place to jealousy or vanity.

I now speak of women who are restrained by principle or prejudice; such women, though they would shrink from an intrigue with real abhorrence, yet, nevertheless, wish to be convinced by the homage of gallantry that they are cruelly neglected by their husbands; or, days and weeks are spent in dreaming of the happiness enjoyed by congenial souls till their health is undermined and their spirits broken by discontent. How then can the great art of pleasing be such a necessary study? it is only useful to a mistress; the chaste wife, and serious mother, should only consider her power to please as the polish of her virtues, and the affection of her husband as one of the comforts that render her task less difficult and her life happier. But, whether she be loved or neglected, her first wish should be to make herself respectable, and not to rely for all her happiness on a being subject to like infirmities with herself.

The worthy Dr. Gregory fell into a similar error. I respect his heart; but entirely disapprove of his celebrated Legacy to his Daughters.

He advises them to cultivate a fondness for dress, because a fondness for dress, he asserts, is natural to them. I am unable to comprehend what either he or Rousseau mean, when they frequently use this indefinite term. If they told us that in a pre-existent state the soul was fond of dress, and brought this inclination with it into a new body, I should listen to them with a half smile, as I often do when I hear a rant about innate elegance. But if he only meant to say that the exercise of the faculties will produce this fondness—I deny it. It is not natural; but arises, like false ambition in men, from a love of power.

Dr. Gregory goes much further; he actually recommends dissimulation, and advises an innocent girl to give the lie to her feelings, and not dance with spirit, when gaiety of heart would make her feel eloquent without making her gestures immodest. In the name of truth and common sense, why should not one woman acknowledge that she can take more exercise than another? Or, in other words, that she has a sound constitution; and why, to damp innocent vivacity, is she darkly to be told that men will draw conclusions which she little thinks of? Let the libertine draw what inference he pleases; but, I hope, that no sensible mother will restrain the natural frankness of youth by instilling such indecent cautions. Out of the abundance of the heart the mouth speaketh; and a wiser than Solomon hath said that the heart should be made clean, and not trivial ceremonies observed, which it is not very difficult to fulfill with scrupulous exactness when vice reigns in the heart.

Women ought to endeavour to purify their heart; but can they do so when their uncultivated understandings make them entirely dependent on their senses for employment and amusement, when no noble pursuit sets them above the little vanities of the day, or enables them to curb the wild emotions that agitate a reed over which every passing breeze has power? To gain the affections of a virtuous man is affectation necessary? Nature has given woman a weaker frame than man; but, to ensure her husband's affections, must a wife, who by the exercise of her mind and body whilst she was discharging the duties of a daughter, wife, and mother, has allowed her constitution to retain its natural strength, and her nerves a healthy tone, is she, I say, to condescend to use art and feign a sickly delicacy in order to secure her husband's affection? Weakness may excite tenderness, and gratify the arrogant pride of man; but the lordly caresses of a protector will not gratify a noble mind that pants for, and deserves to be respected. Fondness is a poor substitute for friendship!

In a seraglio, I grant, that all these arts are necessary; the epicure must have his palate tickled, or he will sink into apathy; but have women so little ambition as to be satisfied with such a condition? Can they supinely dream life away in the lap of pleasure, or the languor of weariness, rather than assert their claim to pursue reasonable pleasures and render themselves conspicuous by practising the virtues which dignify mankind? Surely she has not an immortal soul who can loiter life away merely employed to adorn her person, that she may amuse the languid hours, and soften the cares of a fellow creature who is willing to be enlivened by her smiles and tricks, when the serious business of life is over.

Besides, the woman who strengthens her body and exercises her mind will, by managing her family and practising various virtues, become the friend, and not the humble dependent of her husband; and if she, by possessing such substantial qualities, merit his regard, she will not find it necessary to conceal her affection, nor to pretend to an unnatural coldness of constitution to excite her husband's passions. In fact, if we revert to history, we shall find that the women who have distinguished themselves have neither been the most beautiful nor the most gentle of their sex.

Nature, or, to speak with strict propriety, God, has made all things right; but man has sought him out many inventions to mar the work. I now allude to that part of Dr. Gregory's treatise, where he advises a wife never to let her husband know the extent of her sensibility or affection. Voluptuous precaution, and as ineffectual as absurd. Love, from its very nature, must be transitory. To seek for a secret that would render it constant, would be as wild a search as for the philosopher's stone, or the grand panacea: and the discovery would be equally useless, or rather pernicious to mankind. The most holy band of society is friendship. It has been well said, by a shrewd satirist, "that rare as true love is, true friendship is still rarer."

This is an obvious truth, and the cause not lying deep, will not elude a slight glance of inquiry.

Love, the common passion, in which chance and sensation take place of choice and reason, is, in some degree, felt by the mass of mankind; for it is not necessary to speak, at present, of the emotions that rise above or sink below love. This passion, naturally increased by suspense and difficulties, draws the mind out of its accustomed state, and exalts the affections; but the security of marriage, allowing the fever of love to subside, a healthy temperature is thought insipid, only by those who have not sufficient intellect to substitute the calm tenderness of friendship, the confidence of respect, instead of blind admiration, and the sensual emotions of fondness.

This is, must be, the course of nature. Friendship or indifference inevitably succeeds love. And this constitution seems perfectly to harmonize with the system of government which prevails in the moral world. Passions are spurs to action, and open the mind; but they sink into mere appetites, become a personal and momentary gratification, when the object is gained, and the satisfied mind rests in enjoyment. The man who had some virtue whilst he was struggling for a crown, often becomes a voluptuous tyrant when it graces his brow; and, when the lover is not lost in the husband, the dotard, a prey to childish caprices, and fond jealousies, neglects the serious duties of life, and the caresses which should excite confidence in his children are lavished on the overgrown child, his wife.

In order to fulfil the duties of life, and to be able to pursue with vigour the various employments which form the moral character, a master and mistress of a family ought not to continue to love each other with passion. I mean to say, that they ought not to indulge those emotions which disturb the order of society, and engross the thoughts that should be otherwise employed. The mind that has never been engrossed by one object wants vigour—if it can long be so, it is weak.

A mistaken education, a narrow, uncultivated mind, and many sexual prejudices, tend to make women more constant than men; but, for the present, I shall not touch on this branch of the subject. I will go still further, and advance, without dreaming of a paradox, that an unhappy marriage is often very advantageous to a family, and that the neglected wife is, in general, the best mother. And this would almost always be the consequence if the female mind were more enlarged; for, it seems to be the common dispensation of Providence, that what we gain in present enjoyment should be deducted from the treasure of life, experience; and that when we are gathering the flowers of the day and revelling in pleasure, the solid fruit of toil and wisdom should not be caught at the same time. The way lies before us, we must turn to the right or left; and he who will pass life away in bounding from one pleasure to another, must not complain if he acquire neither wisdom nor respectability of character.

Supposing, for a moment, that the soul is not immortal, and that man was only created for the present scene, I think we should have reason to complain that love, infantine fondness, ever grew insipid and palled upon the sense. Let us eat, drink, and love, for to-morrow we die, would be, in fact, the language of reason, the morality of life; and who but a fool would part with a reality for a fleeting shadow? But, if awed by observing the improbable powers of the mind, we disdain to confine our wishes or thoughts to such a comparatively mean field of action; that only appears grand and important, as it is connected with a boundless prospect and sublime hopes, what necessity is there for falsehood in conduct, and why must the sacred majesty of truth be violated to detain a deceitful good that saps the very foundation of virtue? Why must the female mind be tainted by coquetish arts to gratify the sensualist, and prevent love from subsiding into friendship, or compassionate tenderness, when there are not qualities on which friendship can be built? Let the honest heart shew itself, and *reason* teach passion to submit to necessity; or, let the dignified pursuit of virtue and knowledge raise the mind above those emotions which rather imbitter than sweeten the cup of life, when they are not restrained within due bounds.

I do not mean to allude to the romantic passion, which is the concomitant of genius. Who can clip its wing? But that grand passion not proportioned

enjoyments of life, is only true to the sentiment, and feeds on
ssions which have been celebrated for their durability have always
ınate. They have acquired strength by absence and constitutional
melancholy. The fancy has hovered round a form of beauty dimly seen—but
familiarity might have turned admiration into disgust; or, at least, into indifference, and allowed the imagination leisure to start fresh game. With perfect
propriety, according to this view of things, does Rousseau make the mistress of
his soul, Eloisa, love St. Preux, when life was fading before her; but this is no
proof of the immortality of the passion.

Of the same complexion is Dr. Gregory's advice respecting delicacy of
sentiment, which he advises a woman not to acquire, if she have determined
to marry. This determination, however, perfectly consistent with his former
advice, he calls *indelicate*, and earnestly persuades his daughters to conceal it,
though it may govern their conduct;—as if it were indelicate to have the common appetites of human nature.

Noble morality! And consistent with the cautious prudence of a little soul
that cannot extend its views beyond the present minute division of existence.
If all the faculties of woman's mind are only to be cultivated as they respect her
dependence on man; if, when a husband be obtained, she have arrived at her
goal, and meanly proud rests satisfied with such a paltry crown, let her grovel
contentedly, scarcely raised by her employments above the animal kingdom;
but, if, struggling for the prize of her high calling, she look beyond the present scene, let her cultivate her understanding without stopping to consider
what character the husband may have whom she is destined to marry. Let her
only determine, without being too anxious about present happiness, to acquire
the qualities that ennoble a rational being, and a rough inelegant husband may
shock her taste without destroying her peace of mind. She will not model her
soul to suit the frailties of her companion, but to bear with them: his character may be a trial, but not an impediment to virtue.

If Dr. Gregory confined his remark to romantic expectations of constant
love and congenial feelings, he should have recollected that experience will
banish what advice can never make us cease to wish for, when the imagination
is kept alive at the expence of reason.

I own it frequently happens that women who have fostered a romantic
unnatural delicacy of feeling, waste their[4] lives in *imagining* how happy they
should have been with a husband who could love them with a fervid increasing affection every day, and all day. But they might as well pine married as single—and would not be a jot more unhappy with a bad husband than longing
for a good one. That a proper education; or, to speak with more precision, a
well stored mind, would enable a woman to support a single life with dignity,

I grant; but that she should avoid cultivating her taste, lest her husband should occasionally shock it, is quitting a substance for a shadow. To say the truth, I do not know of what use is an improved taste, if the individual be not rendered more independent of the casualties of life; if new sources of enjoyment, only dependent on the solitary operations of the mind, are not opened. People of taste, married or single, without distinction, will ever be disgusted by various things that touch not less observing minds. On this conclusion the argument must not be allowed to hinge; but in the whole sum of enjoyment is taste to be denominated a blessing?

The question is, whether it procures most pain or pleasure? The answer will decide the propriety of Dr. Gregory's advice, and show how absurd and tyrannic it is thus to lay down a system of slavery; or to attempt to educate moral beings by any other rules than those deduced from pure reason, which apply to the whole species.

Gentleness of manners, forbearance and long-suffering, are such amiable Godlike qualities, that in sublime poetic strains the Deity has been invested with them; and, perhaps, no representation of his goodness so strongly fastens on the human affections as those that represent him abundant in mercy and willing to pardon. Gentleness, considered in this point of view, bears on its front all the characteristics of grandeur, combined with the winning graces of condescension; but what a different aspect it assumes when it is the submissive demeanour of dependence, the support of weakness that loves, because it wants protection; and is forbearing, because it must silently endure injuries; smiling under the lash at which it dare not snarl. Abject as this picture appears, it is the portrait of an accomplished woman, according to the received opinion of female excellence, separated by specious reasoners from human excellence. Or, they[5] kindly restore the rib, and make one moral being of a man and woman; not forgetting to give her all the 'submissive charms.'

How women are to exist in that state where there is to be neither marrying nor giving in marriage, we are not told. For though moralists have agreed that the tenor of life seems to prove that *man* is prepared by various circumstances for a future state, they constantly concur in advising *woman* only to provide for the present. Gentleness, docility, and a spaniel-like affection are, on this ground, consistently recommended as the cardinal virtues of the sex; and, disregarding the arbitrary economy of nature, one writer has declared that it is masculine for a woman to be melancholy. She was created to be the toy of man, his rattle, and it must jingle in his ears whenever, dismissing reason, he chooses to be amused.

To recommend gentleness, indeed, on a broad basis is strictly philosophical. A frail being should labour to be gentle. But when forbearance confounds right and wrong, it ceases to be a virtue; and, however convenient it may be found in a companion—that companion will ever be considered as an inferior, and only inspire a vapid tenderness, which easily degenerates into contempt. Still, if advice could really make a being gentle, whose natural disposition admitted not of such a fine polish, something towards the advancement of order would be attained; but if, as might quickly be demonstrated, only affectation be produced by this indiscriminate counsel, which throws a stumbling-block in the way of gradual improvement, and true melioration of temper, the sex is not much benefited by sacrificing solid virtues to the attainment of superficial graces, though for a few years they may procure the individuals regal sway.

As a philosopher, I read with indignation the plausible epithets which men use to soften their insults; and, as a moralist, I ask what is meant by such heterogeneous associations, as fair defects, amiable weaknesses, &c.? If there be but one criterion of morals, but one archetype for man, women appear to be suspended by destiny, according to the vulgar tale of Mahomet's coffin; they have neither the unerring instinct of brutes, nor are allowed to fix the eye of reason on a perfect model. They were made to be loved, and must not aim at respect, lest they should be hunted out of society as masculine.

But to view the subject in another point of view. Do passive indolent women make the best wives? Confining our discussion to the present moment of existence, let us see how such weak creatures perform their part? Do the women who, by the attainment of a few superficial accomplishments, have strengthened the prevailing prejudice, merely contribute to the happiness of their husbands? Do they display their charms merely to amuse them? And have women, who have early imbibed notions of passive obedience, sufficient character to manage a family or educate children? So far from it, that, after surveying the history of woman, I cannot help, agreeing with the severest satirist, considering the sex as the weakest as well as the most oppressed half of the species. What does history disclose but marks of inferiority, and how few women have emancipated themselves from the galling yoke of sovereign man? So few, that the exceptions remind me of an ingenious conjecture respecting Newton: that he was probably a being of a superior order, accidentally caged in a human body. Following the same train of thinking, I have been led to imagine that the few extraordinary women who have rushed in eccentrical directions out of the orbit prescribed to their sex, were *male* spirits, confined by mistake in female frames. But if it be not philosophical to think of sex when the soul is mentioned, the inferiority must depend on the organs; or the heavenly fire, which is to ferment the clay, is not given in equal portions.

But avoiding, as I have hitherto done, any direct comparison of the two sexes collectively, or frankly acknowledging the inferiority of woman, according to the present appearance of things, I shall only insist that men have increased that inferiority till women are almost sunk below the standard of rational creatures. Let their faculties have room to unfold, and their virtues to gain strength, and then determine where the whole sex must stand in the intellectual scale. Yet let it be remembered, that for a small number of distinguished women I do not ask a place.

It is difficult for us purblind mortals to say to what height human discoveries and improvements may arrive when the gloom of despotism subsides, which makes us stumble at every step; but, when morality shall be settled on a more solid basis, then, without being gifted with a prophetic spirit, I will venture to predict that woman will be either the friend or slave of man. We shall not, as at present, doubt whether she is a moral agent, or the link which unites man with brutes. But, should it then appear, that like the brutes they were principally created for the use of man, he will let them patiently bite the bridle, and not mock them with empty praise; or, should their rationality be proved, he will not impede their improvement merely to gratify his sensual appetites. He will not, with all the graces of rhetoric, advise them to submit implicitly their understanding to the guidance of man. He will not, when he treats of the education of women, assert that they ought never to have the free use of reason, nor would he recommend cunning and dissimulation to beings who are acquiring, in like manner as himself, the virtues of humanity.

Surely there can be but one rule of right, if morality has an eternal foundation, and whoever sacrifices virtue, strictly so called, to present convenience, or whose *duty* it is to act in such a manner, lives only for the passing day, and cannot be an accountable creature.

The poet then should have dropped his sneer when he says,

'If weak women go astray,
'The stars are more in fault than they.'

For that they are bound by the adamantine chain of destiny is most certain, if it be proved that they are never to exercise their own reason, never to be independent, never to rise above opinion, or to feel the dignity of a rational will that only bows to God, and often forgets that the universe contains any being but itself and the model of perfection to which its ardent gaze is turned, to adore attributes that, softened into virtues, may be imitated in kind, though the degree overwhelms the enraptured mind.

If, I say, for I would not impress by declamation when Reason offers her sober light, if they be really capable of acting like rational creatures, let them not be treated like slaves; or, like the brutes who are dependent on the reason of man, when they associate with him; but cultivate their minds, give them the salutary, sublime curb of principle, and let them attain conscious dignity by feeling themselves only dependent on God. Teach them, in common with man, to submit to necessity, instead of giving, to render them more pleasing, a sex to morals.

Further, should experience prove that they cannot attain the same degree of strength of mind, perseverance, and fortitude, let their virtues be the same in kind, though they may vainly struggle for the same degree; and the superiority of man will be equally clear, if not clearer; and truth, as it is a simple principle, which admits of no modification, would be common to both. Nay, the order of society as it is at present regulated would not be inverted, for woman would then only have the rank that reason assigned her, and arts could not be practised to bring the balance even, much less to turn it.

These may be termed Utopian dreams. Thanks to that Being who impressed them on my soul, and gave me sufficient strength of mind to dare to exert my own reason, till, becoming dependent only on him for the support of my virtue, I view, with indignation, the mistaken notions that enslave my sex.

I love man as my fellow; but his scepter, real, or usurped, extends not to me, unless the reason of an individual demands my homage; and even then the submission is to reason, and not to man. In fact, the conduct of an accountable being must be regulated by the operations of its own reason; or on what foundation rests the throne of God?

It appears to me necessary to dwell on these obvious truths, because females have been insulated, as it were; and, while they have been stripped of the virtues that should clothe humanity, they have been decked with artificial graces that enable them to exercise a short-lived tyranny. Love, in their bosoms, taking place of every nobler passion, their sole ambition is to be fair, to raise emotion instead of inspiring respect; and this ignoble desire, like the servility in absolute monarchies, destroys all strength of character. Liberty is the mother of virtue, and if women be, by their very constitution, slaves, and not allowed to breathe the sharp invigorating air of freedom, they must ever languish like exotics, and be reckoned beautiful flaws in nature.

As to the argument respecting the subjection in which the sex has ever been held, it retorts on man. The many have always been enthralled by the few; and monsters, who scarcely have shewn any discernment of human excellence, have tyrannized over thousands of their fellow-creatures. Why have men of superior endowments submitted to such degradation? For is it not universally acknowledged that kings, viewed collectively, have ever been inferior, in abilities and virtue, to the same number of men taken from the common mass of mankind—yet, have they not, and are they not still treated with a degree of reverence that is an insult to reason? China is not the only country where a living man has been made a God. *Men* have submitted to superior strength to enjoy with impunity the pleasure of the moment—*women* have only done the same, and therefore till it is proved that the courtier, who servilely resigns the birthright of a man, is not a moral agent, it cannot be demonstrated that woman is essentially inferior to man because she has always been subjugated.

Brutal force has hitherto governed the world, and that the science of politics is in its infancy, is evident from philosophers scrupling to give the knowledge most useful to man that determinate distinction.

I shall not pursue this argument any further than to establish an obvious inference, that as sound politics diffuse liberty, mankind, including woman, will become more wise and virtuous.

Chap. III
The Same Subject Continued

Bodily strength from being the distinction of heroes is now sunk into such unmerited contempt that men, as well as women, seem to think it unnecessary: the latter, as it takes from their feminine graces, and from that lovely weakness the source of their undue power; and the former, because it appears inimical to the character of a gentleman.

That they have both by departing from one extreme run into another, may easily be proved; but first it may be proper to observe, that a vulgar error has obtained a degree of credit, which has given force to a false conclusion, in which an effect has been mistaken for a cause.

People of genius have, very frequently, impaired their constitutions by study or careless inattention to their health, and the violence of their passions bearing a proportion to the vigour of their intellects, the sword's destroying the scabbard has become almost proverbial, and superficial observers have inferred from thence, that men of genius have commonly weak, or, to use a more fashionable phrase, delicate constitutions. Yet the contrary, I believe, will appear to be the fact; for, on diligent inquiry, I find that strength of mind has, in most cases, been accompanied by superior strength of body—natural soundness of constitution—not that robust tone of nerves and vigour of muscles, which arise from bodily labour, when the mind is quiescent, or only directs the hands.

Dr. Priestly has remarked, in the preface to his biographical chart, that the majority of great men have lived beyond forty-five. And, considering the thoughtless manner in which they have lavished their strength, when investigating a favourite science they have wasted the lamp of life, forgetful of the midnight hour; or, when, lost in poetic dreams, fancy has peopled the scene, and the soul has been disturbed, till it shook the constitution, by the passions that meditation had raised; whose objects, the baseless fabric of a vision, faded before the exhausted eye, they must have had iron frames. Shakespeare never grasped the airy dagger with a nerveless hand, nor did Milton tremble when he led Satan far from the confines of his dreary prison. These were not the ravings of imbecility, the sickly effusions of distempered brains; but the exuberance of fancy, that 'in a fine phrenzy' wandering, was not continually reminded of its material shackles.

I am aware that this argument would carry me further than it may be supposed I wish to go; but I follow truth, and, still adhering to my first position, I will allow that bodily strength seems to give man a natural superiority over woman; and this is the only solid basis on which the superiority of the sex can be built. But I still insist, that not only the virtue, but the *knowledge* of the two sexes should be the same in nature, if not in degree, and that women, considered not only as moral, but rational creatures, ought to endeavour to acquire human virtues (or perfections) by the *same* means as men, instead of being educated like a fanciful kind of *half* being—one of Rousseau's wild chimeras.[6]

But, if strength of body be, with some shew of reason, the boast of men, why are women so infatuated as to be proud of a defect? Rousseau has furnished them with a plausible excuse, which could only have occurred to a man, whose imagination had been allowed to run wild, and refine on the impressions made by exquisite senses—that they might, forsooth, have a pretext for yielding to a natural appetite without violating a romantic species of modesty, which gratifies the pride and libertinism of man.

Women, deluded by these sentiments, sometimes boast of their weakness, cunningly obtaining power by playing on the *weakness* of men; and they may well glory in their illicit sway, for, like Turkish bashaws, they have more real power than their masters: but virtue is sacrificed to temporary gratifications, and the respectability of life to the triumph of an hour.

Women, as well as despots, have now, perhaps, more power than they would have if the world, divided and subdivided into kingdoms and families, were governed by laws deduced from the exercise of reason; but in obtaining it, to carry on the comparison, their character is degraded, and licentiousness spread through the whole aggregate of society. The many become pedestal to the few. I, therefore, will venture to assert, that till women are more rationally educated, the progress of human virtue and improvement in knowledge must receive continual checks. And if it be granted that woman was not created merely to gratify the appetite of man, or to be the upper servant, who provides his meals and takes care of his linen, it must follow, that the first care of those mothers or fathers, who really attend to the education of females, should be, if not to strengthen the body, at least, not to destroy the constitution by mistaken notions of beauty and female excellence; nor should girls ever be allowed to imbibe the pernicious notion that a defect can, by any chemical process of reasoning, become an excellence. In this respect, I am happy to find, that the author of one of the most instructive books, that our country has produced for children, coincides with me in opinion; I shall quote his pertinent remarks to give the force of his respectable authority to reason.[7]

But should it be proved that woman is naturally weaker than man, whence does it follow that it is natural for her to labour to become still weaker than nature intended her to be? Arguments of this cast are an insult to common sense, and savour of passion. The *divine right* of husbands, like the divine right of kings, may, it is to be hoped, in this enlightened age, be contested without danger, and, though conviction may not silence many boisterous disputants, yet, when any prevailing prejudice is attacked, the wise will consider, and leave the narrow-minded to rail with thoughtless vehemence at innovation.

The mother, who wishes to give true dignity of character to her daughter, must, regardless of the sneers of ignorance, proceed on a plan diametrically opposite to that which Rousseau has recommended with all the deluding charms of eloquence and philosophical sophistry: for his eloquence renders absurdities plausible, and his dogmatic conclusions puzzle, without convincing, those who have not ability to refute them.

Throughout the whole animal kingdom every young creature requires almost continual exercise, and the infancy of children, conformable to this intimation, should be passed in harmless gambols, that exercise the feet and hands, without requiring very minute direction from the head, or the constant attention of a nurse. In fact, the care necessary for self-preservation is the first natural exercise of the understanding, as little inventions to amuse the present moment unfold the imagination. But these wise designs of nature are counteracted by mistaken fondness or blind zeal. The child is not left a moment to its own direction, particularly a girl, and thus rendered dependent—dependence is called natural.

To preserve personal beauty, woman's glory! the limbs and faculties are cramped with worse than Chinese bands, and the sedentary life which they are condemned to live, whilst boys frolic in the open air, weakens the muscles and relaxes the nerves. As for Rousseau's remarks, which have since been echoed by several writers, that they have naturally, that is from their birth, independent of education, a fondness for dolls, dressing, and talking—they are so puerile as not to merit a serious refutation. That a girl, condemned to sit for hours together listening to the idle chat of weak nurses, or to attend at her mother's toilet, will endeavour to join the conversation, is, indeed, very natural; and that she will imitate her mother or aunts, and amuse herself by adorning her lifeless doll, as they do in dressing her, poor innocent babe! is undoubtedly a most natural consequence. For men of the greatest abilities have seldom had sufficient strength to rise above the surrounding atmosphere; and, if the page of genius have always been blurred by the prejudices of the age, some allowance should be made for a sex, who, like kings, always see things through a false medium.

Pursuing these reflections, the fondness for dress, conspicuous in women, may be easily accounted for, without supposing it the result of a desire to please the sex on which they are dependent. The absurdity, in short, of supposing that a girl is naturally a coquette, and that a desire connected with the impulse of nature to propagate the species, should appear even before an improper education has, by heating the imagination, called it forth prematurely, is so unphilosophical, that such a sagacious observer as Rousseau would not have adopted it, if he had not been accustomed to make reason give way to his desire of singularity, and truth to a favourite paradox.

Yet thus to give a sex to mind was not very consistent with the principles of a man who argued so warmly, and so well, for the immortality of the soul. But what a weak barrier is truth when it stands in the way of an hypothesis! Rousseau respected—almost adored virtue—and yet he allowed himself to love with sensual fondness. His imagination constantly prepared inflammable fuel for his inflammable senses; but, in order to reconcile his respect for self-denial, fortitude, and those heroic virtues, which a mind like his could not coolly admire, he labours to invert the law of nature, and broaches a doctrine pregnant with mischief and derogatory to the character of supreme wisdom.

• • •

Chap. IX
Of the Pernicious Effects Which Arise from the Unnatural Distinctions Established in Society

From the respect paid to property flow, as from a poisoned fountain, most of the evils and vices which render this world such a dreary scene to the contemplative mind. For it is in the most polished society that noisome reptiles and venomous serpents lurk under the rank herbage; and there is voluptuousness pampered by the still sultry air, which relaxes every good disposition before it ripens into virtue.

One class presses on another; for all are aiming to procure respect on account of their property: and property, once gained, will procure the respect due only to talents and virtue. Men neglect the duties incumbent on man, yet are treated like demi-gods; religion is also separated from morality by a ceremonial veil, yet men wonder that the world is almost, literally speaking, a den of sharpers or oppressors.

There is a homely proverb, which speaks a shrewd truth, that whoever the devil finds idle he will employ. And what but habitual idleness can hereditary wealth and titles produce? For man is so constituted that he can only attain a proper use of his faculties by exercising them, and will not exercise them unless necessity, of some kind, first set the wheels in motion. Virtue likewise can only be acquired by the discharge of relative duties; but the importance of these sacred duties will scarcely be felt by the being who is cajoled out of his humanity by the flattery of sycophants. There must be more equality established in society, or morality will never gain ground, and this virtuous equality will not rest firmly even when founded on a rock, if one half of mankind be chained to its bottom by fate, for they will be continually undermining it through ignorance or pride.

It is in vain to expect virtue from women till they are, in some degree, independent of men; nay, it is vain to expect that strength of natural affection, which would make them good wives and mothers. Whilst they are absolutely dependent on their husbands they will be cunning, mean, and selfish, and the men who can be gratified by the fawning fondness of spaniel-like affection, have not much delicacy, for love is not to be bought, in any sense of the words, its silken wings are instantly shrivelled up when any thing beside a return in kind is sought. Yet whilst wealth enervates men; and women live, as it were, by their personal charms, how can we expect them to discharge those ennobling duties which equally require exertion and self-denial. Hereditary property sophisticates the mind, and the unfortunate victims to it, if I may so express myself, swathed from their birth, seldom exert the locomotive faculty of body or mind; and, thus viewing every thing through one medium, and that a false one, they are unable to discern in what true merit and happiness consist. False, indeed, must be the light when the drapery of situation hides the man, and makes him stalk in masquerade, dragging from one scene of dissipation to another the nerveless limbs that hang with stupid listlessness, and rolling round the vacant eye which plainly tells us that there is no mind at home.

I mean, therefore, to infer that the society is not properly organized which does not compel men and women to discharge their respective duties, by making it the only way to acquire that countenance from their fellow-creatures, which every human being wishes some way to attain. The respect, consequently, which is paid to wealth and mere personal charms, is a true north-east blast, that blights the tender blossoms of affection and virtue. Nature has wisely attached affections to duties, to sweeten toil, and to give that vigour to the exertions of reason which only the heart can give. But, the affection which is put on merely because it is appropriated insignia of a certain character, when its duties are not fulfilled, is one of the empty compliments which vice and folly are obliged to pay to virtue and the real nature of things.

To illustrate my opinion, I need only observe, that when a woman is admired for her beauty, and suffers herself to be so far intoxicated by the admiration she receives, as to neglect to discharge the indispensable duty of a mother, she sins against herself by neglecting to cultivate an affection that would equally tend to make her useful and happy. True happiness, I mean all the contentment, and virtuous satisfaction, that can be snatched in this imperfect state, must arise from well regulated affections; and an affection includes a duty. Men are not aware of the misery they cause, and the vicious weakness they cherish, by only inciting women to render themselves pleasing; they do not consider that they thus make natural and artificial duties clash, by sacrificing the comfort and respectability of a woman's life to voluptuous notions of beauty, when in nature they all harmonize.

Cold would be the heart of a husband, were he not rendered unnatural by early debauchery, who did not feel more delight at seeing his child suckled by its mother, than the most artful wanton tricks could ever raise; yet this natural way of cementing the matrimonial tie, and twisting esteem with fonder recollections, wealth leads women to spurn. To preserve their beauty, and wear the flowery crown of the day, which gives them a kind of right to reign for a short time over the sex, they neglect to stamp impressions on their husbands' hearts, that would be remembered with more tenderness when the snow on the head began to chill the bosom, than even their virgin charms. The maternal solicitude of a reasonable affectionate woman is very interesting, and the chastened dignity with which a mother returns the caresses that she and her child receive from a father who has been fulfilling the serious duties of his station, is not only a respectable, but a beautiful sight. So singular, indeed, are my feelings, and I have endeavoured not to catch factitious ones, that after having been fatigued with the sight of insipid grandeur and the slavish ceremonies that with cumberous pomp supplied the place of domestic affections, I have turned to some other scene to relieve my eye by resting it on the refreshing green every where scattered by nature. I have then viewed with pleasure a woman nursing her children, and discharging the duties of her station with, perhaps, merely a servant maid to take off her hands the servile part of the household business. I have seen her prepare herself and children, with only the luxury of cleanliness, to receive her husband, who returning weary home in the evening found smiling babes and a clean hearth. My heart has loitered in the midst of the group, and has even throbbed with sympathetic emotion, when the scraping of the well known foot has raised a pleasing tumult.

Whilst my benevolence has been gratified by contemplating this artless picture, I have thought that a couple of this description, equally necessary and independent of each other, because each fulfilled the respective duties of their station, possessed all that life could give. Raised sufficiently above abject poverty not to be obliged to weigh the consequence of every farthing they spend, and having sufficient to prevent their attending to a frigid system of economy, which narrows both heart and mind. I declare, so vulgar are my conceptions, that I know not what is wanted to render this the happiest as well as the most respectable situation in the world, but a taste for literature, to throw a little variety and interest into social converse, and some superfluous money to give to the needy and to buy books. For it is not pleasant when the heart is opened by compassion and the head active in arranging plans of usefulness, to have a prim urchin continually twitching back the elbow to prevent the hand from drawing out an almost empty purse, whispering at the same time some prudential maxim about the priority of justice.

Destructive, however, as riches and inherited honours are to the human character, women are more debased and cramped, if possible, by them, than men, because men may still, in some degree, unfold their faculties by becoming soldiers and statesmen.

As soldiers, I grant, they can now only gather, for the most part, vain glorious laurels, whilst they adjust to a hair the European balance, taking especial care that no bleak northern nook or sound incline the beam. But the days of true heroism are over, when a citizen fought for his country like a Fabricius or a Washington, and then returned to his farm to let his virtuous fervour run in a more placid, but not a less salutary, stream. No, our British heroes are oftener sent from the gaming table than from the plow; and their passions have been rather inflamed by hanging with dumb suspense on the turn of a die, than sublimated by panting after the adventurous march of virtue in the historic page.

The statesman, it is true, might with more propriety quit the Faro Bank, or card-table, to guide the helm, for he has still but to shuffle and trick. The whole system of British politics, if system it may courteously be called, consisting in multiplying dependents and contriving taxes which grind the poor to pamper the rich; thus a war, or any wild goose chase, is, as the vulgar use the phrase, a lucky turn-up of patronage for the minister, whose chief merit is the art of keeping himself in place. It is not necessary then that he should have bowels for the poor, so he can secure for his family the odd trick. Or should some shew of respect, for what is termed with ignorant ostentation an Englishman's birth-right, be expedient to bubble the gruff mastiff that he has to lead by the nose, he can make an empty shew, very safely, by giving his single voice, and suffering his light squadron to file off to the other side. And when a question of humanity is agitated he may dip a sop in the milk of human kindness, to silence Cerberus, and talk of the interest which his heart takes in an attempt to make the earth no longer cry for vengeance as it sucks in its children's blood, though his cold hand may at the very moment rivet their chains, by sanctioning the abominable traffick. A minister is no longer a minister, than while he can carry a point, which he is determined to carry. Yet it is not necessary that a minister should feel like a man, when a bold push might shake his seat.

But, to have done with these episodical observations, let me return to the more specious slavery which chains the very soul of woman, keeping her for ever under the bondage of ignorance.

The preposterous distinctions of rank, which render civilization a curse, by dividing the world between voluptuous tyrants, and cunning envious dependents, corrupt, almost equally, every class of people, because respectability is not attached to the discharge of the relative duties of life, but to the station, and when the duties are not fulfilled the affections cannot gain sufficient strength to fortify the virtue of which they are the natural reward. Still there are some loopholes out of which a man may creep, and dare to think and act for himself; but for a woman it is an herculean task, because she has difficulties peculiar to her sex to overcome, which require almost superhuman powers.

A truly benevolent legislator always endeavours to make it the interest of each individual to be virtuous; and thus private virtue becoming the cement of public happiness, an orderly whole is consolidated by the tendency of all the parts towards a common centre. But, the private or public virtue of woman is very problematical; for Rousseau, and a numerous list of male writers, insist that she should all her life be subjected to a severe restraint, that of propriety. Why subject her to propriety—blind propriety, if she be capable of acting from a nobler spring, if she be an heir of immortality? Is sugar always to be produced by vital blood? Is one half of the human species, like the poor African slaves, to be subject to prejudices that brutalize them, when principles would be a surer guard, only to sweeten the cup of man? Is not this indirectly to deny woman reason? for a gift is a mockery, if it be unfit for use.

Women are, in common with men, rendered weak and luxurious by the relaxing pleasures which wealth procures; but added to this they are made slaves to their persons, and must render them alluring that man may lend them his reason to guide their tottering steps aright. Or should they be ambitious, they must govern their tyrants by sinister tricks, for without rights there cannot be any incumbent duties. The laws respecting woman, which I mean to discuss in a future part, make an absurd unit of a man and his wife; and then, by the easy transition of only considering him as responsible, she is reduced to a mere cypher.

The being who discharges the duties of its station is independent; and, speaking of women at large, their first duty is to themselves as rational creatures, and the next, in point of importance, as citizens, is that, which includes so many, of a mother. The rank in life which dispenses with their fulfilling this duty, necessarily degrades them by making them mere dolls. Or, should they turn to something more important than merely fitting drapery upon a smooth block, their minds are only occupied by some soft platonic attachment; or, the actual management of an intrigue may keep their thoughts in motion; for when they neglect domestic duties, they have it not in their power to take the field and march and countermarch like soldiers, or wrangle in the senate to keep their faculties from rusting.

I know that, as a proof of the inferiority of the sex, Rousseau has exultingly exclaimed, How can they leave the nursery for the camp! And the camp has by some moralists been termed the school of the most heroic virtues; though, I think, it would puzzle a keen casuist to prove the reasonableness of the greater number of wars that have dubbed heroes. I do not mean to consider this question critically; because, having frequently viewed these freaks of ambition as the first natural mode of civilization, when the ground must be torn up, and the woods cleared by fire and sword, I do not choose to call them pests; but surely the present system of war has little connection with virtue of any denomination, being rather the school of *finesse* and effeminacy, than of fortitude.

Yet, if defensive war, the only justifiable war, in the present advanced state of society, where virtue can shew its face and ripen amidst the rigours which purify the air on the mountain's top, were alone to be adopted as just and glorious, the true heroism of antiquity might again animate female bosoms. But fair and softly, gentle reader, male or female, do not alarm thyself, for though I have compared the character of a modern soldier with that of a civilized woman, I am not going to advise them to turn their distaff into a musket, though I sincerely wish to see the bayonet converted into a pruning-hook. I only recreated an imagination, fatigued by contemplating the vices and follies which all proceed from a feculent stream of wealth that has muddied the pure rills of natural affection, by supposing that society will some time or other be so constituted, that man must necessarily fulfil the duties of a citizen, or be despised, and that while he was employed in any of the departments of civil life, his wife, also an active citizen, should be equally intent to manage her family, educate her children, and assist her neighbours.

But, to render her really virtuous and useful, she must not, if she discharge her civil duties, want, individually, the protection of civil laws; she must not be dependent on her husband's bounty for her subsistence during his life, or support after his death—for how can a being be generous who has nothing of its own? or, virtuous, who is not free? The wife, in the present state of things, who is faithful to her husband, and neither suckles nor educates her children, scarcely deserves the name of a wife, and has no right to that of a citizen. But take away natural rights, and duties become null.

Women then must be considered as only the wanton solace of men, when they become so weak in mind and body, that they cannot exert themselves, unless to pursue some frothy pleasure, or to invent some frivolous fashion. What can be a more melancholy sight to a thinking mind, than to look into the numerous carriages that drive helter-skelter about this metropolis in a morning full of pale-faced creatures who are flying from themselves. I have often wished, with Dr. Johnson, to place some of them in a little shop with half a dozen children looking up to their languid countenances for support. I am much mistaken, if some latent vigour would not soon give health and spirit to their eyes, and some lines drawn by the exercise of reason on the blank cheeks, which before were only undulated by dimples, might restore lost dignity to the character, or rather enable it to attain the true dignity of its nature. Virtue is not to be acquired even by speculation, much less by the negative supineness that wealth naturally generates.

Besides, when poverty is more disgraceful than even vice, is not morality cut to the quick? Still to avoid misconstruction, though I consider that women in the common walks of life are called to fulfil the duties of wives and mothers, by religion and reason, I cannot help lamenting that women of a superiour cast have not a road open by which they can pursue more extensive plans of usefulness and independence. I may excite laughter, by dropping an hint, which I mean to pursue, some future time, for I really think that women ought to have representatives, instead of being arbitrarily governed without having any direct share allowed them in the deliberations of government.

But, as the whole system of representation is now, in this country, only a convenient handle for despotism, they need not complain, for they are as well represented as a numerous class of hard working mechanics, who pay for the support of royalty when they can scarcely stop their children's mouths with bread. How are they represented whose very sweat supports the splendid stud of an heir apparent, or varnishes the chariot of some female favourite who looks down on shame? Taxes on the very necessaries of life, enable an endless tribe of idle princes and princesses to pass with stupid pomp before a gaping crowd, who almost worship the very parade which costs them so dear. This is more gothic grandeur, something like the barbarous useless parade of having sentinels on horseback at Whitehall, which I could never view without a mixture of contempt and indignation.

How strangely must the mind be sophisticated when this sort of state impresses it! But, till these monuments of folly are levelled by virtue, similar follies will leaven the whole mass. For the same character, in some degree, will prevail in the aggregate of society: and the refinements of luxury, or the vicious repinings of envious poverty, will equally banish virtue from society, considered as the characteristic of that society, or only allow it to appear as one of the stripes of the harlequin coat, worn by the civilized man.

In the superiour ranks of life, every duty is done by deputies, as if duties could ever be waved, and the vain pleasures which consequent idleness forces the rich to pursue, appear so enticing to the next rank, that the numerous scramblers for wealth sacrifice every thing to tread on their heels. The most sacred trusts are then considered as sinecures, because they were procured by interest, and only sought to enable a man to keep *good company*. Women, in particular, all want to be ladies. Which is simply to have nothing to do, but listlessly to go they scarcely care where, for they cannot tell what.

But what have women to do in society? I may be asked, but to loiter with easy grace; surely you would not condemn them all to suckle fools and chronicle small beer! Women might certainly study the art of healing, and be physicians as well as nurses. And midwifery, decency seems to allot to them, though I am afraid the word midwife, in our dictionaries, will soon give place to *accoucheur*, and one proof of the former delicacy of the sex be effaced from the language.

They might, also, study politics, and settle their benevolence on the broadest basis; for the reading of history will scarcely be more useful than the perusal of romances, if read as mere biography; if the character of the times, the political improvements, arts, &c. be not observed. In short, if it be not considered as the history of man; and not of particular men, who filled a niche in the temple of fame, and dropped into the black rolling stream of time, that silently sweeps all before it, into the shapeless void called—eternity. For shape, can it be called, 'that shape hath none?'

Business of various kinds, they might likewise pursue, if they were educated in a more orderly manner, which might save many from common and legal prostitution. Women would not then marry for a support, as men accept of places under government, and neglect the implied duties; nor would an attempt to earn their own subsistence, a most laudable one! sink them almost to the level of those poor abandoned creatures who live by prostitution. For are not milliners and mantua-makers reckoned the next class? The few employments open to women, so far from being liberal, are menial; and when a superiour education enables them to take charge of the education of children as governesses, they are not treated like the tutors of sons, though even clerical tutors are not always treated in a manner calculated to render them respectable in the eyes of their pupils, to say nothing of the private comfort of the individual. But as women educated like gentlewomen, are never designed for the humiliating situation which necessity sometimes forces them to fill; these situations are considered in the light of a degradation; and they know little of the human heart, who need to be told, that nothing so painfully sharpens sensibility as such a fall in life.

Some of these women might be restrained from marrying by a proper spirit or delicacy, and others may not have had it in their power to escape in this pitiful way from servitude; is not that government then very defective, and very unmindful of the happiness of one half of its members, that does not provide for honest, independent women, by encouraging them to fill respectable stations? But in order to render their private virtue a public benefit, they must have a civil existence in the state, married or single; else we shall continually see some worthy woman, whose sensibility has been rendered painfully acute by undeserved contempt, droop like 'the lily broken down by a plow-share.'

It is a melancholy truth; yet such is the blessed effect of civilization! the most respectable women are the most oppressed; and, unless they have understandings far superiour to the common run of understandings, taking in both sexes, they must, from being treated like contemptible beings, become contemptible. How many women thus waste life away the prey of discontent, who might have practised as physicians, regulated a farm, managed a shop, and stood erect, supported by their own industry, instead of hanging their heads surcharged with the dew of sensibility, that consumes the beauty to which it at first gave luster; nay, I doubt whether pity and love are so near akin as poets feign, for I have seldom seen much compassion excited by the helplessness of females, unless they were fair; then, perhaps, pity was the soft handmaid of love, or the harbinger of lust.

How much more respectable is the woman who earns her own bread by fulfilling any duty; than the most accomplished beauty!—beauty did I say?— so sensible am I of the beauty of moral loveliness, or the harmonious propriety that attunes the passions of a well-regulated mind, that I blush at making the comparison; yet I sigh to think how few women aim at attaining this respectability by withdrawing from the giddy whirl of pleasure, or the indolent calm that stupefies the good sort of woman it sucks in.

Proud of their weakness, however, they must always be protected, guarded from care, and all the rough toils that dignify the mind. If this be the fiat of fate, if they will make themselves insignificant and contemptible, sweetly to waste 'life away,' let them not expect to be valued when their beauty fades, for it is the fate of the fairest flowers to be admired and pulled to pieces by the careless hand that plucked them. In how many ways do I wish, from the purest benevolence, to impress this truth on my sex; yet I fear that they will not listen to a truth that dear bought experience has brought home to many an agitated bosom, nor willingly resign the privileges of rank and sex for the privileges of humanity, to which those have no claim who do not discharge its duties.

Those writers are particularly useful, in my opinion, who make man feel for man, independent of the station he fills, or the drapery of factitious sentiments. I then would fain convince reasonable men of the importance of some of my remarks, and prevail on them to weigh dispassionately the whole tenor of my observations. I appeal to their understandings; and, as a fellow-creature, claim, in the name of my sex, some interest in their hearts. I entreat them to assist to emancipate their companion, to make her a *help meet* for them!

Would men but generously snap our chains, and be content with rational fellowship instead of slavish obedience, they would find us more observant daughters, more affectionate sisters, more faithful wives, more reasonable mothers—in a word, better citizens. We should then love them with true affection, because we should learn to respect ourselves; and the peace of mind of a worthy man would not be interrupted by the idle vanity of his wife, nor the babes sent to nestle in a strange bosom, having never found a home in their mother's.

Author's Notes

[1] A lively writer, I cannot recollect his name, asks what business women turned of forty have to do in the world?

[2] Why should women be censured with petulant acrimony, because they seem to have a passion for a scarlet coat? Has not education placed them more on a level with soldiers than any other class of men?

[3] Similar feelings has Milton's pleasing picture of paradisiacal happiness ever raised in my mind; yet, instead of envying the lovely pair, I have, with conscious dignity, or Satanic pride, turned to hell for sublimer objects. In the same style, when viewing some noble monument of human art, I have traced the emanation of the Deity in

the order I admired, till, descending from that giddy height, I have caught myself contemplating the grandest of all human sights—for fancy quickly placed, in some solitary recess, an outcast of fortune, rising superior to passion and discontent.

4 For example, the herd of Novelists.

5 Vide Rousseau, and Swedenborg.

6 'Researches into abstract and speculative truths, the principles and axioms of sciences, in short, every thing which tends to generalize our ideas, is not the proper province of women; their studies should be relative to points of practice; it belongs to them to apply those principles which men have discovered; and it is their part to make observations, which direct men to the establishment of general principles. All the ideas of women, which have not the immediate tendency to points of duty, should be directed to the study of men, and to the attainment of those agreeable accomplishments which have taste for their object; for as to works of genius, they are beyond their capacity; neither have they sufficient precision or power of attention to succeed in sciences which require accuracy: and as to physical knowledge, it belongs to those only who are most active, most inquisitive; who comprehend the greatest variety of objects: in short, it belongs to those who have the strongest powers, and who exercise them most, to judge of the relations between sensible beings and the laws of nature. A woman who is naturally weak, and does not carry her ideas to any great extent, knows how to judge and make a proper estimate of those movements which she sets to work, in order to aid her weakness; and these movements are the passions of men. The mechanism she employs is much more powerful than ours; for all her levers move the human heart. She must have the skill to incline us to do every thing which her sex will not enable her to do herself, and which is necessary or agreeable to her; therefore she ought to study the mind of man thoroughly, not the mind of man in general, abstractedly, but the dispositions of those men to whom she is subject, either by the laws of her country or by the force of opinion. She should learn to penetrate into their real sentiments from their conversation, their actions, their looks, and gestures. She should also have the art, by her own conversation, actions, looks, and gestures, to communicate those sentiments which are agreeable to them, without seeming to intend it. Men will argue more philosophically about the human heart; but women will read the heart of man better than they. It belongs to women, if I may be allowed the expression, to form an experimental morality, and to reduce the study of man to a system. Women have most wit, men have most genius; women observe, men reason: from the concurrence of both we derive the clearest light and the most perfect knowledge, which the human mind is, of itself, capable of attaining. In one word, from hence we acquire the most intimate acquaintance, both with ourselves and others, of which our nature is capable; and it is thus that art has a constant tendency to perfect those endowments which nature has bestowed.—The world is the book of women.' Rousseau's Émile.

I hope my readers still remember the comparison, which I have brought forward, between women and officers.

[7] A respectable old man gives the following sensible account of the method he pursued when educating his daughter. 'I endeavored to give both to her mind and body a degree of vigour, which is seldom found in the female sex. As soon as she was sufficiently advanced in strength to be capable of the lighter labours of husbandry and gardening, I employed her as my constant companion. Selene, for that was her name, soon acquired a dexterity in all these rustic employments, which I considered with equal pleasure and admiration. If women are in general feeble both in body and mind, it arises less from nature than from education. We encourage a vicious indolence and inactivity, which we falsely call delicacy; instead of hardening their minds by the severer principles of reason and philosophy, we breed them to useless arts, which terminate in vanity and sensuality. In most of the countries which I had visited, they are taught nothing of an higher nature than a few modulations of the voice, or useless postures of the body; their time is consumed in sloth or trifles, and trifles become the only pursuits capable of interesting them. We seem to forget, that it is upon the qualities of the female sex that our own domestic comforts and the education of our children must depend. And what are the comforts or the education which a race of beings, corrupted from their infancy, and unacquainted with all the duties of life, are fitted to bestow? To touch a musical instrument with useless skill, to exhibit their natural or affected graces to the eyes of indolent and debauched young men, to dissipate their husband's patrimony in riotous and unnecessary expenses, these are the only arts cultivated by women in most of the polished nations I had seen. And the consequences are uniformly such as may be expected to proceed from such polluted sources, private misery and public servitude.

But Selene's education was regulated by different views, and conducted upon severer principles; If that can be called severity which opens the mind to a sense of moral and religious duties, and most effectually arms it against the inevitable evils of life.' Mr. Day's *Sandford and Merton,* Vol. III.

What to the Slave Is the Fourth of July?

Frederick Douglass
July 5, 1852

Mr. President, Friends and Fellow Citizens: He who could address this audience without a quailing sensation, has stronger nerves than I have. I do not remember ever to have appeared as a speaker before any assembly more shrinkingly, nor with greater distrust of my ability, than I do this day. A feeling has crept over me, quite unfavorable to the exercise of my limited powers of speech. The task before me is one which requires much previous thought and study for its proper performance. I know that apologies of this sort are generally considered flat and unmeaning. I trust, however, that mine will not be so considered. Should I seem at ease, my appearance would much misrepresent me. The little experience I have had in addressing public meetings, in country schoolhouses, avails me nothing on the present occasion.

The papers and placards say, that I am to deliver a 4th [of] July oration. This certainly sounds large, and out of the common way, for it is true that I have often had the privilege to speak in this beautiful Hall, and to address many who now honor me with their presence. But neither their familiar faces, nor the perfect gage I think I have of Corinthian Hall, seems to free me from embarrassment.

The fact is, ladies and gentlemen, the distance between this platform and the slave plantation, from which I escaped, is considerable—and the difficulties to be overcome in getting from the latter to the former, are by no means slight. That I am here to-day is, to me, a matter of astonishment as well as of gratitude. You will not, therefore, be surprised, if in what I have to say, I evince no elaborate preparation, nor grace my speech with any high sounding exordium. With little experience and with less learning, I have been able to throw my thoughts hastily and imperfectly together; and trusting to your patient and generous indulgence, I will proceed to lay them before you.

This, for the purpose of this celebration, is the 4th of July. It is the birthday of your National Independence, and of your political freedom. This, to you, is what the Passover was to the emancipated people of God. It carries your minds back to the day, and to the act of your great deliverance; and to the

signs, and to the wonders, associated with that act, and that day. This celebration also marks the beginning of another year of your national life; and
reminds you that the Republic of America is now 76 years old. I am glad,
fellow-citizens, that your nation is so young. Seventy-six years, though a good
old age for a man, is but a mere speck in the life of a nation. Three score years
and ten is the allotted time for individual men; but nations number their years
by thousands. According to this fact, you are, even now, only in the beginning
of your national career, still lingering in the period of childhood. I repeat, I am
glad this is so. There is hope in the thought, and hope is much needed, under
the dark clouds which lower above the horizon. The eye of the reformer is met
with angry flashes, portending disastrous times; but his heart may well beat
lighter at the thought that America is young, and that she is still in the
impressible stage of her existence. May he not hope that high lessons of wisdom, of justice and of truth, will yet give direction to her destiny? Were the
nation older, the patriot's heart might be sadder, and the reformer's brow heav-
ier. Its future might be shrouded in gloom, and the hope of its prophets go out
in sorrow. There is consolation in the thought that America is young. Great
streams are not easily turned from channels, worn deep in the course of ages.
They may sometimes rise in quiet and stately majesty, and inundate the land,
refreshing and fertilizing the earth with their mysterious properties. They may
also rise in wrath and fury, and bear away, on their angry waves, the accumu-
lated wealth of years of toil and hardship. They, however, gradually flow back
to the same old channel, and flow on as serenely as ever. But, while the river
may not be turned aside, it may dry up, and leave nothing behind but the
withered branch, and the unsightly rock, to howl in the abyss-sweeping wind,
the sad tale of departed glory. As with rivers so with nations.

Fellow-citizens, I shall not presume to dwell at length on the associations
that cluster about this day. The simple story of it is that, 76 years ago, the people of this country were British subjects. The style and title of your "sovereign
people" (in which you now glory) was not then born. You were under the
British Crown. Your fathers esteemed the English Government as the home
government; and England as the fatherland. This home government, you
know, although a considerable distance from your home, did, in the exercise
of its parental prerogatives, impose upon its colonial children, such restraints,
burdens and limitations, as, in its mature judgement, it deemed wise, right
and proper.

But, your fathers, who had not adopted the fashionable idea of this day,
of the infallibility of government, and the absolute character of its acts, presumed to differ from the home government in respect to the wisdom and the

justice of some of those burdens and restraints. They went so far in their excite-
ment as to pronounce the measures of government unjust, unreasonable, and
oppressive, and altogether such as ought not to be quietly submitted to. I
scarcely need say, fellow-citizens, that my opinion of those measures fully
accords with that of your fathers. Such a declaration of agreement on my part
would not be worth much to anybody. It would, certainly, prove nothing, as
to what part I might have taken, had I lived during the great controversy of
1776. To say now that America was right, and England wrong, is exceedingly
easy. Everybody can say it; the dastard, not less than the noble brave, can flip-
pantly discant on the tyranny of England towards the American Colonies. It is
fashionable to do so; but there was a time when to pronounce against England,
and in favor of the cause of the colonies, tried men's souls. They who did so
were accounted in their day, plotters of mischief, agitators and rebels, dangerous men. To side with the right, against the wrong, with the weak against the
strong, and with the oppressed against the oppressor! here lies the merit, and
the one which, of all others, seems unfashionable in our day. The cause of liberty may be stabbed by the men who glory in the deeds of your fathers. But,
to proceed.

Feeling themselves harshly and unjustly treated by the home government,
your fathers, like men of honesty, and men of spirit, earnestly sought redress.
They petitioned and remonstrated; they did so in a decorous, respectful, and
loyal manner. Their conduct was wholly unexceptionable. This, however, did
not answer the purpose. They saw themselves treated with sovereign indifference, coldness and scorn. Yet they persevered. They were not the men to look
back.

As the sheet anchor takes a firmer hold, when the ship is tossed by the
storm, so did the cause of your fathers grow stronger, as it breasted the chill-
ing blasts of kingly displeasure. The greatest and best of British statesmen
admitted its justice, and the loftiest eloquence of the British Senate came to its
support. But, with that blindness which seems to be the unvarying characteristic of tyrants, since Pharoah and his hosts were drowned in the Red Sea, the
British Government persisted in the exactions complained of.

The madness of this course, we believe, is admitted now, even by
England; but we fear the lesson is wholly lost on our present rulers.

Oppression makes a wise man mad. Your fathers were wise men, and if
they did not go mad, they became restive under this treatment. They felt
themselves the victims of grievous wrongs, wholly incurable in their colonial
capacity. With brave men there is always a remedy for oppression. Just here,
the idea of a total separation of the colonies from the crown was born! It was
a startling idea, much more so, than we, at this distance of time, regard it. The

timid and the prudent (as has been intimated) of that day, were, of course, shocked and alarmed by it.

Such people lived then, had lived before, and will, probably, ever have a place on this planet; and their course, in respect to any great change, (no matter how great the good to be attained, or the wrong to be redressed by it), may be calculated with as much precision as can be the course of the stars. They hate all changes, but silver, gold and copper change! Of this sort of change they are always strongly in favor.

These people were called Tories in the days of your fathers; and the appellation, probably, conveyed the same idea that is meant by a more modern, though a somewhat less euphonious term, which we often find in our papers, applied to some of our old politicians.

Their opposition to the then dangerous thought was earnest and powerful; but, amid all their terror and affrighted vociferations against it, the alarming and revolutionary idea moved on, and the country with it.

On the 2nd of July, 1776, the old Continental Congress, to the dismay of the lovers of ease, and the worshippers of property, clothed that dreadful idea with all the authority of national sanction. They did so in the form of a resolution; and as we seldom hit upon resolutions, drawn up in our day whose transparency is at all equal to this, it may refresh your minds and help my story if I read it.

> Resolved, That these united colonies are, and of right, ought to be free and Independent States; that they are absolved from all allegiance to the British Crown; and that all political connection between them and the State of Great Britain is, and ought to be, dissolved.

Citizens, your fathers made good that resolution. They succeeded; and to-day you reap the fruits of their success. The freedom gained is yours; and you, therefore, may properly celebrate this anniversary. The 4th of July is the first great fact in your nation's history—the very ring-bolt in the chain of your yet undeveloped destiny.

Pride and patriotism, not less than gratitude, prompt you to celebrate and to hold it in perpetual remembrance. I have said that the Declaration of Independence is the ring-bolt to the chain of your nation's destiny; so, indeed, I regard it. The principles contained in that instrument are saving principles. Stand by those principles, be true to them on all occasions, in all places, against all foes, and at whatever cost.

From the round top of your ship of state, dark and threatening clouds may be seen. Heavy billows, like mountains in the distance, disclose to the leeward huge forms of flinty rocks! That bolt drawn, that chain broken, and all is lost.

Cling to this day—cling to it, and to its principles, with the grasp of a storm-tossed mariner to a spar at midnight.

The coming into being of a nation, in any circumstances, is an interesting event. But, besides general considerations, there were peculiar circumstances which make the advent of this republic an event of special attractiveness.

The whole scene, as I look back to it, was simple, dignified and sublime.

The population of the country, at the time, stood at the insignificant number of three millions. The country was poor in the munitions of war. The population was weak and scattered, and the country a wilderness unsubdued. There were then no means of concert and combination, such as exist now. Neither steam nor lightning had then been reduced to order and discipline. From the Potomac to the Delaware was a journey of many days. Under these, and innumerable other disadvantages, your fathers declared for liberty and independence and triumphed.

Fellow Citizens, I am not wanting in respect for the fathers of this republic. The signers of the Declaration of Independence were brave men. They were great men too—great enough to give fame to a great age. It does not often happen to a nation to raise, at one time, such a number of truly great men. The point from which I am compelled to view them is not, certainly, the most favorable; and yet I cannot contemplate their great deeds with less than admiration. They were statesmen, patriots and heroes, and for the good they did, and the principles they contended for, I will unite with you to honor their memory.

They loved their country better than their own private interests; and, though this is not the highest form of human excellence, all will concede that it is a rare virtue, and that when it is exhibited, it ought to command respect. He who will, intelligently, lay down his life for his country, is a man whom it is not in human nature to despise. Your fathers staked their lives, their fortunes, and their sacred honor, on the cause of their country. In their admiration of liberty, they lost sight of all other interests.

They were peace men; but they preferred revolution to peaceful submission to bondage. They were quiet men; but they did not shrink from agitating against oppression. They showed forbearance; but that they knew its limits. They believed in order; but not in the order of tyranny. With them, nothing was "settled" that was not right. With them, justice, liberty and humanity were "final;" not slavery and oppression. You may well cherish the memory of such men. They were great in their day and generation. Their solid manhood stands out the more as we contrast it with these degenerate times.

How circumspect, exact and proportionate were all their movements! How unlike the politicians of an hour! Their statesmanship looked beyond the passing moment, and stretched away in strength into the distant future. They seized upon eternal principles, and set a glorious example in their defence. Mark them!

Fully appreciating the hardship to be encountered, firmly believing in the right of their cause, honorably inviting the scrutiny of an on-looking world, reverently appealing to heaven to attest their sincerity, soundly comprehending the solemn responsibility they were about to assume, wisely measuring the terrible odds against them, your fathers, the fathers of this republic, did, most deliberately, under the inspiration of a glorious patriotism, and with a sublime faith in the great principles of justice and freedom, lay deep the corner-stone of the national superstructure, which has risen and still rises in grandeur around you.

Of this fundamental work, this day is the anniversary. Our eyes are met with demonstrations of joyous enthusiasm. Banners and pennants wave exultingly on the breeze. The din of business, too, is hushed. Even Mammon seems to have quitted his grasp on this day. The ear-piercing fife and the stirring drum unite their accents with the ascending peal of a thousand church bells. Prayers are made, hymns are sung, and sermons are preached in honor of this day; while the quick martial tramp of a great and multitudinous nation, echoed back by all the hills, valleys and mountains of a vast continent, bespeak the occasion one of thrilling and universal interest—a nation's jubilee.

Friends and citizens, I need not enter further into the causes which led to this anniversary. Many of you understand them better than I do. You could instruct me in regard to them. That is a branch of knowledge in which you feel, perhaps, a much deeper interest than your speaker. The causes which led to the separation of the colonies from the British crown have never lacked for a tongue. They have all been taught in your common schools, narrated at your firesides, unfolded from your pulpits, and thundered from your legislative halls, and are as familiar to you as household words. They form the staple of your national poetry and eloquence.

I remember, also, that, as a people, Americans are remarkably familiar with all facts which make in their own favor. This is esteemed by some as a national trait—perhaps a national weakness. It is a fact, that whatever makes for the wealth or for the reputation of Americans, and can be had cheap! will be found by Americans. I shall not be charged with slandering Americans, if I say I think the American side of any question may be safely left in American hands.

I leave, therefore, the great deeds of your fathers to other gentlemen whose claim to have been regularly descended will be less likely to be disputed than mine!

The Present

My business, if I have any here to-day, is with the present. The accepted time with God and his cause is the ever-living now.

Trust no future, however pleasant,
Let the dead past bury its dead;
Act, act in the living present,
Heart within, and God overhead.

We have to do with the past only as we can make it useful to the present and to the future. To all inspiring motives, to noble deeds which can be gained from the past, we are welcome. But now is the time, the important time. Your fathers have lived, died, and have done their work, and have done much of it well. You live and must die, and you must do your work. You have no right to enjoy a child's share in the labor of your fathers, unless your children are to be blest by your labors. You have no right to wear out and waste the hard-earned fame of your fathers to cover your indolence. Sydney Smith tells us that men seldom eulogize the wisdom and virtues of their fathers, but to excuse some folly or wickedness of their own. This truth is not a doubtful one. There are illustrations of it near and remote, ancient and modern. It was fashionable, hundreds of years ago, for the children of Jacob to boast, we have "Abraham to our father," when they had long lost Abraham's faith and spirit. That people contented themselves under the shadow of Abraham's great name, while they repudiated the deeds which made his name great. Need I remind you that a similar thing is being done all over this country to-day? Need I tell you that the Jews are not the only people who built the tombs of the prophets, and garnished the sepulchres of the righteous? Washington could not die till he had broken the chains of his slaves. Yet his monument is built up by the price of human blood, and the traders in the bodies and souls of men, shout—"We have Washington to our *father*."—Alas! that it should be so; yet so it is.

The evil that men do, lives after them,
The good is oft' interred with their bones.

Fellow-citizens, pardon me, allow me to ask, why am I called upon to speak here to-day? What have I, or those I represent, to do with your national independence? Are the great principles of political freedom and of natural justice, embodied in that Declaration of Independence, extended to us? and am I, therefore, called upon to bring our humble offering to the national altar, and to confess the benefits and express devout gratitude for the blessings resulting from your independence to us?

Would to God, both for your sakes and ours, that an affirmative answer could be truthfully returned to these questions! Then would my task be light, and my burden easy and delightful. For who is there so cold, that a nation's sympathy could not warm him? Who so obdurate and dead to the claims of gratitude, that would not thankfully acknowledge such priceless benefits? Who so stolid and selfish, that would not give his voice to swell the hallelujahs of a nation's jubilee, when the chains of servitude had been torn from his limbs? I am not that man. In a case like that, the dumb might eloquently speak, and the "lame man leap as an hart."

But, such is not the state of the case. I say it with a sad sense of the disparity between us. I am not included within the pale of this glorious anniversary! Your high independence only reveals the immeasurable distance between us. The blessings in which you, this day, rejoice, are not enjoyed in common.—The rich inheritance of justice, liberty, prosperity and independence, bequeathed by your fathers, is shared by you, not by me. The sunlight that brought life and healing to you, has brought stripes and death to me. This Fourth [of] July is *yours*, not *mine*. *You* may rejoice, *I* must mourn. To drag a man in fetters into the grand illuminated temple of liberty, and call upon him to join you in joyous anthems, were inhuman mockery and sacrilegious irony. Do you mean, citizens, to mock me, by asking me to speak to-day? If so, there is a parallel to your conduct. And let me warn you that it is dangerous to copy the example of a nation whose crimes, towering up to heaven, were thrown down by the breath of the Almighty, burying that nation in irrecoverable ruin! I can to-day take up the plaintive lament of a peeled and woe-smitten people!

> By the rivers of Babylon, there we sat down. Yea! we wept when we remembered Zion. We hanged our harps upon the willows in the midst thereof. For there, they that carried us away captive, required of us a song; and they who wasted us required of us mirth, saying, Sing us one of the songs of Zion. How can we sing the Lord's song in a strange land? If I forget thee, O Jerusalem, let my right hand forget her cunning. If I do not remember thee, let my tongue cleave to the roof of my mouth.

Fellow-citizens; above your national, tumultous joy, I hear the mournful wail of millions! whose chains, heavy and grievous yesterday, are, to-day, rendered more intolerable by the jubilee shouts that reach them. If I do forget, if I do not faithfully remember those bleeding children of sorrow this day, "may my right hand forget her cunning, and may my tongue cleave to the roof of my mouth!" To forget them, to pass lightly over their wrongs, and to chime in with the popular theme, would be treason most scandalous and shocking, and would make me a reproach before God and the world. My subject, then fellow-citizens, is AMERICAN SLAVERY. I shall see, this day, and its popular characteristics, from the slave's point of view. Standing, there, identified with the American bondman, making his wrongs mine, I do not hesitate to declare, with all my soul, that the character and conduct of this nation never looked blacker to me than on this 4th of July! Whether we turn to the declarations of the past, or to the professions of the present, the conduct of the nation seems equally hideous and revolting. America is false to the past, false to the present, and solemnly binds herself to be false to the future. Standing with God and the crushed and bleeding slave on this occasion, I will, in the name of humanity which is outraged, in the name of liberty which is fettered, in the name of the constitution and the Bible, which are disregarded and trampled upon, dare to call in question and to denounce, with all the emphasis I can command, everything that serves to perpetuate slavery—the great sin and shame of America! "I will not equivocate; I will not excuse;" I will use the severest language I can command; and yet not one word shall escape me that any man, whose judgement is not blinded by prejudice, or who is not at heart a slaveholder, shall not confess to be right and just.

But I fancy I hear some one of my audience say, it is just in this circumstance that you and your brother abolitionists fail to make a favorable impression on the public mind. Would you argue more, and denounce less, would you persuade more, and rebuke less, your cause would be much more likely to succeed. But, I submit, where all is plain there is nothing to be argued. What point in the anti-slavery creed would you have me argue? On what branch of the subject do the people of this country need light? Must I undertake to prove that the slave is a man? That point is conceded already. Nobody doubts it. The slaveholders themselves acknowledge it in the enactment of laws for their government. They acknowledge it when they punish disobedience on the part of the slave. There are seventy-two crimes in the State of Virginia, which, if committed by a black man, (no matter how ignorant he be), subject him to the punishment of death; while only two of the same crimes will subject a white man to the like punishment. What is this but the acknowledgement that the slave is a moral, intellectual and responsible being? The manhood of the slave is conceded. It is admitted in the fact that Southern statute books are covered with enactments forbidding, under severe fines and penalties, the teaching of the slave to read or to write. When you can point to any such laws, in reference to the beasts of the field, then I may consent to argue the manhood of the slave.

When the dogs in your streets, when the fowls of the air, when the cattle on your hills, when the fish of the sea, and the reptiles that crawl, shall be unable to distinguish the slave from a brute, *then* will I argue with you that the slave is a man!

For the present, it is enough to affirm the equal manhood of the Negro race. Is it not astonishing that, while we are ploughing, planting and reaping, using all kinds of mechanical tools, erecting houses, constructing bridges, building ships, working in metals of brass, iron, copper, silver and gold; that, while we are reading, writing and cyphering, acting as clerks, merchants and secretaries, having among us lawyers, doctors, ministers, poets, authors, editors, orators and teachers; that, while we are engaged in all manner of enterprises common to other man, digging gold in California, capturing the whale in the Pacific, feeding sheep and cattle on the hill-side, living, moving, acting, thinking, planning, living in families as husbands, wives and children, and, above all, confessing and worshipping the Christian's God, and looking hopefully for life and immortality beyond the grave, we are called upon to prove that we are men!

Would you have me argue that man is entitled to liberty? that he is the rightful owner of his own body? You have already declared it. Must I argue the wrongfulness of slavery? Is that a question for Republicans? Is it to be settled by the rules of logic and argumentation, as a matter beset with great difficulty, involving a doubtful application of the principle of justice, hard to be understood? How should I look to-day, in the presence of Americans, dividing, and subdividing a discourse, to show that men have a natural right to freedom? speaking of it relatively, and positively, negatively, and affirmatively. To do so, would be to make myself ridiculous, and to offer an insult to your understanding.—There is not a man beneath the canopy of heaven, that does not know that slavery is wrong *for him*.

What, am I to argue that it is wrong to make men brutes, to rob them of their liberty, to work them without wages, to keep them ignorant of their relations to their fellow men, to beat them with sticks, to flay their flesh with the lash, to load their limbs with irons, to hunt them with dogs, to sell them at auction, to sunder their families, to knock out their teeth, to burn their flesh, to starve them into obedience and submission to their masters? Must I argue that a system thus marked with blood, and stained with pollution, is *wrong*? No! I will not. I have better employments for my time and strength than such arguments would imply.

What, then, remains to be argued? Is it that slavery is not divine; that God did not establish it; that our doctors of divinity are mistaken? There is blasphemy in the thought. That which is inhuman, cannot be divine! Who can reason on such a proposition? They that can, may; I cannot. The time for such argument is passed.

At a time like this, scorching irony, not convincing argument, is needed. O! had I the ability, and could I reach the nation's ear, I would, to-day, pour out a fiery stream of biting ridicule, blasting reproach, withering sarcasm, and stern rebuke. For it is not light that is needed, but fire; it is not the gentle shower, but thunder. We need the storm, the whirlwind, and the earthquake. The feeling of the nation must be quickened; the conscience of the nation must be roused; the propriety of the nation must be startled; the hypocrisy of the nation must be exposed; and its crimes against God and man must be proclaimed and denounced.

What, to the American slave, is your 4th of July? I answer: a day that reveals to him, more than all other days in the year, the gross injustice and cruelty to which he is the constant victim. To him, your celebration is a sham; your boasted liberty, an unholy license; your national greatness, swelling vanity; your sounds of rejoicing are empty and heartless; your denunciations of tyrants, brass fronted impudence; your shouts of liberty and equality, hollow mockery; your prayers and hymns, your sermons and thanksgivings, with all your religious parade, and solemnity, are, to him, mere bombast, fraud, deception, impiety, and hypocrisy—a thin veil to cover up crimes which would disgrace a nation of savages. There is not a nation on the earth guilty of practices, more shocking and bloody, than are the people of these United States, at this very hour.

Go where you may, search where you will, roam through all the monarchies and despotisms of the old world, travel through South America, search out every abuse, and when you have found the last, lay your facts by the side of the everyday practices of this nation, and you will say with me, that, for revolting barbarity and shameless hypocrisy, America reigns without a rival.

Internal Slave-Trade

Take the American slave-trade, which, we are told by the papers, is especially prosperous just now. Ex-Senator Benton tells us that the price of men was never higher than now. He mentions the fact to show that slavery is in no danger. This trade is one of the peculiarities of American institutions. It is carried on in all the large towns and cities in one-half of this confederacy; and millions are pocketed every year, by dealers in this horrid traffic. In several states, this trade is a chief source of wealth. It is called (in contradistinction to the foreign slave-trade) *"the internal slave trade."* It is, probably, called so, too, in order to divert from it the horror with which the foreign slave-trade is contemplated. That trade has long since been denounced by this government, as piracy. It has been denounced with burning words, from the high places of the nation, as an execrable traffic. To arrest it, to put an end to it, this nation keeps a squadron, at immense cost, on the coast of Africa. Everywhere, in this country, it is safe to speak of this foreign slave-trade, as a most inhuman traffic, opposed alike to the laws of God and of man. The duty to extirpate and destroy it, is admitted even by our DOCTORS OF DIVINITY. In order to put an end to it, some of these last have consented that their colored brethren (nominally free) should leave this country, and establish themselves on the western coast of Africa! It is, however, a notable fact that, while so much execration is poured out by Americans upon those engaged in the foreign slave-trade, the men engaged in the slave-trade between the states pass without condemnation, and their business is deemed honorable.

Behold the practical operation of this internal slave-trade, the American slave-trade, sustained by American politics and American religion. Here you will see men and women reared like swine for the market. You know what is a swine-drover? I will show you a man-drover. They inhabit all our Southern States. They perambulate the country, and crowd the highways of the nation, with droves of human stock. You will see one of these human flesh-jobbers, armed with pistol, whip and bowie-knife, driving a company of a hundred men, women, and children, from the Potomac to the slave market at New Orleans. These wretched people are to be sold singly, or in lots, to suit purchasers. They are food for the cotton-field, and the deadly sugar-mill. Mark the sad procession, as it moves wearily along, and the inhuman wretch who drives them. Hear his savage yells and his blood-chilling oaths, as he hurries on his affrighted captives! There, see the old man, with locks thinned and gray. Cast one glance, if you please, upon that young mother, whose shoulders are bare to the scorching sun, her briny tears falling on the brow of the babe in her arms. See, too, that girl of thirteen, weeping, yes! weeping, as she thinks of the mother from whom she has been torn! The drove moves tardily. Heat and sorrow have nearly consumed their strength; suddenly you hear a quick snap, like the discharge of a rifle; the fetters clank, and the chain rattles simultaneously; your ears are saluted with a scream, that seems to have torn its way to the centre of your soul! The crack you heard, was the sound of the slave-whip; the scream you heard, was from the woman you saw with the babe. Her speed had faltered under the weight of her child and her chains! that gash on her shoulder tells her to move on. Follow the drove to New Orleans. Attend the auction; see men examined like horses; see the forms of women rudely and brutally exposed to the shocking gaze of American slave-buyers. See this drove sold and separated forever; and never forget the deep, sad sobs that arose from that scattered multitude. Tell me citizens, WHERE, under the sun, you can witness a spectacle more fiendish and shocking. Yet this is but a glance at the American slave-trade, as it exists, at this moment, in the ruling part of the United States.

I was born amid such sights and scenes. To me the American slave-trade is a terrible reality. When a child, my soul was often pierced with a sense of its horrors. I lived on Philpot Street, Fell's Point, Baltimore, and have watched from the wharves, the slave ships in the Basin, anchored from the shore, with their cargoes of human flesh, waiting for favorable winds to waft them down the Chesapeake. There was, at that time, a grand slave mart kept at the head of Pratt Street, by Austin Woldfolk. His agents were sent into every town and county in Maryland, announcing their arrival, through the papers, and on flaming "*hand-bills*," headed CASH FOR NEGROES. These men were generally well dressed men, and very captivating in their manners. Ever ready to drink, to treat, and to gamble. The fate of many a slave has depended upon the turn of a single card; and many a child has been snatched from the arms of its mother by bargains arranged in a state of brutal drunkenness.

The flesh-mongers gather up their victims by dozens, and drive them, chained, to the general depot at Baltimore. When a sufficient number have been collected here, a ship is chartered, for the purpose of conveying the forlorn crew to Mobile, or to New Orleans. From the slave prison to the ship, they are usually driven in the darkness of night; for since the antislavery agitation, a certain caution is observed.

In the deep still darkness of midnight, I have been often aroused by the dead heavy footsteps, and the piteous cries of the chained gangs that passed our door. The anguish of my boyish heart was intense; and I was often consoled, when speaking to my mistress in the morning, to hear her say that the custom was very wicked; that she hated to hear the rattle of the chains, and the heart-rending cries. I was glad to find one who sympathized with me in my horror.

Fellow-citizens, this murderous traffic is, to-day, in active operation in this boasted republic. In the solitude of my spirit, I see clouds of dust raised on the highways of the South; I see the bleeding footsteps; I hear the doleful wail of fettered humanity, on the way to the slave-markets, where the victims are to be sold like *horses, sheep,* and *swine,* knocked off to the highest bidder. There I see the tenderest ties ruthlessly broken, to gratify the lust, caprice and rapacity of the buyers and sellers of men. My soul sickens at the sight.

> Is this the land your Fathers loved,
> The freedom which they toiled to win?

Is this the earth whereon they moved?
Are these the graves they slumber in?

But a still more inhuman, disgraceful, and scandalous state of things remains to be presented. By an act of the American Congress, not yet two years old, slavery has been nationalized in its most horrible and revolting form. By that act, Mason & Dixon's line has been obliterated; New York has become as Virginia; and the power to hold, hunt, and sell men, women, and children as slaves remains no longer a mere state institution, but is now an institution of the whole United States. The power is co-extensive with the Star-Spangled Banner and American Christianity. Where these go, may also go the merciless slave-hunter. Where these are, man is not sacred. He is a bird for the sportsman's gun. By that most foul and fiendish of all human decrees, the liberty and person of every man are put in peril. Your broad republican domain is hunting ground for *men*. Not for thieves and robbers, enemies of society, merely, but for men guilty of no crime. Your lawmakers have commanded all good citizens to engage in this hellish sport. Your President, your Secretary of State, your *lords, nobles,* and ecclesiastics, enforce, as a duty you owe to your free and glorious country, and to your God, that you do this accursed thing. Not fewer than forty Americans have, within the past two years, been hunted down and, without a moment's warning, hurried away in chains, and consigned to slavery and excruciating torture. Some of these have had wives and children, dependent on them for bread; but of this, no account was made. The right of the hunter to his prey stands superior to the right of marriage, and to all rights in this republic, the rights of God included! For black men there are neither law, justice, humanity, not religion. The Fugitive Slave *Law* makes mercy to them, a crime; and bribes the judge who tries them. An American judge gets ten dollars for every victim he consigns to slavery, and five, when he fails to do so. The oath of any two villains is sufficient, under this hell-black enactment, to send the most pious and exemplary black man into the remorseless jaws of slavery! His own testimony is nothing. He can bring no witnesses for himself. The minister of American justice is bound by the law to hear but *one* side; and *that* side, is the side of the oppressor. Let this damning fact be perpetually told. Let it be thundered around the world, that, in tyrant-killing, king-hating, people-loving, democratic, Christian America, the seats of justice are filled with judges, who hold their offices under an open and palpable *bribe,* and are bound, in deciding in the case of a man's liberty, *hear only his accusers*!

In glaring violation of justice, in shameless disregard of the forms of administering law, in cunning arrangement to entrap the defenseless, and in diabolical intent, this Fugitive Slave Law stands alone in the annals of tyrannical legislation. I doubt if there be another nation on the globe, having the brass and the baseness to put such a law on the statute-book. If any man in this assembly thinks differently from me in this matter, and feels able to disprove my statements, I will gladly confront him at any suitable time and place he may select.

Religious Liberty

I take this law to be one of the grossest infringements of Christian Liberty, and, if the churches and ministers of our country were not stupidly blind, or most wickedly indifferent, they, too, would so regard it.

At the very moment that they are thanking God for the enjoyment of civil and religious liberty, and for the right to worship God according to the dictates of their own consciences, they are utterly silent in respect to a law which robs religion of its chief significance, and makes it utterly worthless to a world lying in wickedness. Did this law concern the "*mint, anise and cummin*"—abridge the fight to sing psalms, to partake of the sacrament, or to engage in any of the ceremonies of religion, it would be smitten by the thunder of a thousand pulpits. A general shout would go up from the church, demanding *repeal, repeal, instant repeal!*—And it would go hard with that politician who presumed to solicit the votes of the people without inscribing this motto on his banner. Further, if this demand were not complied with, another Scotland would be added to the history of religious liberty, and the stern old Covenanters would be thrown into the shade. A John Knox would be seen at every church door, and heard from every pulpit, and Fillmore would have no more quarter than was shown by Knox, to the beautiful, but treacherous queen Mary of Scotland. The fact that the church of our country, (with fractional exceptions), does not esteem "the Fugitive Slave Law" as a declaration of war against religious liberty, implies that that church regards religion simply as a form of worship, an empty ceremony, and *not* a vital principle, requiring active benevolence, justice, love and good will towards man. It esteems sacrifice above mercy; psalm-singing above right doing; solemn meetings above practical righteousness. A worship that can be conducted by persons who refuse to give shelter to the houseless, to give bread to the hungry, clothing to the naked, and who enjoin obedience to a law forbidding these acts of mercy, is a curse, not a blessing to mankind. The Bible addresses all such persons as "scribes, Pharisees, hypocrites, who pay tithe of *mint, anise,* and *cumin,* and have omitted the weightier matters of the law, judgment, mercy and faith."

The Church Responsible

But the church of this country is not only indifferent to the wrongs of the slave, it actually takes sides with the oppressors. It has made itself the bulwark of American slavery, and the shield of American slave-hunters. Many of its most eloquent Divines, who stand as the very lights of the church, have shamelessly given the sanction of religion and the Bible to the whole slave system. They have taught that man may, properly, be a slave; that the relation of master and slave is ordained of God; that to send back an escaped bondman to his master is clearly the duty of all the followers of the Lord Jesus Christ; and this horrible blasphemy is palmed off upon the world for Christianity.

For my part, I would say, welcome infidelity! welcome atheism! welcome anything! in preference to the gospel, *as preached by those Divines!* They convert the very name of religion into an engine of tyranny, and barbarous cruelty, and serve to confirm more infidels, in this age, than all the infidel writings of Thomas Paine, Voltaire, and Bolingbroke, put together, have done! These ministers make religion a cold and flinty-hearted thing, having neither principles of right action, nor bowels of compassion. They strip the love of God of its beauty, and leave the throng of religion a huge, horrible, repulsive form. It is a religion for oppressors, tyrants, man-stealers, and *thugs*. It is not that "*pure and undefiled religion*" which is from above, and which is "*first pure, then peaceable, easy to be entreated,* full of mercy and good fruits, *without partiality, and without hypocrisy*." But a religion which favors the rich against the poor; which exalts the proud above the humble; which divides mankind into two classes, tyrants and slaves; which says to the man in chains, *stay there*; and to the oppressor, *oppress on*; it is a religion which may be professed and enjoyed by all the robbers and enslavers of mankind; it makes God a respecter of persons, denies his fatherhood of the race, and tramples in the dust the great truth of the brotherhood of man. All this we affirm to be true of the popular church, and the popular worship of our land and nation—a religion, a church, and a worship which, on the authority of inspired wisdom, we pronounce to be an abomination in the sight of God. In the language of Isaiah, the American church might be well addressed, "Bring no more vain ablations; incense is an abomination unto me: the new moons and Sabbaths, the calling of assemblies, I cannot away with; it is iniquity even the solemn meeting. Your new moons and your appointed feasts my soul hateth. They are a trouble to me; I am weary to bear them; and when ye spread forth your hands I will hide mine eyes from you. Yea! when ye make many prayers, I will not hear. YOUR HANDS ARE FULL OF BLOOD; cease to do evil, learn to do well; seek judgment; relieve the oppressed; judge for the fatherless; plead for the widow."

The American church is guilty, when viewed in connection with what it is doing to uphold slavery; but it is superlatively guilty when viewed in connection with its ability to abolish slavery. The sin of which it is guilty is one of omission as well as of commission. Albert Barnes but uttered what the common sense of every man at all observant of the actual state of the case will receive as truth, when he declared that "There is no power out of the church that could sustain slavery an hour, if it were not sustained in it."

Let the religious press, the pulpit, the Sunday school, the conference meeting, the great ecclesiastical, missionary, Bible and tract associations of the land array their immense powers against slavery and slave-holding; and the whole system of crime and blood would be scattered to the winds; and that they do not do this involves them in the most awful responsibility of which the mind can conceive.

In prosecuting the anti-slavery enterprise, we have been asked to spare the church, to spare the ministry; but *how*, we ask, could such a thing be done? We are met on the threshold of our efforts for the redemption of the slave, by the church and ministry of the country, in battle arrayed against us; and we are compelled to fight or flee. From *what* quarter, I beg to know, has proceeded a fire so deadly upon our ranks, during the last two years, as from the Northern pulpit? As the champions of oppressors, the chosen men of American theology have appeared—men, honored for their so-called piety, and their real learning. The Lords of Buffalo, the Springs of New York, the Lathrops of Auburn, the Coxes and Spencers of Brooklyn, the Gannets and Sharps of Boston, the Deweys of Washington, and other great religious lights of the land, have, in utter denial of the authority of *Him*, by whom the professed to he called to the ministry, deliberately taught us, against the example or the Hebrews and against the remonstrance of the Apostles, they teach *"that we ought to obey man's law before the law of God."*

My spirit wearies of such blasphemy; and how such men can be supported, as the "standing types and representatives of Jesus Christ," is a mystery which I leave others to penetrate. In speaking of the American church, however, let it be distinctly understood that I mean the great mass of the religious organizations of our land. There are exceptions, and I thank God that there are. Noble men may be found, scattered all over these Northern States, of whom Henry Ward Beecher of Brooklyn, Samuel J. May of Syracuse, and my esteemed friend on the platform, are shining examples; and let me say further, that upon these men lies the duty to inspire our ranks with high religious faith and zeal, and to cheer us on in the great mission of the slave's redemption from his chains.

Religion in England and Religion in America

One is struck with the difference between the attitude of the American church towards the anti-slavery movement, and that occupied by the churches in England towards a similar movement in that country. There, the church, true to its mission of ameliorating, elevating, and improving the condition of mankind, came forward promptly, bound up the wounds of the West Indian slave, and restored him to his liberty. There, the question of emancipation was a high religious question. It was demanded, in the name of humanity, and according to the law of the living God. The Sharps, the Clarksons, the Wilberforces, the Buxtons, and Burchells and the Knibbs, were alike famous for their piety, and for their philanthropy. The anti-slavery movement *there* was not an anti-church movement, for the reason that the church took its full share in prosecuting that movement: and the anti-slavery movement in this country will cease to be an anti-church movement, when the church of this country shall assume a favorable, instead of a hostile position towards that movement. Americans! your republican politics, not less than your republican religion, are flagrantly inconsistent. You boast of your love of liberty, your superior civilization, and your pure Christianity, while the whole political power of the nation (as embodied in the two great political parties), is solemnly pledged to support and perpetuate the enslavement of three millions of your countrymen. You hurl your anathemas at the crowned headed tyrants of Russia and Austria, and pride yourselves on your Democratic institutions, while you yourselves consent to be the mere *tools* and *body-guards* of the tyrants of Virginia and Carolina. You invite to your shores fugitives of oppression from abroad, honor them with banquets, greet them with ovations, cheer them, toast them, salute them, protect them, and pour out your money to them like water; but the fugitives from your own land you advertise, hunt, arrest, shoot and kill. You glory in your refinement and your universal education yet you maintain a system as barbarous and dreadful as ever stained the character of a nation—a system begun in avarice, supported in pride, and perpetuated in cruelty. You shed tears over fallen Hungary, and make the sad story of her wrongs the theme of your poets, statesmen and orators, till your gallant sons are ready to fly to arms to vindicate her cause against her oppressors; but, in regard to the ten thousand wrongs of the American slave, you would enforce the strictest silence, and would hail him as an enemy of the nation who dares to make those wrongs the subject of public discourse! You are all on fire at the mention of liberty for France or for Ireland; but are as cold as an iceberg at the thought of liberty for the enslaved of America. You discourse eloquently on the dignity of labor; yet, you sustain a system which, in its very essence, casts a stigma upon labor. You can bare your bosom to the storm of British artillery to throw off a threepenny tax on tea; and yet wring the last hard-earned farthing from the grasp of the black laborers of your country. You profess to believe "that, of one blood, God made all nations of men to dwell on the face of all the earth," and hath commanded all men, everywhere to love one another; yet you notoriously hate, (and glory in your hatred), all men whose skins are not colored like your own. You declare, before the world, and are understood by the world to declare, that you *"hold these truths to be self evident, that all men are created equal; and are endowed by their Creator with certain inalienable rights; and that, among these are, life, liberty, and the pursuit of happiness;"* and yet, you hold securely, in a bondage which, according to your own Thomas Jefferson, *"is worse than ages of that which your fathers rose in rebellion to oppose,"* a *seventh part* of the inhabitants of your country.

Fellow-citizens! I will not enlarge further on your national inconsistencies. The existence of slavery in this country brands your republicanism as a sham, your humanity as a base pretence, and your Christianity as a lie. It destroys your moral power abroad; it corrupts your politicians at home. It saps the foundation of religion; it makes your name a hissing, and a bye-word to a mocking earth. It is the antagonistic force in your government, the only thing that seriously disturbs and endangers your *Union.* It fetters your progress; it is the enemy of improvement, the deadly foe of education; it fosters pride; it breeds insolence; it promotes vice; it shelters crime; it is a curse to the earth that supports it; and yet, you cling to it, as if it were the sheet anchor of all your hopes. Oh! be warned! be warned! a horrible reptile is coiled up in your nation's bosom; the venomous creature is nursing at the tender breast of your youthful republic; *for the love of God,* tear away, and fling from you the hideous monster, and *let the weight of twenty millions crush and destroy it forever!*

The Constitution

But it is answered in reply to all this, that precisely what I have now denounced is, in fact, guaranteed and sanctioned by the Constitution of the United States; that the right to hold and to hunt slaves is a part of that Constitution framed by the illustrious Fathers of this Republic.

Then, I dare to affirm, notwithstanding all I have said before, your fathers stooped, basely stooped

> To palter with us in a double sense:
> And keep the word of promise to the ear,
> But break it to the heart.

And instead of being the honest men I have before declared them to be, they were the veriest imposters that ever practiced on mankind. This is the inevitable conclusion, and from it there is no escape. But I differ from those who charge this baseness on the framers of the Constitution of the United States. It is a slander upon their memory, at least, so I believe. There is not time now to argue the constitutional question at length—nor have I the ability to discuss it as it ought to be discussed. The subject has been handled with masterly power by Lysander Spooner, Esq., by William Goodell, by Samuel E. Sewall, Esq., and last, though not least, by Gerritt Smith, Esq. These gentlemen have, as I think, fully and clearly vindicated the Constitution from any design to support slavery for an hour.

Fellow-citizens! there is no matter in respect to which, the people of the North have allowed themselves to be so ruinously imposed upon, as that of the pro-slavery character of the Constitution. In that instrument I hold there is neither warrant, license, nor sanction of the hateful thing; but, interpreted as it ought to be interpreted, the Constitution is a GLORIOUS LIBERTY DOCUMENT. Read its preamble, consider its purposes. Is slavery among them? Is it at the gateway? or is it in the temple? It is neither. While I do not intend to argue this question on the present occasion, let me ask, if it be not somewhat singular that, if the Constitution were intended to be, by its framers and adopters, a slave-holding instrument, why neither slavery, slaveholding, nor slave can anywhere be found in it. What would be thought of an instrument, drawn up, legally drawn up, for the purpose of entitling the city of Rochester to a track of land, in which no mention of land was made? Now, there are certain rules of interpretation, for the proper understanding of all legal instruments. These rules are well established. They are plain, common-sense rules, such as you and I, and all of us, can understand and apply, without having passed years in the study of law. I scout the idea that the question of the constitutionality or unconstitutionality of slavery is not a question for the people. I hold that every American citizen has a fight to form an opinion of the constitution, and to propagate that opinion, and to use all honorable means to make his opinion the prevailing one. Without this fight, the liberty of an American citizen would be as insecure as that of a Frenchman. Ex-Vice-President Dallas tells us that the constitution is an object to which no American mind can be too attentive, and no American heart too devoted. He further says, the constitution, in its words, is plain and intelligible, and is meant for the home-bred, unsophisticated understandings of our fellow-citizens. Senator Berrien tell us that the Constitution is the fundamental law, that which controls all others. The charter of our liberties, which every citizen has a personal interest in understanding thoroughly. The testimony of Senator Breese, Lewis Cass, and many others that might be named, who are everywhere esteemed as sound lawyers, so regard the constitution. I take it, therefore, that it is not presumption in a private citizen to form an opinion of that instrument.

Now, take the constitution according to its plain reading, and I defy the presentation of a single pro-slavery clause in it. On the other hand it will be found to contain principles and purposes, entirely hostile to the existence of slavery.

I have detained my audience entirely too long already. At some future period I will gladly avail myself of an opportunity to give this subject a full and fair discussion.

"Allow me to say, in conclusion, notwithstanding the dark picture I have this day presented of the state of the nation, I do not despair of this country." There are forces in operation, which must inevitably work the downfall of slavery. "The arm of the Lord is not shortened," and the doom of slavery is certain. I, therefore, leave off where I began, with hope. While drawing encouragement from the Declaration of Independence, the great principles it contains, and the genius of American Institutions, my spirit is also cheered by the obvious tendencies of the age. Nations do not now stand in the same relation to each other that they did ages ago. No nation can now shut itself up from the surrounding world, and trot round in the same old path of its fathers without interference. The time was when such could be done. Long established customs of hurtful character could formerly fence themselves in, and do their evil work with social impunity. Knowledge was then confined and enjoyed by the privileged few, and the multitude walked on in mental darkness. But a change has now come over the affairs of mankind. Walled cities and empires have become unfashionable. The arm of commerce has borne away the gates of the strong city. Intelligence is penetrating the darkest corners of the globe. It makes its pathway over and under the sea, as well as on the earth. Wind, steam, and lightning are its chartered agents. Oceans no longer divide, but link nations together. From Boston to London is now a holiday excursion. Space is comparatively annihilated. Thoughts expressed on one side of the Atlantic are distinctly heard on the other. The far off and almost fabulous Pacific rolls in grandeur at our feet. The Celestial Empire, the mystery of ages, is being solved. The fiat of the Almighty, "Let there be Light," has not yet spent its force. No abuse, no outrage whether in taste, sport or avarice, can now hide itself from the all-pervading light. The iron shoe, and crippled foot of China must be seen, in contrast with nature. Africa must rise and put on her yet unwoven garment. "Ethiopia shall stretch out her hand unto God." In the fervent aspirations of William Lloyd Garrison, I say, and let every heart join in saying it:

God speed the year of jubilee
The wide world o'er
When from their galling chains set free,
Th' oppress'd shall vilely bend the knee,
And wear the yoke of tyranny
Like brutes no more.
That year will come, and freedom's reign,
To man his plundered fights again
Restore.

God speed the day when human blood
Shall cease to flow!
In every clime be understood,
The claims of human brotherhood,
And each return for evil, good,
Not blow for blow;
That day will come all feuds to end.
And change into a faithful friend
Each foe.

God speed the hour, the glorious hour,
When none on earth
Shall exercise a lordly power,
Nor in a tyrant's presence cower;
But all to manhood's stature tower,
By equal birth!
That hour will, come, to each, to all,
And from his prison-house, the thrall
Go forth.

Until that year, day, hour, arrive,
With head, and heart, and hand I'll strive,
To break the rod, and rend the gyve,
The spoiler of his prey deprive—
So witness Heaven!
And never from my chosen post,
Whate'er the peril or the cost,
Be driven.

Rerum Novarum
Encyclical on Capital and Labor

Pope Leo XIII

To Our Venerable Brethren the Patriarchs,
Primates, Archbishops, Bishops, and other ordinaries
of places having Peace and Communion with the Apostolic See.

Rights and Duties of Capital and Labor

That the spirit of revolutionary change, which has long been disturbing the nations of the world, should have passed beyond the sphere of politics and made its influence felt in the cognate sphere of practical economics is not surprising. The elements of the conflict now raging are unmistakable, in the vast expansion of industrial pursuits and the marvellous discoveries of science; in the changed relations between masters and workmen; in the enormous fortunes of some few individuals, and the utter poverty of the masses; the increased self reliance and closer mutual combination of the working classes; as also, finally, in the prevailing moral degeneracy. The momentous gravity of the state of things now obtaining fills every mind with painful apprehension; wise men are discussing it; practical men are proposing schemes; popular meetings, legislatures, and rulers of nations are all busied with it—actually there is no question which has taken deeper hold on the public mind.

2. Therefore, venerable brethren, as on former occasions when it seemed opportune to refute false teaching, We have addressed you in the interests of the Church and of the common weal, and have issued letters bearing on political power, human liberty, the Christian constitution of the State, and like matters, so have We thought it expedient now to speak on the condition of the working classes.[1] It is a subject on which We have already touched more than once, incidentally. But in the present letter, the responsibility of the apostolic office urges Us to treat the question of set purpose and in detail, in order that no misapprehension may exist as to the principles which truth and justice dictate for its settlement. The discussion is not easy, nor is it void of danger. It is no easy matter to define the relative rights and mutual duties of the rich and

of the poor, of capital and of labor. And the danger lies in this, that crafty agitators are intent on making use of these differences of opinion to pervert men's judgments and to stir up the people to revolt.

3. In any case we clearly see, and on this there is general agreement, that some opportune remedy must be found quickly for the misery and wretchedness pressing so unjustly on the majority of the working class: for the ancient workingmen's guilds were abolished in the last century, and no other protective organization took their place. Public institutions and the laws set aside the ancient religion. Hence, by degrees it has come to pass that working men have been surrendered, isolated and helpless, to the hardheartedness of employers and the greed of unchecked competition. The mischief has been increased by rapacious usury, which, although more than once condemned by the Church, is nevertheless, under a different guise, but with like injustice, still practiced by covetous and grasping men. To this must be added that the hiring of labor and the conduct of trade are concentrated in the hands of comparatively few; so that a small number of very rich men have been able to lay upon the teeming masses of the laboring poor a yoke little better than that of slavery itself.

4. To remedy these wrongs the socialists, working on the poor man's envy of the rich, are striving to do away with private property, and contend that individual possessions should become the common property of all, to be administered by the State or by municipal bodies. They hold that by thus transferring property from private individuals to the community, the present mischievous state of things will be set to rights, inasmuch as each citizen will then get his fair share of whatever there is to enjoy. But their contentions are so clearly powerless to end the controversy that were they carried into effect the working man himself would be among the first to suffer. They are, moreover, emphatically unjust, for they would rob the lawful possessor, distort the functions of the State, and create utter confusion in the community.

5. It is surely undeniable that, when a man engages in remunerative labor, the impelling reason and motive of his work is to obtain property, and thereafter to hold it as his very own. If one man hires out to another his strength or skill, he does so for the purpose of receiving in return what is necessary for the satisfaction of his needs; he therefore expressly intends to acquire a right full and real, not only to the remuneration, but also to the disposal of such remuneration, just as he pleases. Thus, if he lives sparingly, saves money, and, for greater security, invests his savings in land, the land, in such case, is only his wages under another form; and, consequently, a working man's little estate thus purchased should be as completely at his full disposal as are the wages he receives for his labor. But it is precisely in such power of disposal that ownership obtains, whether the property consist of

land or chattels. Socialists, therefore, by endeavoring to transfer the possessions of individuals to the community at large, strike at the interests of every wage-earner, since they would deprive him of the liberty of disposing of his wages, and thereby of all hope and possibility of increasing his resources and of bettering his condition in life.

6. What is of far greater moment, however, is the fact that the remedy they propose is manifestly against justice. For, every man has by nature the right to possess property as his own. This is one of the chief points of distinction between man and the animal creation, for the brute has no power of self direction, but is governed by two main instincts, which keep his powers on the alert, impel him to develop them in a fitting manner, and stimulate and determine him to action without any power of choice. One of these instincts is self preservation, the other the propagation of the species. Both can attain their purpose by means of things which lie within range; beyond their verge the brute creation cannot go, for they are moved to action by their senses only, and in the special direction which these suggest. But with man it is wholly different. He possesses, on the one hand, the full perfection of the animal being, and hence enjoys at least as much as the rest of the animal kind, the fruition of things material. But animal nature, however perfect, is far from representing the human being in its completeness, and is in truth but humanity's humble handmaid, made to serve and to obey. It is the mind, or reason, which is the predominant element in us who are human creatures; it is this which renders a human being human, and distinguishes him essentially from the brute. And on this very account—that man alone among the animal creation is endowed with reason—it must be within his right to possess things not merely for temporary and momentary use, as other living things do, but to have and to hold them in stable and permanent possession; he must have not only things that perish in the use, but those also which, though they have been reduced into use, continue for further use in after time.

7. This becomes still more clearly evident if man's nature be considered a little more deeply. For man, fathoming by his faculty of reason matters without number, linking the future with the present, and being master of his own acts, guides his ways under the eternal law and the power of God, whose providence governs all things. Wherefore, it is in his power to exercise his choice not only as to matters that regard his present welfare, but also about those which he deems may be for his advantage in time yet to come. Hence, man not only should possess the fruits of the earth, but also the very soil, inasmuch as from the produce of the earth he has to lay by provision for the future. Man's needs do not die out, but forever recur; although satisfied today, they demand fresh supplies for tomorrow. Nature accordingly must have given to man a

source that is stable and remaining always with him, from which he might look to draw continual supplies. And this stable condition of things he finds solely in the earth and its fruits. There is no need to bring in the State. Man precedes the State, and possesses, prior to the formation of any State, the right of providing for the substance of his body.

8. The fact that God has given the earth for the use and enjoyment of the whole human race can in no way be a bar to the owning of private property. For God has granted the earth to mankind in general, not in the sense that all without distinction can deal with it as they like, but rather that no part of it was assigned to any one in particular, and that the limits of private possession have been left to be fixed by man's own industry, and by the laws of individual races. Moreover, the earth, even though apportioned among private owners, ceases not thereby to minister to the needs of all, inasmuch as there is not one who does not sustain life from what the land produces. Those who do not possess the soil contribute their labor; hence, it may truly be said that all human subsistence is derived either from labor on one's own land, or from some toil, some calling, which is paid for either in the produce of the land itself, or in that which is exchanged for what the land brings forth.

9. Here, again, we have further proof that private ownership is in accordance with the law of nature. Truly, that which is required for the preservation of life, and for life's well-being, is produced in great abundance from the soil, but not until man has brought it into cultivation and expended upon it his solicitude and skill. Now, when man thus turns the activity of his mind and the strength of his body toward procuring the fruits of nature, by such act he makes his own that portion of nature's field which he cultivates—that portion on which he leaves, as it were, the impress of his personality; and it cannot but be just that he should possess that portion as his very own, and have a right to hold it without any one being justified in violating that right.

10. So strong and convincing are these arguments that it seems amazing that some should now be setting up anew certain obsolete opinions in opposition to what is here laid down. They assert that it is right for private persons to have the use of the soil and its various fruits, but that it is unjust for any one to possess outright either the land on which he has built or the estate which he has brought under cultivation. But those who deny these rights do not perceive that they are defrauding man of what his own labor has produced. For the soil which is tilled and cultivated with toil and skill utterly changes its condition; it was wild before, now it is fruitful; was barren, but now brings forth in abundance. That which has thus altered and improved the land becomes so truly part of itself as to be in great measure indistinguishable and inseparable from it. Is it just that the fruit of a man's own sweat and labor should be possessed

and enjoyed by any one else? As effects follow their cause, so is it just and right that the results of labor should belong to those who have bestowed their labor.

11. With reason, then, the common opinion of mankind, little affected by the few dissentients who have contended for the opposite view, has found in the careful study of nature, and in the laws of nature, the foundations of the division of property, and the practice of all ages has consecrated the principle of private ownership, as being pre-eminently in conformity with human nature, and as conducing in the most unmistakable manner to the peace and tranquillity of human existence. The same principle is confirmed and enforced by the civil laws-laws which, so long as they are just, derive from the law of nature their binding force. The authority of the divine law adds its sanction, forbidding us in severest terms even to covet that which is another's: "Thou shalt not covet thy neighbour's wife; nor his house, nor his field, nor his man-servant, nor his maid-servant, nor his ox, nor his ass, nor anything that is his."[2]

12. The rights here spoken of, belonging to each individual man, are seen in much stronger light when considered in relation to man's social and domestic obligations. In choosing a state of life, it is indisputable that all are at full liberty to follow the counsel of Jesus Christ as to observing virginity, or to bind themselves by the marriage tie. No human law can abolish the natural and original right of marriage, nor in any way limit the chief and principal purpose of marriage ordained by God's authority from the beginning: "Increase and multiply."[3] Hence we have the family, the "society" of a man's house—a society very small, one must admit, but none the less a true society, and one older than any State. Consequently, it has rights and duties peculiar to itself which are quite independent of the State.

13. That right to property, therefore, which has been proved to belong naturally to individual persons, must in like wise belong to a man in his capacity of head of a family; nay, that right is all the stronger in proportion as the human person receives a wider extension in the family group. It is a most sacred law of nature that a father should provide food and all necessaries for those whom he has begotten; and, similarly, it is natural that he should wish that his children, who carry on, so to speak, and continue his personality, should be by him provided with all that is needful to enable them to keep themselves decently from want and misery amid the uncertainties of this mortal life. Now, in no other way can a father effect this except by the ownership of productive property, which he can transmit to his children by inheritance. A family, no less than a State, is, as We have said, a true society, governed by an authority peculiar to itself, that is to say, by the authority of the father. Provided, therefore, the limits which are prescribed by the very purposes for which it exists be not transgressed, the family has at least equal rights with the

State in the choice and pursuit of the things needful to its preservation and its just liberty. We say, "at least equal rights"; for, inasmuch as the domestic household is antecedent, as well in idea as in fact, to the gathering of men into a community, the family must necessarily have rights and duties which are prior to those of the community, and founded more immediately in nature. If the citizens, if the families on entering into association and fellowship, were to experience hindrance in a commonwealth instead of help, and were to find their rights attacked instead of being upheld, society would rightly be an object of detestation rather than of desire.

14. The contention, then, that the civil government should at its option intrude into and exercise intimate control over the family and the household is a great and pernicious error. True, if a family finds itself in exceeding distress, utterly deprived of the counsel of friends, and without any prospect of extricating itself, it is right that extreme necessity be met by public aid, since each family is a part of the commonwealth. In like manner, if within the precincts of the household there occur grave disturbance of mutual rights, public authority should intervene to force each party to yield to the other its proper due; for this is not to deprive citizens of their rights, but justly and properly to safeguard and strengthen them. But the rulers of the commonwealth must go no further; here, nature bids them stop. Paternal authority can be neither abolished nor absorbed by the State; for it has the same source as human life itself. "The child belongs to the father," and is, as it were, the continuation of the father's personality; and speaking strictly, the child takes its place in civil society, not of its own right, but in its quality as member of the family in which it is born. And for the very reason that "the child belongs to the father" it is, as St. Thomas Aquinas says, "before it attains the use of free will, under the power and the charge of its parents."[4] The socialists, therefore, in setting aside the parent and setting up a State supervision, act against natural justice, and destroy the structure of the home.

15. And in addition to injustice, it is only too evident what an upset and disturbance there would be in all classes, and to how intolerable and hateful a slavery citizens would be subjected. The door would be thrown open to envy, to mutual invective, and to discord; the sources of wealth themselves would run dry, for no one would have any interest in exerting his talents or his industry; and that ideal equality about which they entertain pleasant dreams would be in reality the levelling down of all to a like condition of misery and degradation. Hence, it is clear that the main tenet of socialism, community of goods, must be utterly rejected, since it only injures those whom it would seem meant to benefit, is directly contrary to the natural rights of mankind, and would introduce confusion and disorder into the commonweal. The first and

most fundamental principle, therefore, if one would undertake to alleviate the condition of the masses, must be the inviolability of private property. This being established, we proceed to show where the remedy sought for must be found.

16. We approach the subject with confidence, and in the exercise of the rights which manifestly appertain to Us, for no practical solution of this question will be found apart from the intervention of religion and of the Church. It is We who are the chief guardian of religion and the chief dispenser of what pertains to the Church; and by keeping silence we would seem to neglect the duty incumbent on us. Doubtless, this most serious question demands the attention and the efforts of others besides ourselves—to wit, of the rulers of States, of employers of labor, of the wealthy, aye, of the working classes themselves, for whom We are pleading. But We affirm without hesitation that all the striving of men will be vain if they leave out the Church. It is the Church that insists, on the authority of the Gospel, upon those teachings whereby the conflict can be brought to an end, or rendered, at least, far less bitter; the Church uses her efforts not only to enlighten the mind, but to direct by her precepts the life and conduct of each and all; the Church improves and betters the condition of the working man by means of numerous organizations; does her best to enlist the services of all classes in discussing and endeavoring to further in the most practical way, the interests of the working classes; and considers that for this purpose recourse should be had, in due measure and degree, to the intervention of the law and of State authority.

17. It must be first of all recognized that the condition of things inherent in human affairs must be borne with, for it is impossible to reduce civil society to one dead level. Socialists may in that intent do their utmost, but all striving against nature is in vain. There naturally exist among mankind manifold differences of the most important kind; people differ in capacity, skill, health, strength; and unequal fortune is a necessary result of unequal condition. Such unequality is far from being disadvantageous either to individuals or to the community. Social and public life can only be maintained by means of various kinds of capacity for business and the playing of many parts; and each man, as a rule, chooses the part which suits his own peculiar domestic condition. As regards bodily labor, even had man never fallen from the state of innocence, he would not have remained wholly idle; but that which would then have been his free choice and his delight became afterwards compulsory, and the painful expiation for his disobedience. "Cursed be the earth in thy work; in thy labor thou shalt eat of it all the days of thy life."[5]

18. In like manner, the other pains and hardships of life will have no end or cessation on earth; for the consequences of sin are bitter and hard to bear,

and they must accompany man so long as life lasts. To suffer and to endure, therefore, is the lot of humanity; let them strive as they may, no strength and no artifice will ever succeed in banishing from human life the ills and troubles which beset it. If any there are who pretend differently—who hold out to a hard-pressed people the boon of freedom from pain and trouble, an undisturbed repose, and constant enjoyment—they delude the people and impose upon them, and their lying promises will only one day bring forth evils worse than the present. Nothing is more useful than to look upon the world as it really is, and at the same time to seek elsewhere, as We have said, for the solace to its troubles.

19. The great mistake made in regard to the matter now under consideration is to take up with the notion that class is naturally hostile to class, and that the wealthy and the working men are intended by nature to live in mutual conflict. So irrational and so false is this view that the direct contrary is the truth. Just as the symmetry of the human frame is the result of the suitable arrangement of the different parts of the body, so in a State is it ordained by nature that these two classes should dwell in harmony and agreement, so as to maintain the balance of the body politic. Each needs the other: capital cannot do without labor, nor labor without capital. Mutual agreement results in the beauty of good order, while perpetual conflict necessarily produces confusion and savage barbarity. Now, in preventing such strife as this, and in uprooting it, the efficacy of Christian institutions is marvellous and manifold. First of all, there is no intermediary more powerful than religion (whereof the Church is the interpreter and guardian) in drawing the rich and the working class together, by reminding each of its duties to the other, and especially of the obligations of justice.

20. Of these duties, the following bind the proletarian and the worker: fully and faithfully to perform the work which has been freely and equitably agreed upon; never to injure the property, nor to outrage the person, of an employer; never to resort to violence in defending their own cause, nor to engage in riot or disorder; and to have nothing to do with men of evil principles, who work upon the people with artful promises of great results, and excite foolish hopes which usually end in useless regrets and grievous loss. The following duties bind the wealthy owner and the employer: not to look upon their work people as their bondsmen, but to respect in every man his dignity as a person ennobled by Christian character. They are reminded that, according to natural reason and Christian philosophy, working for gain is creditable, not shameful, to a man, since it enables him to earn an honorable livelihood; but to misuse men as though they were things in the pursuit of gain, or to value them solely for their physical powers—that is

truly shameful and inhuman. Again justice demands that, in dealing with the working man, religion and the good of his soul must be kept in mind. Hence, the employer is bound to see that the worker has time for his religious duties; that he be not exposed to corrupting influences and dangerous occasions; and that he be not led away to neglect his home and family, or to squander his earnings. Furthermore, the employer must never tax his work people beyond their strength, or employ them in work unsuited to their sex and age. His great and principal duty is to give every one what is just. Doubtless, before deciding whether wages are fair, many things have to be considered; but wealthy own-ers and all masters of labor should be mindful of this—that to exercise pres-sure upon the indigent and the destitute for the sake of gain, and to gather one's profit out of the need of another, is condemned by all laws, human and divine. To defraud any one of wages that are his due is a great crime which cries to the avenging anger of Heaven. "Behold, the hire of the laborers... which by fraud has been kept back by you, crieth; and the cry of them hath entered into the ears of the Lord of Sabaoth."[6] Lastly, the rich must religiously refrain from cutting down the workmen's earnings, whether by force, by fraud, or by usu-rious dealing; and with all the greater reason because the laboring man is, as a rule, weak and unprotected, and because his slender means should in propor-tion to their scantiness be accounted sacred. Were these precepts carefully obeyed and followed out, would they not be sufficient of themselves to keep under all strife and all its causes?

21. But the Church, with Jesus Christ as her Master and Guide, aims higher still. She lays down precepts yet more perfect, and tries to bind class to class in friendliness and good feeling. The things of earth cannot be under-stood or valued aright without taking into consideration the life to come, the life that will know no death. Exclude the idea of futurity, and forthwith the very notion of what is good and right would perish; nay, the whole scheme of the universe would become a dark and unfathomable mystery. The great truth which we learn from nature herself is also the grand Christian dogma on which religion rests as on its foundation—that, when we have given up this present life, then shall we really begin to live. God has not created us for the perish-able and transitory things of earth, but for things heavenly and everlasting; He has given us this world as a place of exile, and not as our abiding place. As for riches and the other things which men call good and desirable, whether we have them in abundance, or are lacking in them-so far as eternal happiness is concerned—it makes no difference; the only important thing is to use them aright. Jesus Christ, when He redeemed us with plentiful redemption, took not away the pains and sorrows which in such large proportion are woven together in the web of our mortal life. He transformed them into motives of

virtue and occasions of merit; and no man can hope for eternal reward unless he follow in the blood-stained footprints of his Saviour. "If we suffer with Him, we shall also reign with Him."[7] Christ's labors and sufferings, accepted of His own free will, have marvellously sweetened all suffering and all labor. And not only by His example, but by His grace and by the hope held forth of everlasting recompense, has He made pain and grief more easy to endure; "for that which is at present momentary and light of our tribulation, worketh for us above measure exceedingly an eternal weight of glory."[8]

22. Therefore, those whom fortune favors are warned that riches do not bring freedom from sorrow and are of no avail for eternal happiness, but rather are obstacles;[9] that the rich should tremble at the threatenings of Jesus Christ—threatenings so unwonted in the mouth of our Lord[10]—and that a most strict account must be given to the Supreme Judge for all we possess. The chief and most excellent rule for the right use of money is one the heathen philosophers hinted at, but which the Church has traced out clearly, and has not only made known to men's minds, but has impressed upon their lives. It rests on the principle that it is one thing to have a right to the possession of money and another to have a right to use money as one wills. Private ownership, as we have seen, is the natural right of man, and to exercise that right, especially as members of society, is not only lawful, but absolutely necessary. "It is lawful," says St. Thomas Aquinas, "for a man to hold private property; and it is also necessary for the carrying on of human existence."[11] But if the question be asked: How must one's possessions be used?—the Church replies without hesitation in the words of the same holy Doctor: "Man should not consider his material possessions as his own, but as common to all, so as to share them without hesitation when others are in need. Whence the Apostle with, 'Command the rich of this world . . . to offer with no stint, to apportion largely.'"[12] True, no one is commanded to distribute to others that which is required for his own needs and those of his household; nor even to give away what is reasonably required to keep up becomingly his condition in life, "for no one ought to live other than becomingly."[13] But, when what necessity demands has been supplied, and one's standing fairly taken thought for, it becomes a duty to give to the indigent out of what remains over. "Of that which remaineth, give alms."[14] It is a duty, not of justice (save in extreme cases), but of Christian charity—a duty not enforced by human law. But the laws and judgments of men must yield place to the laws and judgments of Christ the true God, who in many ways urges on His followers the practice of almsgiving—"It is more blessed to give than to receive";[15] and who will count a kindness done or refused to the poor as done or refused to Himself—"As long as you did it to one of My least brethren you did it to Me."[16] To sum up,

then, what has been said: Whoever has received from the divine bounty a large share of temporal blessings, whether they be external and material, or gifts of the mind, has received them for the purpose of using them for the perfecting of his own nature, and, at the same time, that he may employ them, as the steward of God's providence, for the benefit of others. "He that hath a talent," said St. Gregory the Great, "let him see that he hide it not; he that hath abundance, let him quicken himself to mercy and generosity; he that hath art and skill, let him do his best to share the use and the utility hereof with his neighbor."[17]

23. As for those who possess not the gifts of fortune, they are taught by the Church that in God's sight poverty is no disgrace, and that there is nothing to be ashamed of in earning their bread by labor. This is enforced by what we see in Christ Himself, who, "whereas He was rich, for our sakes became poor";[18] and who, being the Son of God, and God Himself, chose to seem and to be considered the son of a carpenter—nay, did not disdain to spend a great part of His life as a carpenter Himself. "Is not this the carpenter, the son of Mary?"[19]

24. From contemplation of this divine Model, it is more easy to understand that the true worth and nobility of man lie in his moral qualities, that is, in virtue; that virtue is, moreover, the common inheritance of men, equally within the reach of high and low, rich and poor; and that virtue, and virtue alone, wherever found, will be followed by the rewards of everlasting happiness. Nay, God Himself seems to incline rather to those who suffer misfortune; for Jesus Christ calls the poor "blessed";[20] He lovingly invites those in labor and grief to come to Him for solace;[21] and He displays the tenderest charity toward the lowly and the oppressed. These reflections cannot fail to keep down the pride of the well-to-do, and to give heart to the unfortunate; to move the former to be generous and the latter to be moderate in their desires. Thus, the separation which pride would set up tends to disappear, nor will it be difficult to make rich and poor join hands in friendly concord.

25. But, if Christian precepts prevail, the respective classes will not only be united in the bonds of friendship, but also in those of brotherly love. For they will understand and feel that all men are children of the same common Father, who is God; that all have alike the same last end, which is God Himself, who alone can make either men or angels absolutely and perfectly happy; that each and all are redeemed and made sons of God, by Jesus Christ, "the first-born among many brethren"; that the blessings of nature and the gifts of grace belong to the whole human race in common, and that from none except the unworthy is withheld the inheritance of the kingdom of Heaven. "If sons, heirs also; heirs indeed of God, and co-heirs with Christ."[22] Such is

the scheme of duties and of rights which is shown forth to the world by the Gospel. Would it not seem that, were society penetrated with ideas like these, strife must quickly cease?

26. But the Church, not content with pointing out the remedy, also applies it. For the Church does her utmost to teach and to train men, and to educate them and by the intermediary of her bishops and clergy diffuses her salutary teachings far and wide. She strives to influence the mind and the heart so that all may willingly yield themselves to be formed and guided by the commandments of God. It is precisely in this fundamental and momentous matter, on which everything depends that the Church possesses a power peculiarly her own. The instruments which she employs are given to her by Jesus Christ Himself for the very purpose of reaching the hearts of men, and drive their efficiency from God. They alone can reach the innermost heart and conscience, and bring men to act from a motive of duty, to control their passions and appetites, to love God and their fellow men with a love that is outstanding and of the highest degree and to break down courageously every barrier which blocks the way to virtue.

27. On this subject we need but recall for one moment the examples recorded in history. Of these facts there cannot be any shadow of doubt: for instance, that civil society was renovated in every part by Christian institutions; that in the strength of that renewal the human race was lifted up to better things—nay, that it was brought back from death to life, and to so excellent a life that nothing more perfect had been known before, or will come to be known in the ages that have yet to be. Of this beneficent transformation Jesus Christ was at once the first cause and the final end; as from Him all came, so to Him was all to be brought back. For, when the human race, by the light of the Gospel message, came to know the grand mystery of the Incarnation of the Word and the redemption of man, at once the life of Jesus Christ, God and Man, pervaded every race and nation, and interpenetrated them with His faith, His precepts, and His laws. And if human society is to be healed now, in no other way can it be healed save by a return to Christian life and Christian institutions. When a society is perishing, the wholesome advice to give to those who would restore it is to call it to the principles from which it sprang; for the purpose and perfection of an association is to aim at and to attain that for which it is formed, and its efforts should be put in motion and inspired by the end and object which originally gave it being. Hence, to fall away from its primal constitution implies disease; to go back to it, recovery. And this may be asserted with utmost truth both of the whole body of the commonwealth and of that class of its citizens-by far the great majority—who get their living by their labor.

28. Neither must it be supposed that the solicitude of the Church is so preoccupied with the spiritual concerns of her children as to neglect their temporal and earthly interests. Her desire is that the poor, for example, should rise above poverty and wretchedness, and better their condition in life; and for this she makes a strong endeavor. By the fact that she calls men to virtue and forms them to its practice she promotes this in no slight degree. Christian morality, when adequately and completely practiced, leads of itself to temporal prosperity, for it merits the blessing of that God who is the source of all blessings; it powerfully restrains the greed of possession and the thirst for pleasure-twin plagues, which too often make a man who is void of self-restraint miserable in the midst of abundance;[23] it makes men supply for the lack of means through economy, teaching them to be content with frugal living, and further, keeping them out of the reach of those vices which devour not small incomes merely, but large fortunes, and dissipate many a goodly inheritance.

29. The Church, moreover, intervenes directly in behalf of the poor, by setting on foot and maintaining many associations which she knows to be efficient for the relief of poverty. Herein, again, she has always succeeded so well as to have even extorted the praise of her enemies. Such was the ardor of brotherly love among the earliest Christians that numbers of those who were in better circumstances despoiled themselves of their possessions in order to relieve their brethren; whence "neither was there any one needy among them."[24] To the order of deacons, instituted in that very intent, was committed by the Apostles the charge of the daily doles; and the Apostle Paul, though burdened with the solicitude of all the churches, hesitated not to undertake laborious journeys in order to carry the alms of the faithful to the poorer Christians. Tertullian calls these contributions, given voluntarily by Christians in their assemblies, deposits of piety, because, to cite his own words, they were employed "in feeding the needy, in burying them, in support of youths and maidens destitute of means and deprived of their parents, in the care of the aged, and the relief of the shipwrecked."[25]

30. Thus, by degrees, came into existence the patrimony which the Church has guarded with religious care as the inheritance of the poor. Nay, in order to spare them the shame of begging, the Church has provided aid for the needy. The common Mother of rich and poor has aroused everywhere the heroism of charity, and has established congregations of religious and many other useful institutions for help and mercy, so that hardly any kind of suffering could exist which was not afforded relief. At the present day many there are who, like the heathen of old, seek to blame and condemn the Church for such eminent charity. They would substitute in its stead a system of relief organized by the State. But no human expedients will ever make up for the

devotedness and self sacrifice of Christian charity. Charity, as a virtue, pertains to the Church; for virtue it is not, unless it be drawn from the Most Sacred Heart of Jesus Christ; and whosoever turns his back on the Church cannot be near to Christ.

31. It cannot, however, be doubted that to attain the purpose we are treating of, not only the Church, but all human agencies, must concur. All who are concerned in the matter should be of one mind and according to their ability act together. It is with this, as with providence that governs the world; the results of causes do not usually take place save where all the causes cooperate. It is sufficient, therefore, to inquire what part the State should play in the work of remedy and relief.

32. By the State we here understand, not the particular form of government prevailing in this or that nation, but the State as rightly apprehended; that is to say, any government conformable in its institutions to right reason and natural law, and to those dictates of the divine wisdom which we have expounded in the encyclical *On the Christian Constitution of the State*.[26] The foremost duty, therefore, of the rulers of the State should be to make sure that the laws and institutions, the general character and administration of the commonwealth, shall be such as of themselves to realize public well-being and private prosperity. This is the proper scope of wise statesmanship and is the work of the rulers. Now a State chiefly prospers and thrives through moral rule, well-regulated family life, respect for religion and justice, the moderation and fair imposing of public taxes, the progress of the arts and of trade, the abundant yield of the land-through everything, in fact, which makes the citizens better and happier. Hereby, then, it lies in the power of a ruler to benefit every class in the State, and amongst the rest to promote to the utmost the interests of the poor; and this in virtue of his office, and without being open to suspicion of undue interference—since it is the province of the commonwealth to serve the common good. And the more that is done for the benefit of the working classes by the general laws of the country, the less need will there be to seek for special means to relieve them.

33. There is another and deeper consideration which must not be lost sight of. As regards the State, the interests of all, whether high or low, are equal. The members of the working classes are citizens by nature and by the same right as the rich; they are real parts, living the life which makes up, through the family, the body of the commonwealth; and it need hardly be said that they are in every city very largely in the majority. It would be irrational to neglect one portion of the citizens and favor another, and therefore the public administration must duly and solicitously provide for the welfare and the comfort of the working classes; otherwise, that law of justice will be violated which

ordains that each man shall have his due. To cite the wise words of St. Thomas Aquinas: "As the part and the whole are in a certain sense identical, so that which belongs to the whole in a sense belongs to the part."[27] Among the many and grave duties of rulers who would do their best for the people, the first and chief is to act with strict justice—with that justice which is called *distributive*—toward each and every class alike.

34. But although all citizens, without exception, can and ought to contribute to that common good in which individuals share so advantageously to themselves, yet it should not be supposed that all can contribute in the like way and to the same extent. No matter what changes may occur in forms of government, there will ever be differences and inequalities of condition in the State. Society cannot exist or be conceived of without them. Some there must be who devote themselves to the work of the commonwealth, who make the laws or administer justice, or whose advice and authority govern the nation in times of peace, and defend it in war. Such men clearly occupy the foremost place in the State, and should be held in highest estimation, for their work concerns most nearly and effectively the general interests of the community. Those who labor at a trade or calling do not promote the general welfare in such measure as this, but they benefit the nation, if less directly, in a most important manner. We have insisted, it is true, that, since the end of society is to make men better, the chief good that society can possess is virtue. Nevertheless, it is the business of a well-constituted body politic to see to the provision of those material and external helps "the use of which is necessary to virtuous action."[28] Now, for the provision of such commodities, the labor of the working class—the exercise of their skill, and the employment of their strength, in the cultivation of the land, and in the workshops of trade—is especially responsible and quite indispensable. Indeed, their co-operation is in this respect so important that it may be truly said that it is only by the labor of working men that States grow rich. Justice, therefore, demands that the interests of the working classes should be carefully watched over by the administration, so that they who contribute so largely to the advantage of the community may themselves share in the benefits which they create-that being housed, clothed, and bodily fit, they may find their life less hard and more endurable. It follows that whatever shall appear to prove conducive to the well-being of those who work should obtain favorable consideration. There is no fear that solicitude of this kind will be harmful to any interest; on the contrary, it will be to the advantage of all, for it cannot but be good for the commonwealth to shield from misery those on whom it so largely depends for the things that it needs.

35. We have said that the State must not absorb the individual or the family; both should be allowed free and untrammelled action so far as is consistent with the common good and the interest of others. Rulers should, nevertheless, anxiously safeguard the community and all its members; the community, because the conservation thereof is so emphatically the business of the supreme power, that the safety of the commonwealth is not only the first law, but it is a government's whole reason of existence; and the members, because both philosophy and the Gospel concur in laying down that the object of the government of the State should be, not the advantage of the ruler, but the benefit of those over whom he is placed. As the power to rule comes from God, and is, as it were, a participation in His, the highest of all sovereignties, it should be exercised as the power of God is exercised—with a fatherly solicitude which not only guides the whole, but reaches also individuals.

36. Whenever the general interest or any particular class suffers, or is threatened with harm, which can in no other way be met or prevented, the public authority must step in to deal with it. Now, it is to the interest of the community, as well as of the individual, that peace and good order should be maintained; that all things should be carried on in accordance with God's laws and those of nature; that the discipline of family life should be observed and that religion should be obeyed; that a high standard of morality should prevail, both in public and private life; that justice should be held sacred and that no one should injure another with impunity; that the members of the commonwealth should grow up to man's estate strong and robust, and capable, if need be, of guarding and defending their country. If by a strike of workers or concerted interruption of work there should be imminent danger of disturbance to the public peace; or if circumstances were such as that among the working class the ties of family life were relaxed; if religion were found to suffer through the workers not having time and opportunity afforded them to practice its duties; if in workshops and factories there were danger to morals through the mixing of the sexes or from other harmful occasions of evil; or if employers laid burdens upon their workmen which were unjust, or degraded them with conditions repugnant to their dignity as human beings; finally, if health were endangered by excessive labor, or by work unsuited to sex or age—in such cases, there can be no question but that, within certain limits, it would be right to invoke the aid and authority of the law. The limits must be determined by the nature of the occasion which calls for the law's interference—the principle being that the law must not undertake more, nor proceed further, than is required for the remedy of the evil or the removal of the mischief.

37. Rights must be religiously respected wherever they exist, and it is the duty of the public authority to prevent and to punish injury, and to protect every one in the possession of his own. Still, when there is question of defending the rights of individuals, the poor and badly off have a claim to especial consideration. The richer class have many ways of shielding themselves, and stand less in need of help from the State; whereas the mass of the poor have no resources of their own to fall back upon, and must chiefly depend upon the assistance of the State. And it is for this reason that wage-earners, since they mostly belong in the mass of the needy, should be specially cared for and protected by the government.

38. Here, however, it is expedient to bring under special notice certain matters of moment. First of all, there is the duty of safeguarding private property by legal enactment and protection. Most of all it is essential, where the passion of greed is so strong, to keep the populace within the line of duty; for, if all may justly strive to better their condition, neither justice nor the common good allows any individual to seize upon that which belongs to another, or, under the futile and shallow pretext of equality, to lay violent hands on other people's possessions. Most true it is that by far the larger part of the workers prefer to better themselves by honest labor rather than by doing any wrong to others. But there are not a few who are imbued with evil principles and eager for revolutionary change, whose main purpose is to stir up disorder and incite their fellows to acts of violence. The authority of the law should intervene to put restraint upon such firebrands, to save the working classes from being led astray by their maneuvers, and to protect lawful owners from spoliation.

39. When work people have recourse to a strike and become voluntarily idle, it is frequently because the hours of labor are too long, or the work too hard, or because they consider their wages insufficient. The grave inconvenience of this not uncommon occurrence should be obviated by public remedial measures; for such paralysing of labor not only affects the masters and their work people alike, but is extremely injurious to trade and to the general interests of the public; moreover, on such occasions, violence and disorder are generally not far distant, and thus it frequently happens that the public peace is imperiled. The laws should forestall and prevent such troubles from arising; they should lend their influence and authority to the removal in good time of the causes which lead to conflicts between employers and employed.

40. The working man, too, has interests in which he should be protected by the State; and first of all, there are the interests of his soul. Life on earth, however good and desirable in itself, is not the final purpose for which man is created; it is only the way and the means to that attainment of truth and that love of goodness in which the full life of the soul consists. It is the soul which

is made after the image and likeness of God; it is in the soul that the sovereignty resides in virtue whereof man is commanded to rule the creatures below him and to use all the earth and the ocean for his profit and advantage. "Fill the earth and subdue it; and rule over the fishes of the sea, and the fowls of the air, and all living creatures that move upon the earth."[29] In this respect all men are equal; there is here no difference between rich and poor, master and servant, ruler and ruled, "for the same is Lord over all."[30] No man may with impunity outrage that human dignity which God Himself treats with great reverence, nor stand in the way of that higher life which is the preparation of the eternal life of heaven. Nay, more; no man has in this matter power over himself. To consent to any treatment which is calculated to defeat the end and purpose of his being is beyond his right; he cannot give up his soul to servitude, for it is not man's own rights which are here in question, but the rights of God, the most sacred and inviolable of rights.

41. From this follows the obligation of the cessation from work and labor on Sundays and certain holy days. The rest from labor is not to be understood as mere giving way to idleness; much less must it be an occasion for spending money and for vicious indulgence, as many would have it to be; but it should be rest from labor, hallowed by religion. Rest (combined with religious observances) disposes man to forget for a while the business of his everyday life, to turn his thoughts to things heavenly, and to the worship which he so strictly owes to the eternal Godhead. It is this, above all, which is the reason arid motive of Sunday rest; a rest sanctioned by God's great law of the Ancient Covenant—"Remember thou keep holy the Sabbath day,"[31] and taught to the world by His own mysterious "rest" after the creation of man: "He rested on the seventh day from all His work which He had done."[32]

42. If we turn not to things external and material, the first thing of all to secure is to save unfortunate working people from the cruelty of men of greed, who use human beings as mere instruments for money-making. It is neither just nor human so to grind men down with excessive labor as to stupefy their minds and wear out their bodies. Man's powers, like his general nature, are limited, and beyond these limits he cannot go. His strength is developed and increased by use and exercise, but only on condition of due intermission and proper rest. Daily labor, therefore, should be so regulated as not to be protracted over longer hours than strength admits. How many and how long the intervals of rest should be must depend on the nature of the work, on circumstances of time and place, and on the health and strength of the workman. Those who work in mines and quarries, and extract coal, stone and metals from the bowels of the earth, should have shorter hours in proportion as their labor is more severe and trying to health. Then, again, the season of the year

should be taken into account; for not unfrequently a kind of labor is easy at one time which at another is intolerable or exceedingly difficult. Finally, work which is quite suitable for a strong man cannot rightly be required from a woman or a child. And, in regard to children, great care should be taken not to place them in workshops and factories until their bodies and minds are sufficiently developed. For, just as very rough weather destroys the buds of spring, so does too early an experience of life's hard toil blight the young promise of a child's faculties, and render any true education impossible. Women, again, are not suited for certain occupations; a woman is by nature fitted for home-work, and it is that which is best adapted at once to preserve her modesty and to promote the good bringing up of children and the well-being of the family. As a general principle it may be laid down that a workman ought to have leisure and rest proportionate to the wear and tear of his strength, for waste of strength must be repaired by cessation from hard work.

In all agreements between masters and work people there is always the condition expressed or understood that there should be allowed proper rest for soul and body. To agree in any other sense would be against what is right and just; for it can never be just or right to require on the one side, or to promise on the other, the giving up of those duties which a man owes to his God and to himself.

43. We now approach a subject of great importance, and one in respect of which, if extremes are to be avoided, right notions are absolutely necessary. Wages, as we are told, are regulated by free consent, and therefore the employer, when he pays what was agreed upon, has done his part and seemingly is not called upon to do anything beyond. The only way, it is said, in which injustice might occur would be if the master refused to pay the whole of the wages, or if the workman should not complete the work undertaken; in such cases the public authority should intervene, to see that each obtains his due, but not under any other circumstances.

44. To this kind of argument a fair-minded man will not easily or entirely assent; it is not complete, for there are important considerations which it leaves out of account altogether. To labor is to exert oneself for the sake of procuring what is necessary for the various purposes of life, and chief of all for self preservation. "In the sweat of thy face thou shalt eat bread."(33) Hence, a man's labor necessarily bears two notes or characters. First of all, it is personal, inasmuch as the force which acts is bound up with the personality and is the exclusive property of him who acts, and, further, was given to him for his advantage. Secondly, man's labor is *necessary*; for without the result of labor a man cannot live, and self-preservation is a law of nature, which it is wrong to disobey. Now, were we to consider labor merely in so far as it is personal,

doubtless it would be within the workman's right to accept any rate of wages whatsoever; for in the same way as he is free to work or not, so is he free to accept a small wage or even none at all. But our conclusion must be very different if, together with the personal element in a man's work, we consider the fact that work is also necessary for him to live: these two aspects of his work are separable in thought, but not in reality. The preservation of life is the bounden duty of one and all, and to be wanting therein is a crime. It necessarily follows that each one has a natural right to procure what is required in order to live, and the poor can procure that in no other way than by what they can earn through their work.

45. Let the working man and the employer make free agreements, and in particular let them agree freely as to the wages; nevertheless, there underlies a dictate of natural justice more imperious and ancient than any bargain between man and man, namely, that wages ought not to be insufficient to support a frugal and well-behaved wage-earner. If through necessity or fear of a worse evil the workman accept harder conditions because an employer or contractor will afford him no better, he is made the victim of force and injustice. In these and similar questions, however—such as, for example, the hours of labor in different trades, the sanitary precautions to be observed in factories and workshops, etc.—in order to supersede undue interference on the part of the State, especially as circumstances, times, and localities differ so widely, it is advisable that recourse be had to societies or boards such as We shall mention presently, or to some other mode of safeguarding the interests of the wage-earners; the State being appealed to, should circumstances require, for its sanction and protection.

46. If a workman's wages be sufficient to enable him comfortably to support himself, his wife, and his children, he will find it easy, if he be a sensible man, to practice thrift, and he will not fail, by cutting down expenses, to put by some little savings and thus secure a modest source of income. Nature itself would urge him to this. We have seen that this great labor question cannot be solved save by assuming as a principle that private ownership must be held sacred and inviolable. The law, therefore, should favor ownership, and its policy should be to induce as many as possible of the people to become owners.

47. Many excellent results will follow from this; and, first of all, property will certainly become more equitably divided. For, the result of civil change and revolution has been to divide cities into two classes separated by a wide chasm. On the one side there is the party which holds power because it holds wealth; which has in its grasp the whole of labor and trade; which manipulates for its own benefit and its own purposes all the sources of supply, and which is not without influence even in the administration of the commonwealth. On

the other side there is the needy and powerless multitude, sick and sore in spirit and ever ready for disturbance. If working people can be encouraged to look forward to obtaining a share in the land, the consequence will be that the gulf between vast wealth and sheer poverty will be bridged over, and the respective classes will be brought nearer to one another. A further consequence will result in the great abundance of the fruits of the earth. Men always work harder and more readily when they work on that which belongs to them; nay, they learn to love the very soil that yields in response to the labor of their hands, not only food to eat, but an abundance of good things for themselves and those that are dear to them. That such a spirit of willing labor would add to the produce of the earth and to the wealth of the community is self evident. And a third advantage would spring from this: men would cling to the country in which they were born, for no one would exchange his country for a foreign land if his own afforded him the means of living a decent and happy life. These three important benefits, however, can be reckoned on only provided that a man's means be not drained and exhausted by excessive taxation. The right to possess private property is derived from nature, not from man; and the State has the right to control its use in the interests of the public good alone, but by no means to absorb it altogether. The State would therefore be unjust and cruel if under the name of taxation it were to deprive the private owner of more than is fair.

48. In the last place, employers and workmen may of themselves effect much, in the matter We are treating, by means of such associations and organizations as afford opportune aid to those who are in distress, and which draw the two classes more closely together. Among these may be enumerated societies for mutual help; various benevolent foundations established by private persons to provide for the workman, and for his widow or his orphans, in case of sudden calamity, in sickness, and in the event of death; and institutions for the welfare of boys and girls, young people, and those more advanced in years.

49. The most important of all are workingmen's unions, for these virtually include all the rest. History attests what excellent results were brought about by the artificers' guilds of olden times. They were the means of affording not only many advantages to the workmen, but in no small degree of promoting the advancement of art, as numerous monuments remain to bear witness. Such unions should be suited to the requirements of this our age—an age of wider education, of different habits, and of far more numerous requirements in daily life. It is gratifying to know that there are actually in existence not a few associations of this nature, consisting either of workmen alone, or of workmen and employers together, but it were greatly to be desired that they should become more numerous and more efficient. We have spoken of them

more than once, yet it will be well to explain here how notably they are needed, to show that they exist of their own right, and what should be their organization and their mode of action.

50. The consciousness of his own weakness urges man to call in aid from without. We read in the pages of holy Writ: "It is better that two should be together than one; for they have the advantage of their society. If one fall he shall be supported by the other. Woe to him that is alone, for when he falleth he hath none to lift him up."[34] And further: "A brother that is helped by his brother is like a strong city."[35] It is this natural impulse which binds men together in civil society; and it is likewise this which leads them to join together in associations which are, it is true, lesser and not independent societies, but, nevertheless, real societies.

51. These lesser societies and the larger society differ in many respects, because their immediate purpose and aim are different. Civil society exists for the common good, and hence is concerned with the interests of all in general, albeit with individual interests also in their due place and degree. It is therefore called a public society, because by its agency, as St. Thomas of Aquinas says, "Men establish relations in common with one another in the setting up of a commonwealth."[36] But societies which are formed in the bosom of the commonwealth are styled *private*, and rightly so, since their immediate purpose is the private advantage of the associates. "Now, a private society," says St. Thomas again, "is one which is formed for the purpose of carrying out private objects; as when two or three enter into partnership with the view of trading in common."[37] Private societies, then, although they exist within the body politic, and are severally part of the commonwealth, cannot nevertheless be absolutely, and as such, prohibited by public authority. For, to enter into a "society" of this kind is the natural right of man; and the State has for its office to protect natural rights, not to destroy them; and, if it forbid its citizens to form associations, it contradicts the very principle of its own existence, for both they and it exist in virtue of the like principle, namely, the natural tendency of man to dwell in society.

52. There are occasions, doubtless, when it is fitting that the law should intervene to prevent certain associations, as when men join together for purposes which are evidently bad, unlawful, or dangerous to the State. In such cases, public authority may justly forbid the formation of such associations, and may dissolve them if they already exist. But every precaution should be taken not to violate the rights of individuals and not to impose unreasonable regulations under pretense of public benefit. For laws only bind when they are in accordance with right reason, and, hence, with the eternal law of God.[38]

53. And here we are reminded of the confraternities, societies, and religious orders which have arisen by the Church's authority and the piety of Christian men. The annals of every nation down to our own days bear witness to what they have accomplished for the human race. It is indisputable that on grounds of reason alone such associations, being perfectly blameless in their objects, possess the sanction of the law of nature. In their religious aspect they claim rightly to be responsible to the Church alone. The rulers of the State accordingly have no rights over them, nor can they claim any share in their control; on the contrary, it is the duty of the State to respect and cherish them, and, if need be, to defend them from attack. It is notorious that a very different course has been followed, more especially in our own times. In many places the State authorities have laid violent hands on these communities, and committed manifold injustice against them; it has placed them under control of the civil law, taken away their rights as corporate bodies, and despoiled them of their property, in such property the Church had her rights, each member of the body had his or her rights, and there were also the rights of those who had founded or endowed these communities for a definite purpose, and, furthermore, of those for whose benefit and assistance they had their being. Therefore We cannot refrain from complaining of such spoliation as unjust and fraught with evil results; and with all the more reason do We complain because, at the very time when the law proclaims that association is free to all, We see that Catholic societies, however peaceful and useful, are hampered in every way, whereas the utmost liberty is conceded to individuals whose purposes are at once hurtful to religion and dangerous to the commonwealth.

54. Associations of every kind, and especially those of working men, are now far more common than heretofore. As regards many of these there is no need at present to inquire whence they spring, what are their objects, or what the means they imply. Now, there is a good deal of evidence in favor of the opinion that many of these societies are in the hands of secret leaders, and are managed on principles ill—according with Christianity and the public well-being; and that they do their utmost to get within their grasp the whole field of labor, and force working men either to join them or to starve. Under these circumstances Christian working men must do one of two things: either join associations in which their religion will be exposed to peril, or form associations among themselves and unite their forces so as to shake off courageously the yoke of so unrighteous and intolerable an oppression. No one who does not wish to expose man's chief good to extreme risk will for a moment hesitate to say that the second alternative should by all means be adopted.

55. Those Catholics are worthy of all praise—and they are not a few—who, understanding what the times require, have striven, by various

undertakings and endeavors, to better the condition of the working class by rightful means. They have taken up the cause of the working man, and have spared no efforts to better the condition both of families and individuals; to infuse a spirit of equity into the mutual relations of employers and employed; to keep before the eyes of both classes the precepts of duty and the laws of the Gospel—that Gospel which, by inculcating self restraint, keeps men within the bounds of moderation, and tends to establish harmony among the divergent interests and the various classes which compose the body politic. It is with such ends in view that we see men of eminence, meeting together for discussion, for the promotion of concerted action, and for practical work. Others, again, strive to unite working men of various grades into associations, help them with their advice and means, and enable them to obtain fitting and profitable employment. The bishops, on their part, bestow their ready good will and support; and with their approval and guidance many members of the clergy, both secular and regular, labor assiduously in behalf of the spiritual interest of the members of such associations. And there are not wanting Catholics blessed with affluence, who have, as it were, cast in their lot with the wage-earners, and who have spent large sums in founding and widely spreading benefit and insurance societies, by means of which the working man may without difficulty acquire through his labor not only many present advantages, but also the certainty of honorable support in days to come. How greatly such manifold and earnest activity has benefited the community at large is too well known to require Us to dwell upon it. We find therein grounds for most cheering hope in the future, provided always that the associations We have described continue to grow and spread, and are well and wisely administered. The State should watch over these societies of citizens banded together in accordance with their rights, but it should not thrust itself into their peculiar concerns and their organization, for things move and live by the spirit inspiring them, and may be killed by the rough grasp of a hand from without.

56. In order that an association may be carried on with unity of purpose and harmony of action, its administration and government should be firm and wise. All such societies, being free to exist, have the further right to adopt such rules and organization as may best conduce to the attainment of their respective objects. We do not judge it possible to enter into minute particulars touching the subject of organization; this must depend on national character, on practice and experience, on the nature and aim of the work to be done, on the scope of the various trades and employments, and on other circumstances of fact and of time—all of which should be carefully considered.

57. To sum up, then, We may lay it down as a general and lasting law that working men's associations should be so organized and governed as to furnish

the best and most suitable means for attaining what is aimed at, that is to say, for helping each individual member to better his condition to the utmost in body, soul, and property. It is clear that they must pay special and chief attention to the duties of religion and morality, and that social betterment should have this chiefly in view; otherwise they would lose wholly their special character, and end by becoming little better than those societies which take no account whatever of religion. What advantage can it be to a working man to obtain by means of a society material well-being, if he endangers his soul for lack of spiritual food? "What doth it profit a man, if he gain the whole world and suffer the loss of his soul?"[39] This, as our Lord teaches, is the mark or character that distinguishes the Christian from the heathen. "After all these things do the heathen seek . . . Seek ye first the Kingdom of God and His justice: and all these things shall be added unto you."[40] Let our associations, then, look first and before all things to God; let religious instruction have therein the foremost place, each one being carefully taught what is his duty to God, what he has to believe, what to hope for, and how he is to work out his salvation; and let all be warned and strengthened with special care against wrong principles and false teaching. Let the working man be urged and led to the worship of God, to the earnest practice of religion, and, among other things, to the keeping holy of Sundays and holy days. Let him learn to reverence and love holy Church, the common Mother of us all; and hence to obey the precepts of the Church, and to frequent the sacraments, since they are the means ordained by God for obtaining forgiveness of sin and for leading a holy life.

58. The foundations of the organization being thus laid in religion, We next proceed to make clear the relations of the members one to another, in order that they may live together in concord and go forward prosperously and with good results. The offices and charges of the society should be apportioned for the good of the society itself, and in such mode that difference in degree or standing should not interfere with unanimity and good-will. It is most important that office bearers be appointed with due prudence and discretion, and each one's charge carefully mapped out, in order that no members may suffer harm. The common funds must be administered with strict honesty, in such a way that a member may receive assistance in proportion to his necessities. The rights and duties of the employers, as compared with the rights and duties of the employed, ought to be the subject of careful consideration. Should it happen that either a master or a workman believes himself injured, nothing would be more desirable than that a committee should be appointed, composed of reliable and capable members of the association, whose duty would be, conformably with the rules of the association, to settle the dispute. Among the several purposes of a society, one should

be to try to arrange for a continuous supply of work at all times and seasons; as well as to create a fund out of which the members may be effectually helped in their needs, not only in the cases of accident, but also in sickness, old age, and distress.

59. Such rules and regulations, if willingly obeyed by all, will sufficiently ensure the well being of the less well-to-do; whilst such mutual associations among Catholics are certain to be productive in no small degree of prosperity to the State. Is it not rash to conjecture the future from the past. Age gives way to age, but the events of one century are wonderfully like those of another, for they are directed by the providence of God, who overrules the course of history in accordance with His purposes in creating the race of man. We are told that it was cast as a reproach on the Christians in the early ages of the Church that the greater number among them had to live by begging or by labor. Yet, destitute though they were of wealth and influence, they ended by winning over to their side the favor of the rich and the good-will of the powerful. They showed themselves industrious, hard-working, assiduous, and peaceful, ruled by justice, and, above all, bound together in brotherly love. In presence of such mode of life and such example, prejudice gave way, the tongue of malevolence was silenced, and the lying legends of ancient superstition little by little yielded to Christian truth.

60. At the time being, the condition of the working classes is the pressing question of the hour, and nothing can be of higher interest to all classes of the State than that it should be rightly and reasonably settled. But it will be easy for Christian working men to solve it aright if they will form associations, choose wise guides, and follow on the path which with so much advantage to themselves and the common weal was trodden by their fathers before them. Prejudice, it is true, is mighty, and so is the greed of money; but if the sense of what is just and rightful be not deliberately stifled, their fellow citizens are sure to be won over to a kindly feeling towards men whom they see to be in earnest as regards their work and who prefer so unmistakably right dealing to mere lucre, and the sacredness of duty to every other consideration.

61. And further great advantage would result from the state of things We are describing; there would exist so much more ground for hope, and likelihood, even, of recalling to a sense of their duty those working men who have either given up their faith altogether, or whose lives are at variance with its precepts. Such men feel in most cases that they have been fooled by empty promises and deceived by false pretexts. They cannot but perceive that their grasping employers too often treat them with great inhumanity and hardly care for them outside the profit their labor brings; and if they belong to any union, it is probably one in which there exists, instead of charity and love, that intes-

tine strife which ever accompanies poverty when unresigned and unsustained by religion. Broken in spirit and worn down in body, how many of them would gladly free themselves from such galling bondage! But human respect, or the dread of starvation, makes them tremble to take the step. To such as these Catholic associations are of incalculable service, by helping them out of their difficulties, inviting them to companionship and receiving the returning wanderers to a haven where they may securely find repose.

62. We have now laid before you, venerable brethren, both who are the persons and what are the means whereby this most arduous question must be solved. Every one should put his hand to the work which falls to his share, and that at once and straightway, lest the evil which is already so great become through delay absolutely beyond remedy. Those who rule the commonwealths should avail themselves of the laws and institutions of the country; masters and wealthy owners must be mindful of their duty; the working class, whose interests are at stake, should make every lawful and proper effort; and since religion alone, as We said at the beginning, can avail to destroy the evil at its root, all men should rest persuaded that main thing needful is to re-establish Christian morals, apart from which all the plans and devices of the wisest will prove of little avail.

63. In regard to the Church, her cooperation will never be found lacking, be the time or the occasion what it may; and she will intervene with all the greater effect in proportion as her liberty of action is the more unfettered. Let this be carefully taken to heart by those whose office it is to safeguard the public welfare. Every minister of holy religion must bring to the struggle the full energy of his mind and all his power of endurance. Moved by your authority, venerable brethren, and quickened by your example, they should never cease to urge upon men of every class, upon the high-placed as well as the lowly, the Gospel doctrines of Christian life; by every means in their power they must strive to secure the good of the people; and above all must earnestly cherish in themselves, and try to arouse in others, charity, the mistress and the queen of virtues. For, the happy results we all long for must be chiefly brought about by the plenteous outpouring of charity; of that true Christian charity which is the fulfilling of the whole Gospel law, which is always ready to sacrifice itself for others' sake, and is man's surest antidote against worldly pride and immoderate love of self; that charity whose office is described and whose Godlike features are outlined by the Apostle St. Paul in these words: "Charity is patient, is kind, . . . seeketh not her own, . . . suffereth all things, . . . endureth all things."[41]

64. On each of you, venerable brethren, and on your clergy and people, as an earnest of God's mercy and a mark of Our affection, we lovingly in the Lord bestow the apostolic benediction.

Given at St. Peter's in Rome, the fifteenth day of May, 1891, the fourteenth year of Our pontificate.

Notes

[1] The title sometimes given to this encyclical, *On the Condiction of the Working Classes*, is therefore perfectly justified. A few lines after this sentence, the Pope gives a more comprehensive definition of the subject of Rerum novarum. We are using it as a title.

[2] Deut. 5:21.

[3] Gen. 1:28.

[4] *Summa theologiae*, IIa–IIae, q. x, art. 12, Answer.

[5] Gen. 3:17.

[6] James 5:4.

[7] 2 Tim. 2:12.

[8] 2 Cor. 4:17.

[9] Matt. 19:23–24.

[10] Luke 6:24–25.

[11] *Summa theologiae*, IIa–IIae, q. lxvi, art. 2, Answer.

[12] Ibid.

[13] Ibid., q. xxxii, a. 6, Answer.

[14] Luke 11:41.

[15] Acts 20:35.

[16] Matt.25:40.

[17] *Hom. in Evang.*, 9, n. 7 (PL 76, 1109B).

[18] 2 Cor. 8:9.

[19] Mark 6:3.

[20] Matt.5:3.

[21] Matt. 11:28.

[22] Rom. 8:17.

[23] 1 Tim. 6:10.

[24] Acts 4:34.

[25] *Apologia secunda*, 39, (*Apologeticus*, cap. 39; PL1, 533A).

[26] See above, pp. 161-184.

[27] *Summa theologiae*, IIa–IIae, q. lxi, are. l, ad 2m.

[28] Thomas Aquinas, *On the Governance of Rulers*, 1, 15 (*Opera omnia*, ed. *Vives*, Vol. 27, p. 356).

[29] Gen. 1:28.

[30] Rom. 10:12.

[31] Exod. 20:8.

[32] Gen. 2:2.

[33] Gen. 3:19.

[34] Eccle. 4:9–10.

[35] Prov. 18:19.

[36] *Contra impugnantes Dei cultum et religionem*, Part 2, ch. 8 (*Opera omnia*, ed. *Vives*, Vol. 29, p. 16).

[37] Ibid.

[38] "Human law is law only by virtue of its accordance with right reason; and thus it is manifest that it flows from the eternal law. And in so far as it deviates from right reason it is called an unjust law; in such case it is no law at all, but rather a species of violence." Thomas Aquinas, *Summa theologiae*, Ia-IIae, q. xciii, art. 3, ad 2m.

[39] Matt. 16:26.

[40] Matt. 6:32-33.

[41] I Cor. 13:4–7.